A PEPPER FOR YOUR THOUGHTS?

A PEPPER FOR YOUR THOUGHTS?

or

How NOT to Start a Gourmet Foods Business

a memoir of a family recipe by

Howard Lev

SPRING **2025**
CHIN MUSIC PRESS
SEATTLE

PUBLISHER:
Chin Music Press
1501 Pike Place #329
Seattle, WA 98101-1542

www.chinmusicpress.com

All Rights Reserved

COVER ART: Julie Paschkis

ORNAMENTAL BREAKS, TAROT ART, & RECIPE HEADERS: Julie Paschkis

INTERIOR PHOTOS (unless otherwise noted) © Howard Lev

COVER & INTERIOR TYPESETTING: Vladimir Verano

Paperback ISBN: 978-1-63405-089-0
Hardback ISBN: 978-1-63405-088-3

Printed in the USA
Library of Congress Control Number: 2024948759
EDITOR'S NOTE: *Go Tribe!*

To Elijah, so he knows the whole story.
And the whole mishpacha, cast and crew.

A PEPPER FOR YOUR THOUGHTS?

FOOD, FAMILY, AND FOLLY

IN 1992, TWENTY YEARS BEFORE THE TV SHOW Portlandia spoofed all the boutique pickle companies sprouting up in Portland, Oregon, in its sketch "We Can Pickle That!" I made the first thirty-three cases (about four hundred jars) of Mama Lil's Peppers in a church kitchen in Seattle. By 1995, I'd made upward of eight hundred cases in a real cannery, which were now being sold in some grocery stores in Seattle. It was the natural next step to expand into Portland, where I'd often spend weekends promoting the peppers.

I was doing my schtick passing out samples of my peppers served on bread in Portland's hip Elephants Delicatessen when a thirty-year-old, spiky-haired, tattooed scenester with a guitar case walked by me. I flung out the pitch line, "The most delicious, pickled peppers on the planet!" Without stopping, he put a sample in his mouth, took three more steps, did an about-face, and came back. He examined my jar of bright orange, red, and yellow pepper ringlets.

"Pickled peppers? I used to be a chef. But these aren't sour like most pickled things." He took another sample. "These are *da bomb!* Wow, the heat's now coming on, yet their flavor is smooth on the palate."

"That's because of the oil," I informed him.

"Cool. How'd you get into peppers?"

"Fear of death. I'm preserving the peppers before their time of dying." It's not the first time I used that line, but this guy actually got my Led Zeppelin reference, as he was smiling when he put a jar in his cart.

Then he asked me, "Can you make a living making peppers?"

I shrugged "Not yet. Can you make a living making music?"

He shrugged. "Not yet. But I will." He gave me his card. His band's name was almost recognizable to me from the underground radio station. Walking away, he called back, "My Aunt Becky's asparagus is *da bomb*, too!"

Two years later at a Portland trade show, I came across that same spiky-haired musician, playing guitar at his booth to lure in folks to taste his Aunt Becky's Preserved Asparagus. The next year at that same show, not only was he back with two more pickled products but so were two other companies who both claimed their one-of-a-kind pickles were based on family recipes.

Now, I'm not saying it was all due to Mama Lil's Peppers that Portland now has a minor-league baseball club named the Portland Pickles, but you get my drift.

Little did I know when I started pickling peppers that when it comes to the American Dream, the hipness factor of turning a family recipe into a business is right up there with being in a successful rock band. And vice versa, as some rock stars aspire to have their own gourmet food products. At one trade show, Bob Weir of the Grateful Dead was in the booth next to me signing bottles of his Snake Oil Hot Sauce for starry-eyed buyers. Luckily for Bob, he has a merch table at his concerts, as his sauce may have sold well at the trade show, but it flopped on the grocery shelves. As for Aunt Becky's (or was it Betty's or Bessie's?), she lasted three years at best—or the lifespan of most gourmet food brands or rock bands whose names have been long forgotten.

Whereas more than thirty years after I sold my first jars, Mama Lil's Peppers not only still exists but is becoming ever more popular in the Pacific Northwest. During a recent trip to a Seattle Costco store, I overheard two elderly women chatting as they put jars of Mama Lil's in their carts. One said to her friend, "I put them in my eggs, religiously, every morning." Her friend one-upped her. "They do amazing things for a roast beef sandwich! In fact, I put them on all my sandwiches!" I was shocked to hear this. These women were hardly the spicy food fans I'd imagined. Had Mama Lil's Peppers gone mainstream?

Now, Mama Lil's is hardly a household name outside of Seattle and Portland, but the fact is they've been sold at one point or another in all fifty states—as well as in Canada, Mexico, England, and Japan. Our peppers have also graced the menus of more than a thousand restaurants. Considering how many gourmet food products I've seen sail on the horizon with such great hopes for success and then sink without a trace, you'd think I must've been doing something right that Mama Lil's has stayed afloat all these years.

The idea to write this book came more than a decade ago when, after lugging a thirty-pound bucket of peppers into the Elysian brewpub, I had a beer with its then owner and master brewer Dick Cantwell. On our second beer, Dick was gloating about how well his new book, *Starting Your Own Brewery,* was selling. By our third beer, Dick told me, perhaps sensing my envy, "You should write the book How to Start a Gourmet Food Business.

"That book's been written," I told Dick. "Besides, I'm the guy to write the book *how not to start a gourmet food business.*"

Now why would I say that about myself?

First off, starting and running any business entails strong organizational skills and a knack for making sound financial decisions. But my shambolic character, I'm afraid, has always lacked those traits. For instance, when I was eleven years old, I went over to my friend Mark Wittow's house to trade baseball cards. Mark's cards were in binders, arranged alphabetically. My cards were stuffed into four paper shopping bags, and I had no idea which bag my Rocky Colavito cards were in. My organizational skills didn't improve as an adult when for ten years I drove a cab and never once kept a trip sheet. Heck, I didn't keep a checkbook until I was forty years old. Luckily—and luck plays a role in all of this—I have a good memory and never bounced a check on anyone. As for Mark, he is still the most organized person I know.

Then there is the issue of making rational financial decisions. At twenty-seven years old with just $700 to my name, I bet $500 at 100-to-1 odds that the Cleveland Indians (now the Guardians) would win the World Series. I was utterly confident that the $50,000 I was going to win would change my life. And that bet did change my life. When my girlfriend told a suitor of hers about what I'd done, he said, "Good, it's decided. Howard's a fool, you're coming with me." She married that guy, and they went on to live happily ever after. While I continued to bet on the Cleveland Indians to win the World Series for the next forty years!

You'd think all this foolishness would be reason enough to discredit my opinion on anything, let alone what product stands a chance of making it in the very competitive world of gourmet foods. It is my hope then that this book may help future food entrepreneurs by warning them in advance how to avoid some of the same wrong turns that I made. Maybe I'll even inspire some of you to think: *If that fool did it, anyone can.* As you'll soon see, when you add up all the blows my business took, the real miracle is that I wouldn't go down. (Like in one of my favorite films, *Raging Bull,* when a dazed Jake LaMotta keeps taking punches from Sugar Ray Robinson, but he stays on his feet. *"You never got me down, Ray!"*)

Perhaps I took to heart that book from kindergarten, *The Little Engine That Could.* It teaches perseverance. No matter how steep a climb or how long a tunnel, believe in yourself and keep on chugging. And if I gleaned any wisdom from my college philosophy courses, it's that dictum by Descartes (or was it, Hegel?): *I fuck up, therefore I am.* Meaning, if you can learn from your mistakes, you might grow in a way you wouldn't have had you not fucked up first. (There you have it, Hegel's theory of dialectics in a nutshell!) This book will expose the many opportunities when I could've made the right business decision, but I clearly fucked up and made the wrong one. Maybe I learned from my mistakes. Or maybe I just fucked up again.

After reading and listening to many entrepreneurial success stories—such as those on the NPR show *How I Built This*—most of the business owners describe their journey as a bumpy ride over a long and winding road, where they just held on tight until they got lucky. But mostly what I got from their stories was they all worked damn hard. Then got lucky. No doubt, I worked hard too. And then got lucky, then unlucky, lucky again, and unlucky once more.

I should confess that I'm a superstitious type who has long suspected that what luck Mama Lil's had in its first twenty years—when I, who had no business running a business, ran one by myself—was also attributable to some spiritual presences who dealt me a magic card or two that enabled me to transcend my entrepreneurial flaws. In mining my memory to write this book, I hoped to locate the source of Mama Lil's luck in anticipation that it's there where I'll spot the magic bubbling to the surface. And like so many fanciful fables about food that depict ancestral traditions kept alive at the dinner table, the teaspoon of magic I'll sprinkle onto my story about a family recipe will come from those familial spirits who, perhaps longing to savor a flavor one last time, found their way back.

I never could have imagined the heartbreak and joy of the wild roller-coaster ride my business took me on, going off the rails on more occasions than I've liked to recall. Magic and spiritual presences aside, Mama Lil's survival was due to the relationships that I forged with the real flesh and blood characters within this book. The farmers, production crews, chefs, restaurateurs, fellow food producers who all brought me joy, camaraderie, and best of all, great food beyond measure. You can taste it in the recipes these characters have generously shared with me and are dispersed between these chapters in this book.

More than anything, I'm thankful to all those folks, spiritual or otherwise, who inspired me to be either courageous or foolish enough to hold on tight, when the rational thing would've been to just let my business go under.

Note: Very few of the recipes in this book are dependent on using Mama Lil's Peppers; the peppers merely take the dish to another level. When I started asking folks for recipes, people would tell me, "A recipe? I just throw Mama Lil's on things." Like any great condiment, the peppers enhance other flavors, and the quantity of peppers called for in each recipe is up to the cook's discretion. But for those who are unfamiliar with Mama Lil's Peppers, each pepper ring is dense with flavor, so a little goes a long way.

PART ONE

THE FOOL

ORIGINS OF A FAMILY RECIPE

PEOPLE HAVE ASKED ME DOZENS of times over the years: What's the secret of longevity in the gourmet food business? To which my favorite answer has become, *Name your business after your mama. Just in case there is an afterlife, you might get lucky, you might get blessed.*

Now, I'm not saying that my mom, Lillian Gordon Lev, had the gentle spirit you'd ever associate with someone who bestowed blessings on people. But she did have the passionate temperament of certain types of saints. And as my childhood friend Jonny Katz once said of her, "Sure your mom was meshuga but if Lil loved you, watch out." Considering how meshuga—Yiddish for crazy—Lil could get at times, seeing her through Jonny's wise eyes when I was a kid made it easier to accept my over-the-top mom. Jonny has since passed away, so I asked his equally astute sister, Kathy—my first unrequited love—what she remembers most about Lil.

Kathy reminisced, "Of course my family loved the abundance of food in Lil's kitchen. But what endeared us to your mom most was Lil's larger-than-life personality. Her bright red hair, and those shiny blue dresses she wore that matched her eyes, and heavily painted eyelids that fluttered wildly when she got excited or was fiercely protecting her large herd. But what amused us most about Lil was her constant agitation with Harry."

When Kathy mentioned my dad, I flashed on a family Passover seder when I must've been nine years old. After asking the requisite four questions ("Why is this night different from all other nights?") I posed a fifth question to my dad: "What's inside a kreplach?" Lil's kreplach were these dough-wrapped meatballs in her beef broth soup that squirted hot, savory juices when you bit into them. Harry, who was as strong as an ox with a girth born of an infinite appetite, spooned two kreplach in his mouth, then hunched his shoulders: "Krep. Krep's in kreplach." I laughed at my dad's joke. But my mom was grimacing when she got up from the table. She'd been the butt of way too many jokes coming out of the mouths of Harry and his brothers.

This being a book about a family recipe, I should shed a little light on the two sides of my family. My father's side, the Levs, emigrated to Youngstown, Ohio, just before World War I from Shchedrin, a shtetl in Belarus (think

Fiddler on the Roof), with rumors of learned rabbis in their ancestry. Lil's family, the Gordons, were shopkeepers who came from eastern Romania, now Moldova, in the village of Tocuz. There's an adage I'd hear growing up about the hierarchy of European Jewry: The German Jews looked down on the Polish Jews, who looked down on the Russian Jews, who looked down on the Romanian Jews, and they all looked down on the Moldovans. Lil's parents, like many Jews from Tocuz, emigrated to Youngstown, where she was born. But her family followed relatives to the big city of Chicago, where her parents had a grocery store with a horse-drawn delivery wagon in the Jewish enclave of Maxwell Street.

Lil's father, Abe Gordon, Chicago, 1924.

In a fit of insecurity, Lil once told me that after she graduated from high school, they—whoever *they* were—wanted to send her "to that college for girls in France. The sore bone." (After hearing this, I'm not sure I ever trusted Lil's version of the truth again.) Not only did my mom not attend college, I doubt she ever read an entire book in her life. Having foregone the Sorbonne, Lil moved to Los Angeles and became a gofer for the former child star Jane Withers and the song-and-dance man Donald O'Connor. My mom reveled in those years during World War II when she got to rub elbows with movie stars. And I'm sure they appreciated Lil's go-getter, stop-at-nothing attitude when she ran their errands on her bicycle, her bright red hair trailing in the wind as she sped down Wilshire Boulevard.

When Harry came home from serving in World War II, instead of going to college like his four brothers did, he moved in with his parents and started building modest homes with his cabinetmaker father, Louie. What my dad had in common with his well-educated brothers was a penchant for telling jokes and funny stories, a trait that I assume they inherited from my grandpa, who I'm told was always making people laugh while standing in line at the lumberyard. My grandma Bessie Lev was savvy and whip-smart, but, in my recollection, a dull cook. I assume that four years of army rations followed by two years of Bessie's boiled chicken may have had something to do with Harry falling in love with Lil, and she moved back to Youngstown.

Being the baby of the family, I was mommy's boy. But as a ten-year-old, the closest I could come to crawling back under mommy's covers was playing gin rummy with her on my parents' spacious bed. Lil loved to play cards. She shuffled with such flair before flinging the deal, and she'd triumphantly throw down her cards when she proclaimed, "Gin!" I was not a good player, and she would let me know it, "It's meshuga you hold on to so many high cards!"

When I was eleven years old, my mom made me stand with her at the stage door of the Packard Music Hall in Warren, Ohio, to meet Donald O'Connor, who was starring in the musical *How to Succeed in Business without Really Trying*. When the door opened, Lil beamed at this short man in heavy makeup. "Hi, Donald, It's Lillian Gordon." When Donald recognized her, my mom was so thrilled that she insisted I shake his hand. Walking away she asked me, "Aren't you glad we knocked on that door?" I wasn't. I was embarrassed. But if I'd inherited just a bit more of Lil's unabashed chutzpah, it sure would have made Mama Lil's sales calls easier for me.

Although Lil was not known for being the sharpest tack in the toolbox, her talent with food was unrivaled by any of my friend's moms. Lil was a real balabusta. (Yiddish for *homemaker extraordinaire*—although I always assumed it meant a ballsy *and* busty woman.) Of all the classic Eastern European Jewish comfort foods Lil made (and she made them all), what I loved most was her variety of dumplings—like her large matzoh balls that defied gravity by floating among the celery, carrots, and turnips in her chicken soup. My very favorite meal of Lil's was the ultimate mommy food: chicken and dumplings. I've eaten many moms' versions in my life, but none has come close to the sumptuousness of my mom's chicken and dumplings.

Besides cooking for my own family of voracious appetites, Lil was a committed soldier for our synagogue, where she'd cater weddings, bar mitzvahs, Purim parties, you name it. Typically, she used our basement kitchen with her mother's old gas stove for these big jobs. For one event, Lil had to drive through a blizzard across town to the one store that carried the off-season fruit and melons to make a large fruit salad bowl. When my mom got home, she was stressed out and ordered my brother and me to bring everything from her car into the basement.

Inside Lil's trunk was a watermelon the size of a dinosaur egg. My brother and I tenderly carried it together through the kitchen toward the basement steps. But being teenage boys who played a lot of catch with each other, my brother gently tossed the melon to me when, *oops,* the melon dropped and splattered all the way down the basement stairs. When Lil saw the carnage, she shrieked. "Oy vey!" then cocked her arm, cantaloupe in hand. "Don't throw it, Mom!" I pleaded. When she set the cantaloupe down, I reached over and grabbed a chunk of melon. When *WHOOSH!* A melon rind flew by my head, nailing my brother who slid down the steps, wailing. Our balabusta mama had gone stark raving meshuga! With tears streaming down her face Lil was hurling chunks of melon down at us, screaming.

"That was the last watermelon in town!"

"C'mon, Mom! There's gotta be one more watermelon in Youngstown."

But there's no making peace with meshuga. *SPLAT!* A chunk of melon nailed me on my head, and I slid down the steps. My brother and I locked ourselves in the bathroom to wait out the storm. Friends who never met Lil have asked me if I take after her in any way, and in a fit of passion, I'll admit I've been known to throw some watermelon in my day. Anyway, my dad must have found the *very* last melon in town on his way home from work, as my next memory is being in the backseat of her car cradling a huge bowl of fruit salad with bits of melon still in my hair.

Lightning-quick temper and inferiority complex aside, Lil was a proud woman who carried herself with her chin up, chest out, and shoulders back. She even proudly told folks she was from Youngstown, the epitome of the Rust Belt's decline. Most of all, Lil showed her pride in how hard she could work, be it catering extravagant parties, scrubbing a stubborn stain out of an heirloom tablecloth, or getting a tough job done for my dad's construction business.

When my dad wasn't throwing his weight around on the handball courts, he was always at work on his construction business. Especially at the dinner table. Perhaps it's from watching Harry eat that I learned how to multitask in my own small business. With the rotary phone holding down the want-ads, he had the receiver tucked in his chin as he juggled a pencil, fork, and glass of milk, all while negotiating to buy a used backhoe. With a mouthful of mashed potatoes he barked into the phone, "Fuck you, too!" Then he slammed the receiver down, and told my brother and me, "Sometimes the best deals are the ones you don't make." Do I take after my dad in any way? I certainly inherited his appetite, table manners, and large nose. And like those bits of mashed potatoes on Harry's nose, food has always found a way onto mine.

My fondest recollection of my parents as a team was on warm August nights seeing them work with such gusto in their large garden behind our suburban home. My dad would pause with his shovel to devour a beefsteak tomato in two bites. Lil, crouched and hidden by cornstalks, would yell, "Look!" Then she'd stand tall to proudly show off two plump eggplants and a handful of red, orange, and yellow goat horn–shaped peppers. Those were the peppers she used to make what would become known as Mama Lil's Peppers. I paid no attention to how she made them except that it took up lots of space

My parents, Lil and Harry, early 1980s.

in the kitchen. The next day, the jars of pepper rings were back in their box and taken down to her cellar pantry to "cure" for a couple months.

But the memories I cherish most of Lil making food from her garden are not of the hot peppers in oil, but rather of a Romanian eggplant recipe, called salata. In her bathrobe, Lil would descend into the basement at 4 a.m. to roast eggplant on the burners of her mother's old gas stove. My family would awaken to the pungent smokiness of charred eggplant wafting through the house. When I'd come home for dinner after my paper route, Lil would be spinning the crank on her mother's countertop grinder as she stuffed roasted eggplant and fresh bell peppers into it.

Our neighbor, Aaron Grossman, whose heritage was also Moldovan, would be at the kitchen table with Harry, impatiently waiting with forks in hand. This memory must be from 1969, the year of the moon landing. I was fourteen years old and didn't quite get the joke my dad told Grossman as they dug into the plates of salata that Lil set in front of them.

The astronaut looks out his window. A woman is spinning the crank of a meat grinder. The astronaut goes outside and asks the woman, "What are you making?"

"I'm making children," she says as she spins the grinder's crank.

"That's how you make chopped liver, not children," the astronaut tells her.

"So how do you make children?"

"I'll show you." The astronaut climbs out of his space suit, and right there on the moon, they do it. It's over quick.

"So, where's my children?" the woman kvetches.

The astronaut tells her, "It takes nine months to make children."

"So why'd you stop?"

14

Lil laughed at that one. Then she unclamped the grinder from her counter and with a turn of a screw, broke it down into its four pieces, washed and dried them, then before reassembling it, rubbed them with oil. Of all the objects passed down from her own mother, Lil put the most care into preserving this countertop meat grinder made in 1921, the year she was born. The quantity of chopped liver and eggplant salata that grinder churned out in eighty years was enough, to quote a favorite phrase of Lil's, to feed an army. My most indelible memory of Lil's kitchen is how, when the lights were turned off, that grinder was still glistening with oil.

To set the record straight, before I started Mama Lil's Peppers, I had never once called my mother Mama Lil. Heck, I'm not sure I ever called her Mama. Even though my hometown of Youngstown had a reputation for being a tough Mafia town with an Italian-dominant food culture, I was a Jewish kid who went to a Jewish Sunday school and played at the Jewish Community Center. As far as I knew, none of my Jewish friends called their mommy "mama."

Not to be an unreliable narrator, but as for the pepper recipe, I should clarify that it was not passed down from Lil's Jewish Romanian heritage as I initially assumed; it's a hometown recipe. The variety of chile peppers that Lil used, that everybody used was Hungarian hot wax peppers, which the farmers called *goathorns* because of their shape. (Since Hungary borders Romania, I assumed it one of Lil's Romanian recipes.) Naming my business *Mama Lil's* made it sound Italian—which it is, I suppose. The hot-peppers-in-oil recipe originated in the Italian region of Abruzzo, a hundred or so miles east of Rome. This recipe became—and still is—popular in the sister cities of Youngstown and Warren, Ohio, because the Mahoning Valley had one of the largest pockets of Abruzzo Italians in the country. The hot peppers in oil were nonexistent in the nearby Italian culinary cultures of Pittsburgh and Cleveland, which had much larger Italian populations but far fewer Abruzzesi.

The Abruzzo Italians were the primary restaurateurs in the Youngstown-Warren area. (Whereas the Sicilians and Neapolitans owned dark bars with secretive back rooms.) The first restaurant in the region to serve hot peppers in oil was then known as Abruzze's 422 (now Café 422), located on the Route 422 strip in Warren. It opened its doors in 1939, and word has it that from day one, the second you sat down, a bowl of yellow, orange, and red pepper rings in oil would appear on the table with a basket of soft Italian bread. For free! Like Jewish delicatessens that gave you dill pickles once you were seated, these peppers drew folks into Abruzze's with the promise of instant gratification. And if you ran out of peppers and wanted more, you raised your bowl, and the waitress brought you more. For free! (Those were the days!)

These sweet, spicy, garlicky peppers in oil were so adored by Abruzze's customers that every other restaurant on the strip in Warren—Alberini's, the Living Room, Salvatore's, Jimmy Chieffo's, Leo's, and Enzo's, to name but a few—copycatted them by serving the hot peppers in oil as a gratis appetizer. I wouldn't be surprised if the only restaurant back in the day that didn't serve the peppers in oil in the area was the Ding Ho on Market Street.

When I was a teenager, Jonny Katz's family went out to dinner with my family at the Living Room in Warren. Moments after sitting down, we were brought a bowl of hot peppers in oil and a basket of bread. As we all dug in, Jonny observed "Everyone here is eating these peppers. And no one can stop eating them." And he was right. As I looked around waitresses with bowls of peppers in hand were constantly dropping them at all the tables. Honestly, I hadn't put together yet that the peppers served by these restaurants were the same recipe that Lil made.

Over time, almost everyone who grew up in the Mahoning Valley developed a craving for these hot peppers in oil. Yet for some reason, no business made them to be sold commercially in stores—meaning that you either made them in your own kitchen or became friendly with someone who did. My uncle Irv Lev, who was a bit of a nemesis to Lil, made his hot peppers in oil from peppers he grew in his garden. Like Lil, Irv didn't pasteurize his jars. Nor for that matter did my cousin Ray Lev, a dentist who also made them. But at least Ray was science-minded enough to refrigerate his jars after packing them.

While visiting my folks a few years after I started my business, I took a sauna with my old and hobbled father at the Jewish Community Center. A man I knew from childhood, David Luntz, sat down next to us. When I reminded Luntz how far I'd hit his fastball in an epic neighborhood game thirty years ago—the only home run I ever hit in my life—he said under his breath, "Gaylord was playing shallow. So, what are you doing with your life?"

My father proudly spoke up: "Howie's making the hot peppers in oil!"

Luntz was unimpressed. "Who doesn't make the hot peppers in oil?" Whereupon two other men in the sauna said they also made the peppers. Fact is, although its origins might be in the Abruzzo region of Italy, the only people I knew who made them (besides Lil) were middle-aged Jewish men with paunches. But I later learned it was Lil's Serbian friend Dessa who taught Lil how to make the peppers. But Dessa said it was Irina from Ukraine who taught her. When I asked Irina about the peppers, she said she learned how to make them from Maja, who was Slovenian. And all these people made the peppers just a little differently. And some of them thought the hot peppers in oil may have been from their own ancestral culinary cultures.

How American is that?

As it turns out, Steubenville, a small mill town on the Ohio River seventy miles below Youngstown—best known for being the hometown of Dean

Martin, the King of Cool—also had a large Abruzzo community that emigrated from the Italian hill towns of L'Aquila and Sulmona. Jerry Mascio, the king of polenta, was born in Sulmona and puts on the San Gennaro Festival every year on the same street where his parents started a fresh pasta business in the Georgetown neighborhood of Seattle in the 1950s. Jerry brings a wedding band, Ray Massa's EuroRhythms, all the way from Steubenville to add to the Abruzzo ambience. A couple of years back, I was at the festival helping at a booth serving porchetta sandwiches when Ray Massa himself stopped by between sets. "That's amore!" he said upon taking a healthy bite of his sandwich. When Ray lifted the bun and saw the colorful pepper rings, he bragged, "The Steubenville peppers! Cool."

At Jerry's urging, I visited the Abruzzo towns of Sulmona and L'Aquila to trace the hot peppers in oil to their source. I poked my head into a dozen restaurants while I was there and ate at a few of them. None of them served the hot peppers in oil—let alone gave them away for free. I went to the Sulmona farmers' market twice, and no one was selling anything close to the hot peppers in oil. Is it possible that this recipe originated from one or two families, and when they emigrated from these hill towns that, like the twins Romulus and Remus, one landed in the Mahoning Valley and the other in Steubenville?

Who knows? The hot peppers in oil recipe may have originated from the Abruzzo region of Italy, but now, generations later, it's an American recipe.

In Youngstown, the peppers were eaten one way.

Pasta e ceci

Natalia Lepore Hagan

Natalia grew up in Youngstown, Ohio, in an artsy family who origi-
nally emigrated from the town of Sulmona in the Abruzze region
of Italy. Natalia spent her 20's dancing and singing up a storm on
Broadway. But when the shows stopped during the pandemic, she
fashioned a new identity for herself when she started cooking up
a storm. She presently resides in Philly where she is sharing all her
culinary secrets with her Midnight Pasta classes.

Ingredients

One 1 lb. box of orecchiette
1 16 oz. can of chickpeas
A handful of rosemary sprigs
Three garlic cloves, diced
Crushed red pepper flakes
Half of a 12 oz. jar of Mama Lil's Mildly Spicy Peppers in Oil

Process

Bring a pot of heavily salted water to a boil.
Heat a deep sided Dutch oven to medium high heat. Add some
nice extra virgin olive oil, a tablespoon of Mama Lil's oil, the garlic,
two sprigs of rosemary, and red pepper flakes to your pan. Stir frequently until aromatic.
Add two cans of chickpeas with their juices to the oil and herbs and
bring to a simmer.
Once the pot of salted water is at a rolling boil add the orecchiette
and cook for half the suggested time on the package.
Strain the pasta straight from the water to the chickpeas and continue to cook the pasta in the Dutch oven on medium high heat.
Reserve the pasta water and add as needed to continue to cook
through the orecchiette.
Chop 2-4 tablespoons of Mama Lil's Peppers in Oil and stir into the
pasta.
Add olive oil and salt to taste.
Pairs well with a nice Montepulciano.

FOLLOW THE BOUNCING JAR
OF PEPPERS

BEFORE I STARTED MAMA LIL'S PEPPERS, I spent a decade of my life working as a cabbie while I stubbornly tried to break into the movies by writing screenplays. I didn't succeed with my writing (although I was an excellent cabdriver). But I learned a thing or two about the storytelling trade, such as finding the inciting incident, or when the plot is set into motion and the hero—or in my case, the fool—trips his way into the action. As I reflect on the start of my pepper journey, several incidents dating back to my adolescence helped me recognize that the hot peppers in oil I'd taken for granted my whole life were, in fact, quite special.

Once her kids left the nest, Lil would regularly send us (along with other goodies, of course) jars of her hot peppers in oil. She may have felt these jars strengthened our attachment to her, lest we never come back—much like the Youngstown restaurants gave away their peppers to its customers to make sure they came back. In 1970, my family took a road trip to drive my older sister, Bobbi, to Boston for her senior year at college. Our trunk was loaded with Bobbi's suitcases, as well as a cooler and a box of food for her dorm room. I was in the backseat between my brother and sister reading the Kurt Vonnegut novel *God Bless You, Mr. Rosewater,* which my friend Mark Wittow had loaned me for the trip, writing his name in it to make sure he got his book back. I loved Mr. Rosewater and would quote him to my quibbling family: "God damn it, you've got to be kind!"

With a day to kill, we took a side trip to Cape Cod. Lil was driving and Harry was the navigator, trying to get us to where he could feast on lobster. By then I was starting to read Vonnegut's story collection, *Welcome to the Monkey House.* In the book's introduction, Vonnegut states that he lives on Cape Cod in the town of Barnstable. Just then we passed a sign, "Barnstable 2 miles."

I let slip out, "Kurt Vonnegut lives in Barnstable,"

My mom asked, "Kurt who?"

Bobbi knew Lil all too well. "I like Vonnegut's books, but we're not going to his house." After stopping in the town square to ask for directions, we pulled into a driveway and parked next to an Alfa Romeo sports car with Eugene McCarthy bumper stickers on it.

"Now what?" I asked my mom.

Lil burst out, "I know. Give him a jar of peppers. Everybody likes those."

Bobbi protested. "That's my jar of peppers!"

Before my mother could make a move to the trunk, I walked through the tall hedges to the front door with my older brother, Bruce, tagging along behind me. As I stood at the door, I could see inside the window where an attractive middle-aged woman was standing at the kitchen sink. When I knocked, my brother ran off—the coward. I was about to join him when the woman opened the door drying her hands with a dish towel. I weakly asked her, "Is... Kurt home?"

The woman spotted my brother hiding in the hedges and started chuckling. "My husband is home. But he's taking a shower. Then he's catching a flight to a peace conference. I'm sorry."

"No, I'm sorry for bothering you." Embarrassed, I started to walk away.

She called after me, "But if you want my husband's autograph, take your book to the back porch where our friends are eating lunch. They'll have Kurt sign it for you."

I ran back to the car, grabbed the copy of *God Bless You, Mr. Rosewater,* and then bolted through the hedges toward the back porch as Lil called after me, "Did you meet the author?"

From my fifteen-year-old perspective, their two friends on the backyard patio were the spitting image of Boris Badenov and Natasha Fatale from *Rocky and Bullwinkle.* The woman was tall and wore a halter top, with hair down to her waist. Boris, bearded, plump, and smoking a cigar, even had a thick European accent when he asked, "Vat are you doing here?" When I showed him my book, he waved me away. "Go away. Kurt's not here."

"But Kurt's wife said he's taking a shower ... and you'll have him sign it for me." Boris looked perturbed but he took my book and walked into the house. I assumed he'd sign Kurt's name himself. Which was fine by me as what was I doing here anyway? It was my mom's idea, not mine. A minute later, Boris came back out and took his seat. *Hey, where's my book,* I wondered.

A man's welcoming voice called out, "Hi there. Thanks for stopping by." Walking toward me was a shaggy, dripping-wet Kurt Vonnegut Jr. in a velour pullover, corduroy pants, and unlaced tennis shoes. Kurt handed me the copy of *God Bless You, Mr. Rosewater,* shook my hand, and then with the kindest eyes told me, "Sorry I've got to leave so soon. But thank you for stopping— " Kurt looked over my shoulder and started grinning as he asked, "And who are you?" I turned, expecting to see my timid brother but, oy, it was my very untimid mother.

"I'm Lil Lev. And Kurt, I gotta tell you my kids just love your books."

With his kind eyes twinkling, Kurt told my mom, "Lil, my books aren't only for kids. They're written for adults too."

"I know that. My daughter Bobbi reads your books too. She's twenty-one years old! And she wanted you to have this." Before I could stop her, Lil handed Kurt a jar of her peppers. I grabbed for the jar, and we had a brief tug-of-war until I realized Kurt really wanted it and I let go. Kurt then twisted the lid off, fished out a pepper ring, put it into his mouth and savored it. "Lil, these are delicious! " Then he held up the jar to admire it. "And spicy! Too bad you weren't here earlier. We just ate lunch. These would have been perfect on my wife's tuna melts."

When we were back in the car, Lil couldn't wait to tell Bobbi, "He loved them. He invited us for lunch. Maybe we'll stop back at Kurt's when we pick you up in the spring? He's such a nice man, isn't he Howie?"

"Just like Mr. Rosewater said, 'God damn it, you've got to be kind.'" That's when I came upon the page in the book with Vonnegut's inscription and read it out loud to my family: "*Peace & Plenty! To Mark Wittow—Kurt Vonnegut.*" My dad laughed.

But Lil spoke the only word: "Oy!"

If my overbearing balabusta mother wasn't meshuga enough, when I was sixteen years old, I made her even more meshuga when I started hitchhiking across the country every chance I got,

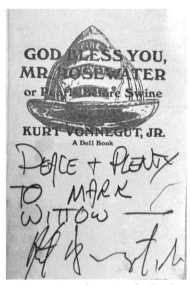

Damn it, you've got to be kind.

to visit my Uncle Dan in Seattle or my cousin Sharon in Los Angeles. So that Lil couldn't say no, I used excuses like I was making a road movie or practicing my photography. On one trip Lil dropped me off at the freeway entrance and handed me a heavy double-layered paper bag. With a tear in her eye, she told me, "If you're still hungry later I put something extra in your backpack." Twelve hours later, I was rolling out my sleeping bag in Wisconsin below a freeway underpass. By then I'd polished off six pastrami sandwiches, two cans of Coke, a bag of potato chips, and a Snickers bar. But I was still hungry. I went through my backpack hoping to find my mom's chocolate chip cookies. But I found a small loaf of bread and a jar of peppers. I didn't open it.

Twenty hours later, my last ride talked me into hopping a freight train in Billings, Montana. A dozen sketchy men were milling about in an encampment near the tracks. I made friends with a hippie going in the opposite direction who gave me pointers about which of these characters I should avoid, "Some of these dudes would throw you off the train just to steal a dollar from you." Before we crawled into our sleeping bags, I opened that jar of peppers and broke bread with him. Next thing I knew, the hippie was shaking me awake and a minute later I was climbing into an empty boxcar. It was noisy as hell but when I finally fell back to sleep, I didn't awaken until the sun was shining on my face. Then, as we slowly glided through glistening mountains, I experienced the pure joy of taking a leak out the open boxcar door.

"Hey, you!" a voice shouted over the clanging of the train. I jumped in fright. Two dirt-encrusted thirty-year-old men were staring at me like scavengers who'd encountered weak prey. "We're hungry," one hobo lamented. The other snarled, "And we're *dead* broke."

Not the adjective I wanted to hear. And I didn't want them to even think I had a wallet. "I do have some food, and you're welcome to it," I said, unzipping my backpack. Oy. The lid had wriggled loose from the jar I opened last night, and all the peppers and oil had spilled out into my backpack. "I'm so sorry," I said, showing them the oily mess of peppers in my pack. One of the hobos thrust his filthy fingers inside, grabbed a handful of peppers and bread, and jammed it into his mouth. As he chewed it, oil mixed with dirt and dust ran down his face. The other hobo watched intently. Was it edible? The hobo swallowed and burst out, "They're good!" Then his friend reached in and grabbed a fistful of peppers and stuffed it into his mouth. "They ARE good!" Those two hobos took turns sopping up every drop of oil with the bread. Then to thank me, as if I weren't dirty enough, insisted I shake their oily hands.

Then it all went black. A hobo lamented, "Fuck. The tunnel for the Continental Divide!"

Being in that tunnel was scary as hell but after a few minutes I was finally able to relax. Until we hit a bump of such force that it threw me to the steel floor. Dazed, I stood back up and braced myself, only to have the next bump hurl me to the back of the boxcar. I thought for sure the train would derail and so did the hobos as I heard screams of terror coming from somewhere. Then the train came to a long, screeching stop and didn't budge for at least ten eerie minutes. When we started moving again, we were going backward! Then forward, then backward, then forward again, punctuated by earth-rattling bumps and more screams from the hobos. When we eventually emerged into the light, having traveled a mere half mile in over an hour, the hobos were right next to me clinging to each other in a tight embrace. One of them opened his eyes and smiled when he saw me. "I was scared! So, I focused on that nice spicy flavor on the back of my throat. Man, oh man, I was wishing there were more!"

I suppose the hobos changing their tune toward me after tasting Lil's peppers is memorable enough to call it an inciting incident. But in hindsight, I'd also like to suggest that the most overused cliché in the English language, *the light at the end of the tunnel,* might be the best metaphor for the worst experience I ever had with Mama Lil's. It's probably the same reason why when folks ask me for advice on starting a gourmet food business, I usually tell them that unless they have a lifetime supply of stubborn stick-to-itiveness in their disposition to weather the terrifying uncertainty that spans the continental divide between success and failure, they should NOT start a gourmet food business. As all too many restaurateurs will be sure to tell you, some tunnels are just drainpipes that lead down into the sewer.

When I went off to study photography at Hampshire College in Amherst, Massachusetts, sure enough, Lil sent me care packages that always included a jar of peppers. When I shared the peppers with my dormmates, the gal who liked them most became my girlfriend. As for my education, I tried to get into an advanced photography class, but unfortunately, only one spot was available for the two of us waiting to be interviewed by the instructor. I was not the one chosen. So, blame it on that other guy, Ken Burns, that I gave up on becoming the next Henri Cartier-Bresson, dropped out of college then moved back to Youngstown.

After eight months of pounding nails for my dad, I realized carpentry wasn't my calling either. But I rediscovered the hot peppers in oil at all those wonderful Italian restaurants while I was there. After saving up $2,000, I transferred to the University of Washington where my uncle Dan Lev taught politics. A thousand miles into the Amtrak ride to Seattle I woke up to an empty train. Where was everybody? In the bar of course. When I opened the jar of peppers my mother had given me, I instantly made friends with fun-loving peoplewho all had the same destination: Reno, Nevada.

"Cal Neva's got great slots. Play a roll of quarters and see where it goes." College didn't start for two weeks, and there'd be another train in twenty-four hours, so I followed my friends inside the Cal Neva casino. And never saw them again. But they were right about the slot machines—in no time, one roll of quarters turned into ten rolls. Then twenty rolls. And when I moved to the blackjack table, I turned those quarters into four hundred silver dollars!

Then blame it on old-fashioned bad luck. Or blame it on my waitress's cleavage or the whiskey sours she kept bringing me, because at one point the tables turned. I noticed a security guard watching over me just in case I went berserk. Which was a distinct possibility, as I'd lost $1,000 of my hard-earned money by making silly bets to try and win all my money back. And I still had ten hours before the next train out of Reno! With my backpack on my weary shoulders, I moped around Reno lashing at myself for being that fool who soon parted with his money. I sat in the train station to wait out the last hour, misery mounting with every tick of the station clock. Then I heard myself say out loud, "I got $1,000 left. If I lose it, it can't feel any worse than this!"

In a trance-like state, I walked back to Club Cal Neva, cashed in all my travelers checks for ten $100 chips, then took a seat at an empty maximum-bet blackjack table. The dealer was in her mid-fifties, about my mom's age.

When she saw desperate me fighting back tears as I slid my ten $100 chips toward her, she asked with such genuine maternal concern, "You okay, hon?"

"I worked so hard for the money I lost. I've got to win it back!" As I was telling her this, I noticed another security guard standing behind me. The dealer looked me in the eye.

"Hon, sometimes the best thing is to cut your losses. Trust me. I've been at this a while." I looked in her eyes, and I trusted her. I slid my $1,000 bet off the table and in its place put down the minimum bet of two silver dollars. The dealer nodded; I'd done the right thing. Then she dealt me…

A jack of clubs in the hole. Then face up, an ace of spades. Blackjack!

Whatever Lady Luck looks like, it was not my dealer. She wouldn't even look at me. The only thing worse than losing my money was what just happened when I could've won it all back, plus $500 more! There was nothing for me to do or say but cash in my $1,003 of chips and run for the train before I had to spend twenty-four more hours in Reno.

I'm telling this story because I've always heard that entrepreneurs have a knack for trusting their gut instincts and making intuitive but well-educated guesses. But my tendency is to be too trusting, and to guess wrong. And when I second-guess myself, I'm usually doubly wrong. I've known this about myself from playing cards with my mom: I've always had a propensity for wishful thinking by making silly bets and taking foolish risks. A character flaw that's gotten my business into trouble time and time again, as you'll soon see.

Perhaps my most impressive accomplishment during my next foray in college besides watching nearly a thousand classic movies, was revealed on a Friday afternoon when I was running late for my campus job and got pulled over by a policeman for making a California stop. I was sitting in the back-seat of the cop car when the scratchy police radio announced, "Mr. Lev has a warrant for his arrest. Get this, for ninety-nine unpaid parking tickets." The cop whistled. "Ninety-nine parkers? Judgment Day!"

I knew I had lots of parkers but not that many. My father once accused me of being a scofflaw and maybe he was right. I had little respect for rules, especially when no parking spots were available. I spent the weekend in jail and on Monday was ordered to pay $4,000. I didn't pay it. Instead, I dropped out of college again, then found a job as a deckhand on a Mississippi River tugboat where I'd figured I have the time to catch up on my reading and memorize Keats' great odes.

Considering that I'd been living with ten southern men and a very off-limits thirty-year-old Cajun chef named Verna, there's a lot I could say about my year on the river. But I'll limit it to when a supply boat pulled alongside us while I was chipping paint on the stern, and was handed the mail. Which included a box. For me.

"Mom, how'd you find me in Natchez, Mississippi?"

I knew Verna was a fan of spicy foods, so that night after I mopped the galley floor, the two of us polished off one of those jars of peppers as we told funny stories about our moms. But when Captain Floyd Fontenot walked in and saw us flirting, he slammed the galley door on the way out. I loved reading Mark Twain while going up and down the river, and Verna's gumbo had become my favorite food, but when the captain threatened to cut my heart out the next day, I realized Life on the Mississippi was probably not for me, either. I jumped ship in St. Louis, flew back to Seattle, and crashed at my uncle Dan's house.

That's when I met Linda who lived in a bungalow right above the freeway on lower Capitol Hill. Linda of course loved the peppers and when my mom sent more jars to her place and not my uncle's, she asked me to move in with her. (Now that I think about it Lil's peppers had always been a form of romantic currency for me.) Even though the freeway was noisy, our place had a great view of the Space Needle and the Olympic Mountains. With binoculars from my front porch I could see if my cab was in the taxi lot two miles away on Dexter Avenue. That view is now long gone obscured by towering skyscrapers.

Now I can't entirely blame my silly $500 bet on the Cleveland Indians as to why Linda married the other guy four years later, but it didn't help when I told her, "I love the Indians so much that when they lose, I wanna lose with them." Neither did coming home broke for the second time after losing my night's wages at the cab lot poker game. The deciding factor was when Linda had to bail me out of jail for those ninety-nine parkers I never paid off.

When my sister, Bobbi, was diagnosed with cancer in 1985, I sublet what was now my rental home so I could be near her. Initially, I crashed at the New York City Bowery loft of my college buddy Patrick Lango, who like me was an aspiring screenwriter, but made his living naming lipsticks for an advertising firm. My only payment to Pat was three jars of Lil's peppers that he put in his pantry. At a dinner party, I met his friends, the budding screenwriter Tony Gilroy (of later *Bourne* fame) and his wife, Susan, an actress. Upon tasting the peppers, Susan told me, "You should start a business with these peppers." I assumed Susan was trying to disincline me from my screenwriting ambitions, as heck, her uber-talented husband was still tending bar.

I told Susan, "I have no idea how to make the peppers. Or how to run a business."

Perhaps Susan had acted in *Medea* in college because when she warned me, "Then learn how. If you don't do it, someone else will!" She sounded like the Oracle of Delphi.

Fortune tellers!

My sister Bobbi really was a fortune teller. For a living, she interpreted astrology charts and read tarot cards for scores of clients who relied on her advice. When I'd visit her on weekends, she'd go over my astrology chart and

Bobbi in 1985.

have me throw the tarot. Bobbi knew I was struggling with choosing a calling, so when the Fool card kept appearing, she'd assuage my concerns by assuring me, "The Fool means new beginnings."

"Aren't I getting old for new beginnings?" I asked her, only to feel horrible for having said that. I had my whole life ahead of me. Bobbi, most likely not. As her illness progressed, I moved into Bobbi's apartment in Cambridge to be her caregiver. Lil, who spelled me at times, brought a case of peppers that she enjoyed giving to Bobbi's friends when they visited her.

But Bobbi was not dying in peace. She was angry that her life was being cut short and was clinging to it by the thinnest of threads and would not let go. A friend of hers mentioned that she knew Ram Dass, who lived in the neighborhood, and perhaps he could come by to have a chat with Bobbi. Ram Dass, back when he was Richard Alpert, had researched psychedelics with Timothy Leary at Harvard. After traveling to India in the late 1960s, Alpert reinvented himself as Baba Ram Dass, one of the first mindfulness gurus, when he authored his bestselling book Be Here Now. Amid the AIDS crisis of the 1980s, Ram Dass dedicated himself to the Dying Project by helping teach folks like Bobbi—too young to die—how to find peace and let go.

When I told Bobbi that Baba Ram Dass is coming by, she was as excited as a kid who'd been told that the real Santa Claus would be sliding down the chimney. When I answered the door, Ram Dass even looked like Santa, his broad smile beaming through his full gray-white beard. When I led him into Bobbi's room and Ram Dass kissed her hand, it was as if he had given Bobbi a ticket to the afterlife. She couldn't wait for the ride to begin. As he held her hand, the great spiritual master told her a story about being at his mother Gertrude's memorial service.

"I saw my mom looking down at me from the roof beams of the temple. And she told me, we will see each other again." As Bobbi listened intently, her smile began to fade. But Ram Dass, absorbed in telling his story, was inattentive to her as his voice took on a mysterious tone. "Two years later, on the streets of Calcutta, a woman was walking toward me. I just knew…" and he turned to look directly in Bobbi's eyes and whispered, "She was my mother!"

Bobbi's face contorted with anguish. "You mean I'm going see my mother… again?"

As I walked Ram Dass to the door, he asked me, "Did I say something wrong?"

To assuage his bruised magisterial ego, I told him, "Unlike your mom Gertrude, Lil is no angel." Then I went to the kitchen and grabbed the last jar we had of Lil's peppers. When I presented it to Ram Dass, he bowed graciously, then admired the jar of colorful peppers.

"This is beautiful. And it looks delicious. Did you make these?"

"No, my mom made it."

Ram Dass handed the jar back. "Give it to someone more deserving."

After Bobbi died (peacefully, I believe), I inherited her Ford Pinto and drove to Ohio, stopping on the way at Pat Lango's family farm near Buffalo, New York. When I stepped into Pat's kitchen with that jar of peppers, he was fussing over a cast-iron pot, the source of a mouth-watering aroma coming into being. "After we finish the chores in eight hours," Pat proclaimed, "this nine-pound leg of lamb will be the most delicious piece of meat you'll have ever eaten in your life." Then he took the jar of peppers from me and set it on the dining room table. "And your mom's peppers might be perfect with it."

As we crisscrossed his farm for eight hours—milking cows, sweeping manure, bailing hay—Pat made pit stops to tend to that lamb, at one point, cooing, "It's now caramelizing in its fats!" When we finally sat down and deliriously dug into that succulent meat there was simply no stopping us. Granted, we'd worked hard and hadn't eaten all day, but as long as we had peppers to eat with the lamb, we ate every last morsel of it.

On the sublime drive along the Allegheny River back to my parents, I thought about those nine pounds of lamb we devoured. In Youngstown, the hot peppers in oil were eaten one way—as an appetizer served on bread. But as my friend and I had just experienced, it was their symbiotic relationship with other foods that made the hot peppers in oil truly remarkable. That slow-cooked lamb was no doubt delicious, but the peppers' mellow spiciness and their silky, savory oil made it even much more so. And although I didn't know it then, the trace of the acidic vinegar in the pickled peppers was helping break down the lamb so it was easier to digest in our bellies.

Stepping into Lil's kitchen, I saw that, in addition to chicken and dumplings bubbling on the stove and some freshly made eggplant salata, my father had grilled some tenderloin steaks. I urged my parents to try the peppers as a condiment with the steak. From then on, a jar of peppers came to the table every time my parents ate meat. While packing to go back to Seattle, I found a stash of my mother's jars in the basement pantry. When Lil caught me sneaking three jars into my suitcase, she acted as if I'd wounded her. "If you only knew how much work it takes to make them…oh, just take them. Saves me the trouble of mailing them to you."

In 1986, Seattle's economy was but a fraction of what it is today. Sure, Microsoft was already manufacturing millionaires, but Starbucks had only six or seven stores. I assume Bezos was still in college. Back then, it seemed Seattle had an inferiority complex compared to other large West Coast cities like LA or San Francisco, where serious people went to make things really happen. Yet Seattle's regional identity was expressing itself in all the rock clubs that were sprouting around town. Local television commercials appealed to this generation: "You got roommates, a part-time job, you're in two bands. You need a phone line to fit your lifestyle."

My new girlfriend, Maggie, had an interesting lifestyle. She was an actress who was in a rock band. But back then, who wasn't in a band in Seattle or Portland, or at least had a partner who was? My new next-door neighbor, Chris, even had a band who practiced in his house. Because of the constant noise from the freeway below us, his band could get away with practicing any time of the day or night. But I just couldn't get into their heavy metal vibe. On hot days, they'd open the windows, but if I was trying to concentrate on writing a screenplay, I'd go over and shut them. But they were nice guys who would always apologize when I did.

On the gorgeous summer solstice evening of 1987, my new friend, Jeffrey—a frenetic hedonist whose Jewfro gave him the look of a mad scientist—came by when I was watching the sunset from my porch while my neighbor's band was jamming with the windows wide open. Speaking of wide-open windows, Jeffrey pulled out a baggie and said, "It's such a lovely evening, why don't we eat some of these." He started nibbling on some dried mushrooms that made him curl his nose. "I forgot how bitter these are." I went into the kitchen and along with a couple of beers I brought out one of the two jars I had of my mom's peppers.

I told Jeffrey, "Try those with these."

Upon forking some peppers in his mouth, Jeffrey proclaimed, "These peppers would make shit taste good." As we watched the streaming trails of freeway lights, it seemed like the sun would never go down. All this time, Jeffrey kept snacking out of the baggie and the jar of peppers and at one point enthusiastically announced, "They're making my throat have an orgasm!" Soon Jeffrey—with some help from me—was into my mom's second jar. And whoops, just like that nine pounds of lamb, as long as we had peppers to eat with them, we'd eaten the whole baggie of magic mushrooms!

The loud music from next door shifted, settling into a dark, seductive groove with heavy wailing vocals that seemed to pull the sun below the jagged ridge of the Olympic Mountains. The sky burst into dying orange flames. The Space Needle started glowing in all its phallic glory. And below us the cosmic flow of red and white freeway lights and hiss of traffic was totally in sync with the music blaring next door. So much loud energy was, strangely, so peaceful.

Suddenly, the peace was punctured by an ambulance with its spinning red lights weaving around cars on the freeway. Its piercing siren got louder and louder as it raced towards us. Or was it the rock and roll scream roaring out of my neighbor's throat that harmonized with the siren in a soaring crescendo that lasted the length of, well, an orgasm. The ambulance raced away, and the siren and my neighbor's scream trailed off.

Jeffrey marveled, "Wow! That was synchronicity incarnate!" Then Jeffrey shrugged the psychedelic miracle off and stuck his fork back in the jar. When his fork came out empty, Jeffrey demanded, "We need more peppers."

"You ate my last two jars! My mom won't send me more peppers until October, earliest."

"Don't tell me that! Our concert isn't over, our trip isn't over, and I don't want this sensation in my throat to be over yet, either! Hey, you know how to make these, right?"

"Nope, I've never made them before." I told Jeffrey.

"Then we gotta learn how…in fact, we should start a business making these peppers," Jeffrey implored.

This notion of starting a business based on Lil's pepper recipe was becoming a running theme, so I asked Jeffrey, who was a contractor like my dad, "How do you start a business?"

"You just start it. Like you start a rock band. Get some musicians together, start jamming. Speaking of which, your neighbor's band is fuckin' awesome! Do they even have a name?"

Yep. That loud, gorgeous solstice evening of 1987 is when the seeds finally germinated in my brain that I really should start a business based on this pepper recipe that I'd been eating my whole life. And considering I'd been listening to my neighbor's band practice nonstop for over a year now, it was also the night I realized that Soundgarden kicked butt!

Mama Lil's Roast Chicken

Jeffrey Baron

Jeffrey is quite the foodie. At his home, he cures meat and fish and ferments veggies. And to this day he still pickles peppers with me.

Serves 4

1 organic, never-frozen (3- to 4-pound) chicken

½ of a 12-ounce jar Mama Lil's Peppers, oil reserved*

Coarse kosher salt and freshly ground black pepper

8 garlic cloves, unpeeled

5 sprigs thyme, plus ½ teaspoon chopped leaves

3 sprigs oregano, plus ½ teaspoon chopped leaves

8 small potatoes, halved

3 large yellow onions, quartered

Preheat the oven to 425°F.

Rub 2 teaspoons of the Mama Lil's oil on the outside of the chicken, followed by 1 teaspoon of salt. Place the garlic and the thyme and oregano springs inside the chicken cavity, followed by 1/8 teaspoon black pepper, 1/8 teaspoon salt, and 2 teaspoons Mama Lil's pepper oil. Sprinkle ¼ teaspoon salt and ¼ teaspoon black pepper on the outside of the bird.

Coat the inside of a roasting pan with some more Mama Lil's pepper oil. Spread 2 tablespoons of Mama Lil's Peppers evenly around the pan. Place the chicken in the pan.

In a large bowl, combine the potatoes and onions with 2 tablespoons Mama Lil's pepper oil and toss to coat lightly. Arrange the potatoes, onions, and garlic cloves in the pan around the chicken. Heap 4 more tablespoons of peppers (6 ounces in all) on top of this potato con- coction.

In a small bowl, combine the chopped thyme, chopped oregano, ¼ teaspoon black pepper, and ½ teaspoon salt. Sprinkle this mixture over the chicken, potatoes, and Mama Lil's Peppers.

Roast the chicken until a meat thermometer—inserted into the thick- est part of the chicken—reads 160°F, about 45 minutes or 1 hour, and the skin has nicely browned. Turn off the heat and let the chicken sit in the oven for about 10 minutes. Take it out of the oven, let it rest for 5 minutes. When you cut up the chicken, capture the juices, and deglaze the pan with them and stir, scraping up the brown bits. Pour this gravy over the chicken, potatoes, and onions, or serve alongside. You should have a juicy, fragrant bird with great skin.

WHERE NOT TO PICKLE PEPPERS

LATER THAT SUMMER OF 1987, AN ARTICLE RAN in the Sunday edition of the *Seattle Times* about a U-pick farm in the Yakima Valley called Krueger Pepper Gardens. Folks from all over the Pacific Northwest would make pilgrimages to their farm to pick from the hundred different varieties of chile peppers grown there. I called my mom to ask her what variety of pepper she used, how she cut them, and would she write down her recipe for me. I received an envelope a week later with a baggie of pepper rings, but her handwritten recipe got soggy from the peppers and was illegible.

Five of us and three dogs squeezed into Maggie's VW van to drive over the mountains to pick peppers. The affable, ruddy-faced farmer, Gayle Krueger, was at his farmstand serving slices of a Jerusalem melon that was so juicy it hydrated us all afternoon. Our dogs happily ran around the field as we picked two hundred pounds of the most colorful and firm Hungarian goathorn peppers I'd ever seen. We then piled back in the van, where the dogs slept the whole way home on top of four burlap bags, each stuffed with fifty pounds of peppers.

By the time I drove my cab to Jeffrey's place where we were going to do all the pickling and canning, my friends had begun slicing the peppers without me—using a Cuisinart. I was peeved. "Why'd you use a Cuisinart? The pepper rings are sliced too thin!" When I looked more closely, I became even more incensed. "And you didn't scoop out the seeds with a butter knife like you were supposed to."

A thin, intense man whom I'd never met before snapped at me, "I don't see Travis Bickle scooping out seeds with a fuckin' butter knife." As it turns out, this man, Brad, was a chef at the Pink Door restaurant where a friend of ours was a bartender. He bragged that he was a master at canning and had been enlisted to help us. But Brad had no more of an idea what he was doing than the rest of us. We hadn't even figured out where we were going to pickle the peppers yet. Then Brad suggested, "People make wine in bathtubs. Pickle the peppers in the tub."

Jeffrey seconded the idea, and our two hundred pounds of too thinly sliced peppers with too many seeds went into the tub that we filled with a salty vinegar solution to pickle overnight. I emphasized to my partners that according to Lil, draining the peppers was the most crucial step in making the peppers taste right. Jeffrey was instructed to pull the plug at 5 a.m. so they could drain for at least twelve full hours before we packed them into jars.

When I arrived back at Jeffrey's the next day after my cab shift, Brad was filling jars with peppers, then turning the jar over to drain the vinegar out. Meaning: The vinegar had not drained at all! "You guys didn't drain the fuckin' vinegar out!" I screamed at Brad.

Jeffrey walked in. "If you wanna see what the fuckin' vinegar took out, follow me."

A layer of the bathtub's enamel had peeled off, thanks to the corrosiveness of the salty pickling brine. When Brad saw the black scars on the tub, he pulled off his prep gloves like a surgeon whose patient had flatlined on him, then split. Not ready to admit defeat, Jeffery and I drained the peppers with a salad spinner. Following Lil's instructions, we sterilized the jars and lids in boiling water. Then we seasoned the peppers with garlic and oregano, packed them into jars, filled them with oil, screwed on the lids, then hoped for the best.

A day later, we had reason to be hopeful. Most of the lids on the one hundred and twenty jars that covered every surface of Jeffrey's kitchen had been sucked in and were sealed. Jeffrey held up a jar to the light to admire the vibrantly colorful pepper rings then opened the jar and forked some peppers into his mouth. "They're not bad…ouch!" Digging into his mouth, he pulled out a small white particle, examined it on his finger.

"Is it a pepper seed?" I asked. "Or garlic?"

"No!" Jeffrey lamented. "It's fuckin' fleck of bathtub enamel!" Upon inspecting more jars and seeing more white flecks, we concluded the best move was *out of sight, out of mind,* and we unloaded them at the dump. It cost about a buck a jar to throw them away.

I learned a good lesson, though. Vinegar is an acid; the technical term for pickling is *acidification.* And when you add salt, it gets even stronger. Vinegar is potent and excellent for cleaning toilets and tubs. But don't let it sit overnight in them. Over the course of this book, I'm going to teach you how to make Lil's peppers. And the first thing to do is buy a pickling crock.

So much for my first stab at starting a pepper business. But lo and behold, a screenplay I'd written, called *A Midsummer Night's Game,* about a cabbie who discovers he has the power to determine the outcomes of the Cleveland Indians games—now where would I come up with a silly idea like that?—garnered attention from a producer who'd made a film with Tom Hanks. Hanks was a fan of the Cleveland Indians and of Shakespeare. Maybe he'd like my movie idea. The producer suggested that I should "come down to L.A. and do lunch."

My childhood friend Jonny Katz, who was by then living in Los Angeles, had read my screenplay and wanted to talk about it with me before my meeting. I'd just read Jonny's story, "The Extraction of the Stone," which gave the impression of revealing kabbalistic mysteries, so I was embarrassed to discuss my trivial screenplay with him. But Jonny liked my script and was encouraging. "Our stories have similarities. Both are about fools. And your fool is based on the greatest fool of them all, Bottom from *Midsummer Night's Dream*. And this is what the last line of your screenplay should be, 'Just wait until next year. They'll be right back on the bottom.'"

Lunch with the producer went well—and she loved Jonny's idea for the last line. I came back to Seattle sky-high with expectations an option for $20,000 would soon be in my mailbox.

NOT!

I didn't have to wait a year to land right back on the bottom. When the option arrived two weeks later, the check wasn't for $20,000—it was for $20. When I called the producer, she told me, "This will be a hard sell. A baseball movie called *Major League* about the Cleveland Indians is in pre-production. And then there's another baseball movie coming out called *Field of Dreams*. I'm afraid you've been beaten to the punch."

So much for my Hollywood dreams coming true. To the contrary, my life spiraled into a cascading run of bad luck. My rock-and-roll girlfriend married her drummer. My dog died. The house I'd rented for the last eight years was torn down and replaced by twenty luxury condos, all with beautiful views. Even though I couldn't afford it, I started looking to buy a house. Not that I want to compare being a first-time home buyer with starting a gourmet food business, but in both instances, I employed some magic to make it happen. A smoke-and-mirrors kind of magic.

In 1989, Seattle home prices were a fraction of what they are now, but I had no income to show the bank, as I had never kept trip sheets as a cabbie. Instead, I filled out my tax forms with the numbers my loan officer told me to, and my friend who was a manager at Yellow Cab vouched for me. While waiting for the bank to approve my loan, which unsurprisingly took forever, I sublet a room a couple of doors down from the house I was trying to buy.

Luckily for me, the seller, a tall, handsome ninety-year-old black man named Reverend Franklin James, wasn't in a hurry to move out. During this time the Reverend often invited me over for a lunch of rice, collard greens, and fried chicken. Reverend James loved to tell stories about his family, his hunting dogs, and his faith where he'd inevitably quote from the Old Testament, which he assumed because I was Jewish, I was more acquainted with than I was.

Considering the Reverend's age, he was in excellent shape. Which was surprising, due to his diet. Inside his kitchen next to his bedroom door were three tall towers of empty Crisco cans stacked within one another, reaching just below the ten-foot ceiling. The Reverend fried *a lot* of chicken. For one lunch, I brought him a jar of my mother's peppers. I debated whether I should give it to him, as I was down to my last jar and I hated to waste it on someone who might not appreciate it. The next time I saw him, he just couldn't wait to tell me, "I *love* your mom's peppers. I eat them with my eggs almost every morning. Sparingly, of course."

When I told the Reverend I intended to turn his house into a duplex so I could afford to live there, he started preaching to me about the spiritual value of hard work and even bragged about the fifty postholes he had recently dug around his Pentecostal church. "Are you a hard worker, Howard?" Then he stared me in the eye and sternly asked, "Why aren't you married? Why no children?" He winked at me. "Maybe this house will bring you luck with that."

I wanted to believe this holy man's house *would* bring me luck, but we had different ideas of what luck was. Selling a screenplay would be a stroke of luck for me. A more likely miracle would be the Cleveland Indians winning the World Series. Finally, after the interest rates rose a couple of points, the bank loan was set to go through. All I needed was to have the Reverend sign the final paperwork, get the key from him, and then the house would be mine.

When the big day came, the door was open, so I walked right into the kitchen looking for the Reverend. He wasn't there, so I knocked on his bedroom door off the kitchen. As I stood there, I noticed that one of the towers of Crisco cans had mysteriously grown taller and now turned the ceiling's corner. I knocked again. Getting no response, I opened the door.

The Reverend was lying on his back in bed, arms folded across his chest, with his old cat Goldie lying on his stomach. As I entered, I was hoping the Reverend would sense my presence and wake up. When he didn't, I whispered into his ear, "Reverend James. It's Howard. I'm here to get the key." Still no response, so I nudged him. Neither the Reverend nor his cat moved. I nervously backed out of his room into the kitchen and bumped into a stack of Crisco cans. Fumbling to catch them, I lost my balance, and *tim-ber,* all three towers toppled down with me. You'd think the racket of one hundred cans crashing would've woken the dead. But neither the Reverend nor his cat stirred. That grease *had* done him in and at the worst moment!

The Reverend's granddaughter came running up from the basement, expecting the worst. When she saw me on my knees with those cans rolling around, she was laughing. "You alright?"

"I'm okay. But I couldn't wake your granddaddy. Is he okay?"

Her giggle subsided into a warm smile. "My granddaddy probably got his hearing aids out. He's been praying in his room all morning long, blessing this house for you, Howard." Right on cue, Reverend James walked into the kitchen with his cat Goldie in his arms. When he saw me on the floor amidst those cans, he started chuckling, too.

"Howard, you brought down my towers of Jericho!"

"I thought I was Samson pulling down the pillars of the temple."

The day after the Reverend moved out, I started converting the house into a duplex. I was living in the basement, which was inundated with mice. I assume his cat Goldie must've been blessing the house for me too, as I had just begun interviewing potential house cats when a young stray found her way through my basement window and took care of those mice in no time. Until she went blind seventeen years later, Marion leapt through that window down into my basement office not only to keep me company, but also to keep the rodents away. Which is a good thing if you're in the food business.

Reverend James and his cat Goldie, and my cat, Marion.

Reverend James stopped by three months later to check on my remodel. I'd removed the interior walls on the second floor, so as he climbed the familiar winding stairway, sunlight was pouring in where it never had before. When he reached the step where the sun washed over his face, he looked down at me and said, "I know I blessed this house, but I didn't think I blessed it this good. That's the Lord's truth."

To turn around the phrase, the house I bought from Reverend James is not the house that Mama Lil's built, but rather, it's the house that helped me build Mama Lil's. For twenty years, I had an office in its basement where I stored enough cases of peppers in the crawl space to make deliveries without driving to the warehouse first, saving me hundreds of hours a year. And for better or worse, when I needed money to help me grow my business, I borrowed, sometimes heavily, against my house that Reverend James blessed.

In the spring of 1992, when I finally finished the remodel on my home, Lil told me she's coming out to teach me how to make the important stuff. And after hearing about our bathtub fiasco, she was also determined to show me how *she* made the peppers. When I picked Lil up from the airport, she had a large, heavy suitcase, and her purse felt like it had a bowling ball in it. When she squeezed into my 1966 Volvo 122 wagon and I stretched the manual seatbelt across her chest, she was scowling until we got to my home. But within seconds of being in my kitchen, Lil had an apron on and was inspecting the chicken, carrots, onions, and celery I had on hand.

Lil shrieked, "Oy! Where's the turnips?!"

"Mom, turnips weren't on your list."

"Of course they were. You can't make chicken soup without turnips. Go back to the store and get us two of them." I was out the door when another "Oy!" stopped me in my tracks. Magician-like, Lil pulled two softball-size turnips from her purse. After getting the chicken soup going, and charring eggplant over the burners of my gas stove, she showed me how she removed the seeds from the peppers with a serrated butter knife and sliced them into rings that went into a pickling crock, which we poured a vinegar-salt solution over. The next morning, we drained the pickled peppers in colanders. Before bed, we added garlic and oregano to them, then packed the peppers into three jars and filled them with oil.

"Mom, I was told you have to boil the jars of peppers for twenty minutes."

Lil shook her head confidently as she twisted on the lids with her aging fingers. "They're pickled, so you don't have to. All I do is sterilize the jars— and I've never had one spoil on me. We have just enough time to make salata." Then she clamped the meat grinder to my counter.

"Mom, my Cuisinart might not be good for the peppers, but it should be perfect for salata."

"No, the raw peppers and roasted eggplant," Lil said adamantly, "must be fed through the grinder at the same time for their flavors to blend." After making the salata, she cleaned the four pieces of the grinder, rubbed them with vegetable oil, reassembled it then wrapped it in a towel and put it in her suitcase. When she came out of the bedroom all packed and ready to go, she presented me with a housewarming gift: her own 1975 edition of *Joy of Cooking*. On the way to the airport, I realized that she'd forgotten to show me how to make chicken and dumplings. "Next time," my mom said, tugging on her seatbelt, "maybe you'll have a better car so you can take me shopping. I'll teach you to make chicken and dumplings then."

Portland Avocado Toast

Reverend Cynthia Lena Breen

I first met Lil Lev in 1990 at my sister's Pink Door restaurant in the Pike Place Market, which now that I think about it, may have been where I met her son. I introduced her to folks that day as Mama Lil even though Mama Lil's Peppers was two years away from being born. Over a long lunch Lil and I talked about food, our offspring and the many blessings family can bring. I appreciated her immensely as she was spicy, colorful and great fun. The peppers do her justice.

Ever since we made that first batch at the church kitchen, Mama Lil's Peppers in Oil have been a staple for my family, and we have found countless ways to spice up our favorite family recipes with them. However, after enjoying the peppers for 32 years, I found that a simple way of eating them is best. Below is a breakfast we eat regularly as the peppers do go great with eggs!

Ingredients

1 large slice of sourdough bread (preferably homemade)
1 clove of garlic
½ ripe avocado
Squeeze of lemon juice
Salt and pepper to taste
1 egg
2 slices of cooked bacon (optional)
2 tablespoons of Mama Lil's Peppers, drained.

Making the toast

Toast bread in the oven, when done rub garlic on bread while still warm.
Cook egg any style of your liking, fried with a runny yolk is best.
While the egg is cooking, mash up avocado, add lemon juice and season with salt and pepper. Layer the avocado on the toast,(add bacon if using) add the layer of egg. Then add a few of the pepper rings on top, and you are ready to eat.
Serve with tea or coffee of your choice. Or on Sundays, enjoy it with some champagne.

STARTING OUT—REALLY, THIS TIME

IN 1992, A UNITARIAN MINISTER FRIEND of mine named Cynthia married Nick, who'd been living the last twenty-five years in Canada. In coming back to the States, Nick was starting anew and needed a job. I was thirty-seven years old and by now my cabbie/screenwriter schtick was wearing thin. Since you've got to start somewhere, the three of us hatched the idea of packing a few hundred jars of Lil's pepper recipe in the Unitarian church's commercially licensed kitchen.

On a hot Labor Day weekend, the five of us—me, Cynthia, her daughter, Nick, and his two sons—drove to Krueger's farm to pick Hungarian goathorn peppers. What Cynthia's daughter Leah remembers most about that day, was two things: "It was hot! And on the way home with my new brothers, I smoked pot for the first time as we listened to Pearl Jam's first album over and over." Yep, that was 1992.

I initially tried to talk Nick into slicing the peppers by hand, but he told me, "It's the twentieth century. We're using a Cuisinart." It was 2 a.m. before we got the peppers—once again too thinly sliced—into the pickling brine. The next morning, we were back in the church kitchen to drain the peppers in cheesecloth. Ten hours later, with the pressure of an incoming wedding party upon us, we packed thirty-three cases of jars and then pasteurized the jars for twenty-one minutes in boiling water. Nick's idea. As far as I was concerned, we didn't need to pasteurize the jars.

While loading the cases of still warm jars into my station wagon Nick suggested, "Let's call them, 'Mama Lil's Hungarian Hots.'"

"Really?" I said skeptically. "I've never even called my mom Mama."

Cynthia seconded the idea. "Lil's gonna love being Mama Lil."

My extremely handy artist friend, Don Blevins, helped me convert the crawl space at the bottom of my basement steps into a closet to store all these cases. While putting down plywood over the dirt floor, I discovered two cases of jars of very unappetizing peaches. I assumed they were Reverend James's and might have been there for twenty years. The dust suggested longer.

Don laughed. "I hope these jars don't foreshadow the fate of *your* jars."

I reminded Don, "The Reverend blessed my house, he didn't curse it."

First pack, Unitarian Church, 1992.   *First label.*

Don designed the first label for Mama Lil's Hungarian Hots, and he even helped me hand-cut and paste them onto the jars. When all was tabulated, those thirty-three cases cost us $1,400 to make, or $4 per jar. And we didn't need to pay for the use of the church kitchen.

What allowed me to go forward with my business was that other sage advice for artists and other dreamers: "Don't quit your day job!" In fact, my very first sale was to a passenger in my cab, a dentist from Alaska, who bought a case from me when he saw it on the front seat. For twenty years, I'd deliver cases to a dental lab, where they'd be flown up to Alaska with his other orders. You've got to love those steady customers who pay retail prices and shipping.

While taking a break between cab trips one night, I met the sausage impresario Tony Cascioppo hanging out at the cabaret bar of the Pink Door restaurant. His sister Julie was performing that night, channeling Tom Jones with her character, Sam Turner, who was crooning and mingling with the crowd. When Tony told me he had a storefront where they sold jars of stuff, I cracked open a jar of peppers for him. Tony was inhaling the savory aroma of the peppers just as his sister walked past us, thrusting her hips to flaunt a large phallic prosthesis. Tony reached into her pants and pulled out a baguette! Breaking off a piece, he laid some peppers on the bread and took his first bite. Cascioppo's was the first store to sell Mama Lil's Peppers.

I went into DeLaurenti Food & Wine, Seattle's premier Italian food store in the Pike Place Market, a few times to give its managers samples. But finally, after I opened a jar in front of them and made them taste the peppers, they said yes, becoming the second store to sell Mama Lil's. Thirty years later, our whole line of jars still graces DeLaurenti's shelves.

The third store to sell the peppers was European Vine Selections, my neighborhood wine shop. One of the store's owners was and still is the amusing and ever-amused Doug Nufer. Doug, who writes novels while he tends to his shop, has a discerning palate and is always the first person to sniff out a cork-tainted bottle of wine at a tasting. He is known to be a tough critic, but he liked the peppers and bought a case. Two weeks later, I got a reorder for four more cases. When I delivered them, I asked him why he wanted so many jars. Doug showed me an article he'd written for the local weekly alternative paper, *The Stranger*. In praising the peppers' versatility, he coined the word *peppatunities*. Now he expected to have a run on the jars, as his wine shop was one of only three places in town that sold them.

Thirty years later, Doug's shop still sells Mama Lil's. I asked him recently how many jars he sells versus how many he eats for himself. Doug confessed, "Half and half. By selling the jars I'm just covering my habit."

The fourth place in Seattle to sell Mama Lil's jars was a hybrid store/café called Plenty, located in Seattle's Madrona neighborhood. Plenty's chef and owner, the friendly and erudite Jim Watkins, made everything at Plenty from scratch. But Jim knew that my peppers would be tough to replicate, and he happily put some jars on his shelves. Sometimes he even used my peppers in the food he created. When Lil visited me that first real year of Mama Lil's, I took her to Plenty to impress her. She was perusing the menu when Jim came to take our order.

"Bring us whatever you feel like cooking," I told Jim. Lil started to protest, but I told him to ignore her. Jim assumed Lil liked spicy foods. In fact, I thought Lil liked spicy foods.

When Jim brought us two mouthwatering plates of lamb couscous, Lil looked at her plate suspiciously. With Jim standing over us, I dug in and egged my mother on to try it. Cautiously, she took a bite, started gagging, and could not stop. Poor Jim led Lil to the restroom where he stood outside the door experiencing a chef's ultimate nightmare as Lil retched for minutes on end. When she emerged, with her face as red as a beet, she walked straight out the café's door. When I opened my car door for her, she snarled, "Now you're making me get into *this*."

Succulent Lamb and Vegetable Couscous with Mama Lil's Sauce

Jim Watkins

Before Plenty, Jim was the first chef at the renowned Café Flora. After Plenty he graced Seattle for years with splendid food at a few restaurants, and dormitories. On that day when Lil dined at Plenty Café, Jim used harissa in his couscous, which made Lil gag. Thereafter he used Mama Lil's instead, making it so much better. Serves about 6.

½ of a 12-ounce jar Mama Lil's Peppers, oil included
½ cup extra-virgin olive oil, plus 1 tablespoon
2 tablespoons fresh lemon juice
5 tablespoons butter
1 tablespoon extra-virgin olive oil
1 large sweet onion, thinly sliced
1 large pinch saffron threads
4 meaty lamb shanks, about 1 pound each
Salt and freshly ground black pepper
1 tablespoon sweet paprika, plus more for dusting
2 teaspoons ground cumin
Large pinch of cayenne pepper
3 large plum tomatoes, peeled, seeded, and quartered
3½ quarts water
10 parsley sprigs and 1 large thyme sprig, tied with kitchen string
3 medium waxy potatoes (red or yellow), cut into 1½-inch chunks
3 large celery ribs, cut into 2-inch lengths
2 large carrots, cut into 2-inch lengths
2 large red bell peppers, cut into ½-inch pieces
2 to 3 medium zucchinis, cut into ¼-inch pieces (about 3 cups)
2 cups fresh or frozen peas
2 cups Israeli couscous (also called pearl couscous)
¼ cup slivered fresh mint leaves

To make the Mama Lil's sauce:

Empty the jar of Mama Lil's Peppers and its oil into the bowl of a food processor (alternatively, use an immersion blender and a medium, steep-sided bowl). Add ½ cup of the olive oil and the lemon juice, then process until a fairly smooth purée forms. Taste and adjust the seasoning as needed. Set aside.

To make the stew:

In a very large, enameled cast-iron pot over medium heat, melt 3 tablespoons of the butter with the remaining 1 tablespoon olive oil. Add the onion and cook, stirring occasionally, until just softened, about 5 minutes. In a small bowl, crumble the saffron into 2 tablespoons of hot water and let stand for at least 10 minutes.

Season the lamb shanks with salt and black pepper and dust with the paprika. Add the shanks to the pot and cook over medium heat, turning them occasionally, until they are well browned, about 7 minutes. Sprinkle the shanks with the remaining 1 tablespoon of paprika plus the cumin and cayenne. Continue to cook, turning the pieces, until they become fragrant, about 1 minute.

Add the tomatoes and 3 quarts of the water; bring to a boil over medium-high heat. Skim off any fat that floats to the surface, then add the saffron and its soaking liquid, the parsley bundle, and a couple of large pinches of salt. Reduce the heat to low, cover partially, and simmer for at least 2 hours, or until the lamb is very tender.

Transfer the shanks to a large plate and tent with aluminum foil. Put the potatoes, celery, and carrots into the pot with the liquid. Cover and simmer over medium heat until almost tender, about 10 minutes. Add the bell peppers and zucchini and simmer uncovered until all the vegetables are tender, about 10 minutes longer. Remove from the heat and discard the parsley bundle. Set aside 1 cup of the cooking liquid, then add the peas to the pot.

Remove the meat from the bones and cut it into ¾-inch pieces. Return the meat to the stew. Stir gently, then taste and season with more salt and pepper as needed.

To make the couscous:

In a large saucepan over medium heat, melt the remaining 2 tablespoons of butter. Add the couscous and cook, stirring gently, until it is lightly toasted, about 3 minutes. Add the remaining 2 cups of water, the reserved 1 cup of cooking liquid, and a large pinch of salt, and bring to a boil. Cover, remove from the heat, and let stand until the liquid has been absorbed, about 10 minutes. Fluff with a fork.

To serve, mound the couscous on a large, high-sided platter. Ladle one-third of the lamb and vegetables around the couscous then moisten everything with some of the cooking liquid. Sprinkle with the fresh mint. Serve a bowl of extra stew on the side, then pass the Mama Lil's sauce at the table.

There wasn't a lot for me to do with my pepper business at this point, as I couldn't make another batch of jars until the harvest of 1993. But those jars of peppers went everywhere with me. Toward the end of my cab shifts, I also hung out at the bar at Campagne, a fancy French restaurant in Pike Place Market where an artist friend of mine, Bryan Yeck, worked as its bartender. On slow nights, I could always count on Bryan to hook me up with a customer.

But one night while I was in there, they were very busy, and the stressed-out manager pointed at a table where some long-haired hippies were having too good of a time, I guess. He told Bryan, "That table of guys don't belong here. Tell them to go somewhere else."

While I was driving these happy bohemians to another bar, I recognized the man in the front seat. He was a barista at a nearby coffee shop who'd made me many a latte in the day. He saw the case of peppers on the seat and pulled out a jar. "These look delicious. What are they?"

"Hot peppers in oil. I'm trying to start a business based on my mom's recipe."

"Cool. Our band's named after his grandma's recipe."

"What kind of recipe?" I asked as I looked at his bandmates in the rearview mirror.

One of them said, rather drolly, "Jam." It was 1992 and the music scene's stars weren't so recognizable to everybody. Yet. A month later, I spotted Pearl Jam back at Campagne, but this time with a privacy rope around them, as they drank cognac and feasted on plates of charcuterie and cassoulet with, if not their biggest fan, certainly one of their tallest—basketball star and bad-boy-turned-international ambassador Dennis Rodman. Family recipe or not, that barista's band climbed to fame as fast as Starbucks. And ten million times faster than Mama Lil's.

The more typical customers I'd encounter at Campagne were the restaurant employees and chefs who'd hang out there at the end of their shifts. Everyone knew me as a likeable cabbie, and they seemed to like my peppers as they never turned me down when I gave them jars. But there was one chef who was there with his sous chef. The sous liked my peppers and told me so. But when it was pointed out to his chef that I was the maker of the peppers, I'm not sure that his "meh" response was because he didn't like my peppers, or he didn't like the looks of me.

I was almost embarrassed when I gave a jar to Tamara Murphy, (R.I.P.) Campagne's extremely talented chef who'd just won the James Beard award for Best Chef in the Northwest. When Tamara bought a case to have around Campagne's kitchen, it felt like a first feather in my cap. (While slow-roasting in a sauna with her former sous chef Daisley Gordon, he divulged to me, "For a lunch entrée at Café Campagne, Tamara would cut a pork tenderloin into three pieces, cover them with plastic wrap, hammer the hell out of them with a meat mallet, grill them, and then serve them on a warm potato bun with some Bonne Maman apricot preserve on one side and your peppers and a pile of greens on the other.")

I also persuaded the Czech restaurateur Peter Cipra of Labuznik to try my peppers while he was hanging at Campagne one late night. Many people, including my uncle Dan, considered Labuznik—where many movers and shakers in town dined—to be one of the finest restaurants in Seattle at the time. Peter was known as a tyrant in his kitchen, and I expected him not to like me or my peppers. But upon trying them, his face lit up. "These would be *great* served with lamb."

I boasted to Peter, "A friend and I once ate nine pounds of lamb in one sitting. As long as we had peppers to put on each bite, we kept eating that lamb until it was gone." Peter sized me up and must've assessed I wasn't exaggerating, as Labuznik became the second restaurant to order my peppers. Peter, who has since passed away, once told me he never used Mama Lil's in any recipes but rather, he just impulsively threw them on things. The Pink Door, also in Pike Place Market, was the third restaurant to buy a case. That was an easy sell, as its owner Jackie was the sister of Cynthia, the minister at the church where we had made the peppers.

On another night at Campagne's bar, a man in his late thirties with a polished air of success noticed some of us snacking from my jar and asked if he could try them. As it turns out he owned a food brokerage company in Chicago, and he offered me some advice: "Get a new label so you can see more of the colorful peppers in the jar. And if you're interested in making a go of it, you should walk the floor of the Fancy Food Show. See if you fit in. While you're at it, check out your competition."

A lesson for all newbies: Know your competition. Frankly, sometimes you can't compete.

When the 1993 Summer Fancy Food Show sent me an application, I checked the box on its paperwork that said Mama Lil's was a store. It also asked if I had "buying authority." That seemed like a good box to check, too. A month later, I was strolling the aisles in the Philadelphia convention center, grazing on samples of mouthwatering foods from everywhere in the world. It was like a rolling cocktail party without the booze—or like I was a tourist walking through the red-light district in Amsterdam, as attentive vendors squinted to read my badge. When they saw I was a buyer, I got the hard sell—that is, until they realized I was just window shopping.

One booth was serving samples of pasta in tomato sauce, along with paper cups of wine. They were small cups, so I took a second one. Someone tightly grabbed my forearm. It was a stout sixty-year-old man who released my arm to shake my hand so hard that my knees buckled. The man pointed at what looked like an Oscar statuette. "My sauce is contender for best in the show. You're a buyer—if you know what's good for you, buy my sauce! In fact, take a jar home with you." The man handed me a jar of…LaMotta's Tomatta Sauce. He was no other than the boxing legend Jake LaMotta, played by Robert De Niro in the Martin Scorsese *film Raging Bull!*

"Thanks, Jake. It's a great sauce. But I'm not really a buyer. I'm just starting out and scoping out the show. Got any advice for me?"

Jake raised his fists. "Yeah, don't get beaten to the punch."

As I walked the aisles absorbing what this business of gourmet foods was about, tasting dozens of olives, pickles, peppers, and various condiments, I tried to imagine competing in this unfamiliar yet intriguing world. I didn't look or dress like these people. I wasn't a chef or a foodie even, and I certainly didn't have the star power of the Raging Bull. But this much I knew: My peppers were comparatively first-rate. I could see myself competing in this world.

That is, until I came upon a booth that had a product that looked similar to mine. They were colorful pepper rings in oil. I tasted them. Oy. They even tasted like my peppers. Maybe they weren't quite as good, but they were good. I asked the women at the booth where their peppers were grown and where their cannery was. The woman read my badge, then told me scornfully, "Mama Lil's *Peppers*? Are you even a buyer? Move along. We need to focus on our real customers." I was devastated that this product existed. As the Oracle of Delphi had predicted years ago and as the Raging Bull had presciently warned me minutes ago, I'd been beaten to the punch, yet again. Salerno Turci's Peppers was way ahead of me in establishing itself as a brand.

I found Salerno Turci's Peppers in a grocery store in Seattle and monitored the jars on the shelves. They weren't selling well. The next year their peppers were green, so not as attractive or tasty as before and the jars were soon remaindered. The following year, they were out of business.

That's when I began to realize that climate made a huge difference in the quality of the peppers. Lil told me that summers in Ohio were more humid than before, and no one could get their peppers to turn orange and red anymore, which is when the peppers get sweet. But because of the Yakima Valley's rich volcanic soil, excellent irrigation from the snowpack of the Cascade mountains, and a perfectly arid summer climate that typically stretched deep into October, the Hungarian goathorns grew more consistently colorful in the Yakima Valley—meaning that they were able to fully ripen and become sweeter while still staying crisp and firm—than anywhere else in the country. Due to these ideal growing conditions, I had a distinct competitive advantage over Salerno Turci's Peppers.

And Mama Lil's stood a chance of becoming a contender.

THE 63 GOLD BUFF TWIST

IN THE SUMMER OF 1993, I WENT TO a potluck party where I met the children's book illustrator and artist, Julie Paschkis, who I was told might be able to come up with a new label for Mama Lil's jars. The first thing Julie told me about herself was, "My strength is that I'm fast. My weakness is I'm fast." My contribution to the potluck was of course a jar of Mama Lil's Hungarian Hots. When Julie tasted them, her eyes lit up. "These are good. What kind of peppers are they?"

"Hungarian goathorns." I told her.

Julie looked to the right, to the left, then back at me. "I know what your label looks like." As it turns out this was right down Julie's alley. Her art is influenced by Eastern European folk art, often featuring simply drawn animals on a black background. I visited her studio two days later, where she showed me a drawing of a goat in a classic children's book, *The Poppy Seed Cakes*, illustrated by Maud and Miska Petersham. Then Julie showed me her idea. It was a drawing of two goats facing each other over a dark background.

I took Julie's drawing to my friend Tom Kleifgen, a fastidious graphic designer who earned his reputation by making a dry-soup cup jump off the shelves. Tom tweaked Julie's color palette to make the label look Italian *and* Hungarian. Then he took me to Olshen's Packaging in Seattle's Sodo industrial area, where Tom helped me choose the jar. For the harvest of 1993, Mama Lil's had a new label, a new jar, and a *half-ton* of peppers being grown by Gayle Krueger.

But—small detail—the Unitarian Church kitchen was no longer available. I had no idea where to make my jars. Every city has incubator commercial kitchens where you can rent a space for several hours at a time. I looked at all of them in Seattle, but none could accommodate us. We needed too much space for too many hours at a stretch. I was clueless at how to proceed.

As fate would have it, I was walking near my house when a cyclist rode past me and shouted out my name. David Lee, an intense man with large probing eyes, had been a line cook at a restaurant where a girlfriend of mine used to work. We hadn't seen each other in years, but he recalled tasting my mom's peppers years ago one night after work. The next day, Nick and I toured the Essential Foods manufacturing facility where David was the operations manager. It was equipped with stainless-steel worktables and cutting boards to prep the peppers, containers to pickle the peppers in, and most importantly, according to Nick, commercial pressure cookers for pasteurizing the jars. I still wasn't sold on the concept of pasteurization—Lil never pasteurized hers—but luckily, Nick's judgment superseded mine and he said they'd work fine.

For the price of $500 and one case of peppers to Essential's owner, we could use his facility on the condition we'd complete the whole process in forty-eight hours: from Friday at 6 p.m. when his crew knocked off to Sunday at 6 p.m. when they came back to work. The process of making the peppers typically took sixty hours, so I knew we'd be cutting corners.

When I squeezed twenty of these fifty-pound burlap bags into my Volvo station wagon for the 150-mile drive from Wapato to Seattle, there were three bags in the passenger seat with one of them partially on my lap. Upon arriving with the peppers at the Essential Food facility, a pallet of jars and lids, and a pallet of oil and vinegar awaited me. We were ready to rock.

Or should I say, rock-climb. It was slow going. For the physical act of cutting the peppers, I was determined NOT to use a Cuisinart this year, so I called every friend who had the least bit of talent with a knife. Nick's job that day was mixing the pickling brine as he wanted nothing to do with slicing the peppers by hand. Slicing entailed three jobs: Cut the stems off the peppers. Scoop the seeds out. And slice the peppers into rings—a task reserved for the chefs among my artisan crew of artists, chefs, actors, and singer-songwriters wielding knives that day. My job was the worst one, which no one else wanted to do—sticking a butter knife into the destemmed pepper, breaking the seed membrane, and scooping the seeds out. I was proud at how fast I could scoop out those seeds.

The goathorns seemed especially hot this year, so I urged my slicers to wear two layers of food prep gloves. Also, when the seeds contact water, they emit a gas that irritates some people's throats and lungs. (But not mine! If that had been the case, I'd have been out of this business long ago.) Some of my crew said they couldn't breathe. Can't argue with that. It was such a beautiful day outside that nobody was motivated to stay too long.

Luckily, David Lee was watching over us when he was there experimenting with his own food product that in a few years would be named *Field Roast*. Knowing I had a tight window to get the job done, he kept feeding me with workers. Only later did David show me the spot just north of Pike Place Market called the Millionair Club—now called Uplift Northwest—where recent immigrants looking for part-time work flagged down cars.

But some people just have no business working with food. Like the middle-aged man with a thick Texas accent David brought me. Not only wouldn't he take his cowboy hat off to put a hairnet on, but he refused to wear the protective gloves. Two hours later, when he went upstairs to use the restroom, there was a scream so loud we all looked up in fright. And we never saw him come down. Not even to get paid. He must've self-ignited and shot right through the roof.

Finally, we had a thousand pounds of sliced peppers soaking in pickling brine. When I'd ask my mom how long she pickled her peppers, her answer was always, "Overnight." Which was rather unspecific, depending on whether you're a night owl or not. We were pinched for time, so after fifteen hours, by using a pocket pH meter that never gave us the same reading twice, Nick and I deemed the peppers were pickled. Then we bound those pickled peppers in cheesecloth and hung them to drain.

As my mother preached and I no doubt will be mentioning repeatedly throughout this book, the most important step in making pickled peppers in oil taste great is to *thoroughly drain the peppers of the pickling brine*. But when I'd ask Lil how long I should drain them for, she'd tell me, "Overnight." When we returned the next day, the peppers had drained for twelve hours. Then, with Bob Marley spurring us on, my crew of friends and sons and daughters of friends, started *jammin' till the jam is through*. We seasoned and packed all those brightly colored peppers into a thousand jars that covered the entire surface of all the available prep tables. After we filled those jars with oil, *(stir it up!)* a luscious aroma of peppers, garlic, and oregano was released, saturating all of our senses.

It was a ribbon-cutting moment when my friend the gentle giant actor, Jean Sherrard, dramatically sliced open the box of lids and handed me the first one. But that first lid was too small, so I asked Jean for another. He reached into the box and handed me a second lid. It was too small. And for that matter so was the third lid. And the fourth. When the fifth lid didn't fit, Jean's eyes and mouth opened very wide. When we wrote screenplays together, Jean made that same look of ecstatic surprise when inspired with a great idea. Honestly, I was expecting Jean to give me a great marketing concept. I misread Jean's face entirely. Jean realized that all the lids were too small! The label on the box read, "59 ml gold buff twists," not the "63 ml gold buff twist" lids I'd ordered. Thankfully, we had another box. Only to find out they were also filled with the wrong, 59 gold buff twists.

With the Essential Foods crew due to start its shift in a few hours, I was starting to panic. I called David Lee to alert him, but he was out hiking. I called Olshen's Packaging. No one answered. Why would they answer? It was a gorgeous Sunday afternoon. Any sane person would be off hiking. I should've been hiking. Jean drove to scout Olshen's. He reported that my only hope was a phone number for the security firm that monitored the building. I called the number twice, leaving frantic messages like, "I'm going to huff and puff and blow your door down!" Then lo and behold I somehow found the residential phone number for Aaron Olshen, the owner of Olshen's. This kind old man's voice on his answering machine said, "I'll get back to you soon." I was rejoicing as I just knew that Aaron would come to my rescue, and soon. Until I discovered—Aaron's obituary! He had died just last week. And I was now mourning him.

Jean called me back from Olshen's warehouse. "I almost hate to tell you this. There's a small window up the wall that's partially cracked open." Twenty minutes later, I was standing on Jean's shoulders, pulling myself up to the narrow vent window. I pushed it open as wide as it would go and started to climb through. But I'm a big guy, and I got stuck. Like, really stuck. I was wedged in so tightly I couldn't get in or out. But out seemed easier than in. I was almost back out the window, when I realized, *If I don't get these lids, the jars would be kaput. Mama Lil's would be— kaput!* Then according to Jean who witnessed this from below the window, my hips wriggled so furiously that I eventually slipped through—with my head dropping straight toward the toilet. When I broke my fall on that porcelain with my forearms, I felt invincible.

But when I walked out the bathroom door, I set off a deafening alarm, which really set my adrenaline off. The warehouse was pitch dark, but with my heightened senses I found the bank of light switches and I lit that warehouse up! But where were the boxes of lids? I desperately dashed up and down the aisles until I spotted the boxes on racks ten feet off the ground. I found a two-by-four, then began knocking the boxes onto the floor. One box burst open when it hit the floor. And mercy, dozens of 63 ml gold buff twists were rolling on the ground beneath me!

Minutes later, with two boxes of 63 gold buff twists tucked under my arms, I ran out into the glaring sunlight. Over the sound of the building's alarm and another siren that was getting louder, I threw the boxes in Jean's trunk. Which is when the source of the siren swung into the parking lot. I was not a thief. But in my filthy white shirt I must've looked like one to the two cops who hopped out of their car with hands on their holsters. "What did you put in the trunk?!"

I was trying to explain the situation to the skeptical cops when the cavalry arrived in the form of Olshen's manager, who told the police he'd handle it from there. The manager looked at me incredulously. He could not believe I'd gone to such lengths to get those 63 gold buff twists. On parting, he told me, "I've seen a lot of businesses come and go, but you might have what it takes."

All's well that ends well. Not only did we get the jars packed with seconds to spare, but that fuckup by the bottle company garnered Mama Lil's a short bugle blast of publicity. When the Seattle Times gossip columnist Jean Godden caught wind of my escapade, she told the tale of Mama Lil's survival in her weekly column. This accounted for a noticeable spike in sales for Mama Lil's jars, well, for a week anyway.

A few months later Nick and I tried to come up with a business plan. His first question to me was, "How long until we're each making 100K a year?"

I told him, "If we sell these thousand jars for $5 a jar, we'll have $500 profit between us. For the year. If we double our profits every year, which is a good goal to have, ten years from now, we might each earn $50,000 a year." Ten years was a long time away—and I was only guessing. As self-deceptive as I was, I knew enough about the difficulty of making these peppers that I had no delusions of hitting it big. That was what writing screenplays and betting on the Cleveland Indians was for. Making peppers was an interesting hobby. But Nick was in a new marriage and couldn't afford to dabble with hobbies. He needed to earn a living, and now.

In 1994, Essential Foods allowed me to pack for two weekends, so I could double our output of jars over last year. My friend Jean was there and so was my bartender friend Bryan Yeck, who was considering becoming my partner. Now, Bryan may have sliced a thousand lime wedges in his day, but he was not prepared for how brutal it was to hand slice a thousand pounds of peppers. When Bryan grabbed the tenth burlap sack of peppers and yelled, "Hallelujah! I see the

Bryan Yeck, Jean Sherrard, Tikka Sears.

bottom of the pallet!" he sounded like a mariner who spotted land after months at sea. When I pointed to Bryan where the other pallet of peppers was, he fell to his knees in despair. There was another ocean to cross.

An hour later, Bryan was in the emergency room after nearly slicing a finger off. It may have been intentional, at least unconsciously. Rumor has it my grandfather Louie Lev shot off his big toe to avoid becoming cannon fodder on the Russian front in the first World War. And Bryan was certainly at war with the peppers. In the end, his finger healed fine, and he went on to open Zeitgeist Coffee, one of Seattle's great independent coffee shops, which I'm proud to say used Mama Lil's Peppers on its sandwiches for more than twenty years.

For the second weekend at Essential Foods, I convinced Cynthia's son, Orion Breen—who had honed his knife skills at his aunt Jackie's Pink Door restaurant—into gathering a group of his high school buddies to help me get to the finish line. In writing this, I was trying to remember if that was the last pepper-slicing day of 1993 or 1994. But then I recalled those teenagers were playing Soundgarden's 1994 album, *Superunknown,* for twelve hours straight. When their energy waned and they threatened to leave, I inspired them onward by telling them when Soundgarden's lead singer was my neighbor, our landlord ordered us to clear the overgrown blackberry brambles on our shared walkway. "Chris Cornell and I had a race. I used a motorized hedge trimmer. Chris attacked the brambles with a machete. It was like Paul Bunyan versus the chainsaw! And Chris won, handily! That man has *energy!*"

One measure of success in my first three years in business, where I managed to double the output each year, was that I sold or gave away all the jars we made. What is also true is that I didn't pay myself a dime. But luckily cabdriving paid my bills and tenants helped me pay my mortgage. Besides, I still considered myself a screenwriter. At the time, I was dating a psychotherapist who'd read one of my scripts and she liked it enough (or so she said). But after tasting the peppers, she said that now that I was forty years old, if I focused on them instead of my screenplays, she might consider me as marriage material. But I wasn't ready to give up on my Hollywood ambitions—and besides, I wasn't sure if she was marriage material either.

But she may have been a savvier shrink than I gave her credit for—by using reverse psychology on me. Now when I'd submit my screenplays, I'd include a jar, hoping they'd like the peppers and feel compelled to read my play. Back then, my personal phone line was also my business line so when calls came in, I would answer with an upbeat chirp, "Mama Lil's!"

A bubbly woman's voice said, "Hi. This is Linda at Brillstein-Grey. Please hold for Brad." I was shocked to hear back from Brad Grey, the Hollywood super-agent to whom on a lark I'd sent a jar along with my screenplay, *All the Fish in the Sea.*

"Howie baby! Brad Grey. How the hell are you?"

"I'm great! Brad, thanks for calling…so, did you like *All the Fish in the Sea?*"

"Howie, I'm not calling about fish. It's those peppers. Where can I buy more jars in LA?"

"Uh…nowhere. Yet."

"Then ship me a case. Pronto."

"Sure, but my screenplay. Have you read—"

"Right, I'll read, uh…*It All Sounds Fishy to Me* this weekend. Send me a case of those jars! I'll have Linda send you a check."

I followed through from my end. But Brad Grey soon became president of Paramount Pictures, so I doubt he ever read a word of *It All Sounds Fishy to Me,* or whatever that screenplay was called. But the message was coming in loud and clear from too many sources to ignore. I needed to reverse my priorities. Writing screenplays would now become my hobby. I needed to turn the peppers into a job.

Cheesy Crabby Cakes

Tom Douglas

Tom, the James Beard award winning chef and restauranteur of Serious Pie, Half-Shell, and Dahlia Bakery among many others, started out in the 1980's by focusing his food, cookbooks, gourmet products and local radio show, on what is grown, caught and eaten in the Pacific Northwest. By doing so Tom helped define the Northwest's culinary milieu perhaps as much as Tom Robbins did its cultural zeitgeist. Tom is also the most generous food entrepreneur I've met, both personally and civically, as best demonstrated to me in the recession of 2009 when at the last minute he stepped in to sponsor the annual Lake Union fireworks celebration to make sure that the show went on.

Makes 4 portions or about 24 appetizers.

1 egg
1/4 cup sour cream
2 teaspoons chili powder
1/4 teaspoon kosher salt
1½ cups grated cheddar cheese
3 tablespoons coarsely chopped Mama Lil's Peppers
1 pound Dungeness crabmeat, drained, picked clean of shells (do not break up larger chunks)
½ cup breadcrumbs
4 tablespoons butter

In a large bowl, use a whisk to beat the egg with the sour cream, chili powder, and salt. Add the cheddar cheese and Mama Lil's Peppers. Gently fold in the crabmeat and mix to combine. Divide the mixture into eight portions and form them into hamburger-like patties. Pour the breadcrumbs into a shallow cake pan and dredge the crab cakes in as many crumbs as will adhere to them. At this point, it's best to refrigerate these for 4 hours or up to 1 day.
Line a serving plate with paper towels. In a medium frying pan over medium heat, warm the butter until it begins to turn foamy. Add four of the crab cakes to the pan and cook for 2 to 3 minutes on each side until browned. Don't fuss with them...they will break apart if you try to turn them too much. They're finished when they reach an internal temp of 150°F with an instant-read thermometer. Transfer the crab cakes to the prepared plate to drain and repeat with the remaining cakes. Serve hot with fries or salad.

WOLF PACK: THE EARLY YEARS

If by chance you stumbled on my book while looking for a real how-to guide on starting and running a gourmet food business—complete with graphs, facts, figures, and sourcing guides—I recommend the extremely thorough *From Kitchen to Market: Selling Your Gourmet Food Specialty* by Stephen F. Hall. That book has been the bible for gourmet food entrepreneurs since it came out in 1992.

In 1995, I finally got around to reading Hall's book. I must admit, if I'd read it *before* I started my business instead of after, I might've known better about the nitty-gritty of profit margins and not embarked on my pepper journey at all! The back cover verbiage was promising: "Learn how to turn kitchen creations into profits." But when I read the chapter on pricing, I was disheartened. It states that there are several tiers of middlemen for getting your products into retailers, and it's hard to go around them, especially with the larger corporate-owned stores.

It's the sales broker who sells your products to the store's buyer, and they take a 10 to 20 percent commission on each sale. But the broker doesn't deliver your products. That's the distributor's job, and they take another 25 to 35 percent commission. By the time the middlemen took their cuts, the jars I sold for $4 (my cost of goods) would cost $11 on the shelf. Stores told me no one would pay that price, no matter how good my peppers are! The economics of this arrangement is a bit like why your therapist refuses to accept payment from your insurance company. It pays the equivalent of distributor pricing. No wonder so many therapists refuse to take insurance. And why so many gourmet food companies only sell directly to stores.

Back then, my goal was to get my peppers on grocery store shelves, with the caveat that I would be my own middleman. Now I wasn't the only vendor who delivered his own product, but I know for a fact I was the only one doing it out of my cab. It was while I was waiting to check my products in at stores that I picked the brains of other small producers who, like me, were trying to cobble together a living. A man who was delivering his own salsa told me about Wolf Pack, a cannery in the town of Gold Bar, in the foothills of the Cascades mountains.

When I first called Wolf Pack's number, the din of the machinery was so loud I could barely make out the gruff voice shouting into the phone: "If you wanna pack here, come see me in Gold Bar. Follow the sign for Wallace Falls across the railroad tracks. Then turn left on Moonlight Drive."

"Moonlight Drive" was one of my favorite Doors songs, so I played it as I drove fifty miles to the cannery. But this Moonlight Drive was not what that hopeful song suggested…*Let's swim to the moon…parked beside the ocean on our moonlight drive.* It was a potholed road lined with trailer-park homes with junked cars in their yards. But at the end of it lay the serene Wallace River. This was more like it! *We've stepped into a river…as I watch you glide, falling through wet forests on our moonlight drive.* I followed the road along the stream until I came upon the large, green aluminum barn-like structure that housed the cannery. Even though Wolf Pack was a long drive from Seattle, its tranquil location was alluring. Not only did it sit on the edge of a forest and river, but it was right below Mount Stickney, where you could see the magnificent 265-foot drop of Wallace Falls.

Outside the cannery lay a graveyard of antique canning equipment in various states of rust and disrepair. Whoever George Wolf was, he'd been at it for a while. I slid the heavy sliding barn door open. And whoa! Rivers of steam were shooting out of two aluminum tunnels and billowing up into the rafters. As a pungent smell of cooked tomatoes infiltrated my nostrils, I heard a voice uttering a burst of "Goddamits!" It was so loud inside the cannery, I didn't know where those "Goddamits" were coming from, until a large man clutching a giant crescent wrench rolled out from underneath one of the steam tunnels, with fogged-up glasses and a grease-stained undershirt. I helped him to his feet. He was at least sixty years old, stood 6 feet, 6 inches tall, and had to weigh close to 300 pounds. "George Wolf here."

I shook his giant paw. "George Wolf? I mistook you for my friend, George Bear." My lame joke garnered the first of a thousand groans George would aim at me over the years.

With George Wolf at Wolf Pack, 1995

George then led me on a tour of his cannery that he built himself. Back then, Wolf Pack had two employees—his eternally disaffected twenty-year-old grandson, who was hosing down the cannery floor, and his grandson's young wife, who was at the end of the pasteurization tunnel with heatproof gloves catching hot jars of salsa off the conveyor belt.

Behind the tunnel was George's one-room living quarters that doubled as his lab. When I stepped inside this windowless room, the first thing I saw was a king-size bed that took up half of the space. The second thing I noticed was a glass-enclosed gun rack. Seeing those half dozen old hunting rifles, I knew exactly who George Wolf reminded me of: John Wayne.

"Show me your product!" George demanded, as if asking me to draw my gun. I handed him a jar I made last year. George shook his head dismissively, "Mama Lil's, huh? You know how many sauces I've made here named after someone's mama? Mama Mia's, Mama Melina's, Mama Mary's." He turned my jar over to inspect it. "What's your production process?" When I described my process, George's face contorted into a pained sneer. "You mean you put the vinegar in, then take it out? Where does all that vinegar go? Down my drain? County charges me for that. Now, a liquid like a sauce, salsa, or jam even, we use my filling machines. Looks like your pepper rings need to be hand-packed, then filled with oil. By hand. What a fuckin' pain in the ass."

I couldn't really argue with George; the peppers in oil were a fuckin' pain in the ass. There's another lesson for newbies: *The easier your product goes into the jar, the better. Hand-packing is slow. Liquids fill fast and are easy to get into jars. Dried spices or rubs, even more so.*

"So, what's the pH of your peppers?"

"Not sure of that either. Our pH meter was a little unreliable."

George looked at me like I was an idiot. "Your product is being sold in stores and you don't know its pH?" He twisted the lid off the jar, emptied it in a colander to separate the oil from the peppers, then in George-speak "comminuted" them in a blender. Sliding out a real pH meter from his kitchen counter, he stuck its probe into the minced peppers. The numerical display started at 4.22, then slowly went down, settling on 3.43. I didn't know if this was a good number or not. But George was smiling when he told me, "That's a nice low pH you got here. Makes my job a little easier. So, what was the center temperature you pasteurized this jar to?"

"I'm not sure of that either. We cooked these in a pressure cooker. They got overcooked. I'm not sure these need to be cooked. My mother never does. And her jars never go bad on her."

George raised an eyebrow. "Maybe your mama's a witch who puts a magic spell on her jars. We apply science around here. You read about Louie Pasteur in eighth-grade science?"

There's a lesson I learned too late. Know the science of your product before plunging in. Acidification and pasteurization are chemistry experiments that could blow up in your face.

I told George, "I just want my jars pasteurized to the lowest temperature, no more."

George howled, "For cryin' out loud, you pasteurized your jars in a pressure cooker and now you're worried about me overcooking them. We can do a trial run, but your product sounds like a pain in the ass. Now, I'm in charge of all the pasteurization and keeping the logs. But we won't help you slice peppers. You'll have to bring your own crew out here. You up for that?"

Rounding up a crew and then driving an hour to slice peppers was going to be a pain in the ass. The whole damn process of canning Mama Lil's, even in this beautiful location, even in this real cannery, *was* going to be a pain in the ass. But Wolf Pack was my only option. Needing this to work, I told George, "Luckily, I love to drive. In fact, I'm a professional driver."

George gave me another once-over. "You don't look like a race car driver."

"One step above. I drive a cab. No one can get from point A to point B faster than me."

Fortuitously, an old friend and former roommate, Michael Brooks, let me know he was looking for both a place to live and a job. Michael was a tall, thin Black man who'd worked at restaurants where I hung out, so I knew he was a diligent, steady worker. But more importantly, considering all the time we'd be spending together, Michael was wise and well-read, making him a good companion on the drives out to the cannery.

My 1966 Volvo 122 station wagon was a dependable workhorse that came my way cheap, but recently, when it was parked on the street outside the Club Rock Candy —where my friend Terry Lee Hale was opening for the Screaming Trees—my car got plowed into by a car being pursued by police. The bid to repair the door was so high that I didn't fix it. Instead, I stretched bungee cords between the door handles to keep the damaged door closed. On that first morning when Michael and I pulled up to the Millionair Club to round up the crew, a dozen Hispanic men pounced on my car. Within seconds, six men were sitting on top of each other in the back seat. After a brief argument among them, two men got out and Michael stretched the bungee across their four bellies and hooked it on the handle.

One of the men asked, "Qué pasa?"

Michael told him, "Seatbelt." Strangely, all the men nodded in understanding as if they'd worn this *Mexican* seatbelt before.

That first day at Wolf Pack, the six of us hand-sliced a half-ton of peppers, filling all of George's thirty food-prep tubs. The next day Michael and I drained them of the brine for which I used George's giant plastic colanders that filled up the cannery's walk-in refrigerator to its gills. The next morning, when I opened the walk-in door, George was standing amid the colanders of peppers shaking his arms at me. "Goddamit! There's a sea of fuckin' peppers in here!"

"Where else am I going to drain the fuckin' peppers, George?" I implored. That same day while we were packing jars, George was in his shop constructing—out of vats used for brining fish he had lying around—what would become my pickling vats for years to come. By drilling hundreds of holes in stainless steel plates, he created a method to drain the peppers right inside the vat, saving all sorts of space in his walk-in refrigerator.

We repeated our routine every three days: I'd drive to Krueger's farm in Wapato in my station wagon, pick up twenty burlap sacks of peppers and drive four hours to Wolf Pack to drop the peppers off, so I had an empty car the next morning when Michael and I rounded up a crew and drove back out to Wolf Pack to slice and pickle the peppers. The following day Michael and I drove back out to drain the peppers. The next day, with George's crew of two stationed at the pasteurization tunnels, Michael and I packed the peppers into jars and filled them with oil. And that oil got everywhere. George was a sight to see as he gingerly walked the slippery cannery floors, cursing. "For fuckin' crying out loud, how'd oil get on my fuckin' toilet seat?"

By the third round of slicing peppers at Wolf Pack, just two men were willing to get into my car at the Millionair Club. When George saw how slow-going it was for the four of us that day, he turned me on to a company that sliced vegetables with sophisticated Urschel slicing machines. For the fourth round of peppers, I borrowed George's van and brought a ton (literally two thousand pounds) of goathorns to this company. A day later they were sliced and packed into seventy-five plastic bags weighing twenty pounds each. This was the first time I calculated that I lost 25 percent of the peppers' weight in stems and seeds. It wasn't cheap having the peppers sliced by this company, but I was happy not to be doing the slicing myself. But the next time I brought them a ton of peppers, the next day my forty burlap sacks of peppers were waiting for me. The crew refused to slice them again because they were hacking from the fumes.

It was too late to drive back to Seattle and round up a crew, so Michael and I drove to Wolf Pack and started de-seeding and slicing the peppers by ourselves. After two hours we'd barely made a dent. Then, in my anxious state of trying to do the impossible, I had the best idea I'd ever had in my life (which, I'm afraid to say, includes all my movie inspirations). It was a simple idea. *If I didn't take the seeds out, the peppers would be hotter. And maybe I'd have a second product, which was just a hotter version of my first one. This second product would save on the labor of taking the seeds out, and the peppers would lose less weight.* I'm no economist, but by leaving the seeds in, I realized my yield would increase as my cost of goods and labor decreased. But here's the cleverest part of my idea: To distinguish between the seedless *milder* version and the *hotter* version with seeds, we'd put a different color lid on the jar and then on the label we'd turn the goats around, so they're kicking each other instead of facing each other.

I told Michael, "And I'll call them *Kick-Ass* Peppers!"

Michael hated scooping the seeds out with a butter knife, so he was easily won over by my idea. I then called three friends to get their opinions, and they all came to the same conclusion: "They shouldn't be *kick-ass* peppers—they should be called *kick-butt* peppers." The poet Ron Dakron preferred the word "butt" with the reasoning: "An ass is a donkey, not a goat. Besides, goats *butt* each other. Always go with the double entendre."

But merely leaving the seeds in was not enough for the Kick Butt Peppers to be a viable second product. They needed to be much hotter than the Mildly Spicy Peppers. Gayle Krueger had me try a very hot Romanian pepper, and I bought every one of them for a batch of Kick Butts. For the next batch I purchased all the hot cayenne peppers he grew. My last batch I bought all of his Scotch bonnet peppers and like a Cracker Jack surprise, buried a whole pepper in each jar. As far as I recall the only customer complaint was: "They are hot. Going in. And going out!"

Michael Brooks, Wolf Pack, 1995.

Although making Kick Butt Peppers sped up our prep time by not having to take the seeds out, it didn't make hand-packing the jars go any faster. After each packing day, George would look at my meager output and shake his head. George got paid based on units produced, so he wasn't making much money out of me. I was perplexed, too. How did so many peppers turn into so few jars? As it turns out, not only was I losing 25 percent of the weight in stems and seeds, but after draining the peppers, I also lost 25 percent of their water weight. George told me that most gourmet foods made at Wolf Pack added water to their products. But the salt in my pickling brine pulled the water *out* of my peppers, making for an abysmal recovery rate.

It was then I realized that this must be what the Peter Piper nursery rhyme was about. ("If Peter Piper picked a peck of pickled peppers, how many pickled peppers did Peter Piper pick?"). It was a labor dispute. Peter was a disgruntled employee for good reason. Since he was picking "pickled" peppers, for every two pounds Peter picked, he got paid for only one. After four years of pickling peppers, I was coming to terms with the fact that I was making something that shouldn't even exist, at least not as a commercial product. I should've known this from the start. In Youngstown, no commercial manufacturers made the peppers to be sold in stores. In fact, people almost never bought the peppers in oil. The jars were always a gift from someone.

Sure, in 1995 I'd made progress by adding the less expensive Kick Butt Peppers to my line. And I tripled the number of jars I'd made the year before to eight hundred cases. I was pepper-rich—and dead broke. And I knew, after selling all these jars, that my profits would be negligible at best. Then lo and behold, the Cleveland Indians made it into the World Series. To the tune of $5000, they could win big for me!

NOT! Ten days later, I was in a catatonic state on my couch after having watched the Indians lose the *last* game of the World Series to the Braves. When my phone rang, I wondered who would dare call me in this time of profound grief. Lil knew better than that. But it was my childhood friend Jonny Katz, whom I hadn't talked to in years. After we consoled each other about the Indians, he asked me if I had a new script going.

I told Jonny, "Nope. I started a business making the hot peppers-in-oil."

"What are you naming your business?" he asked. "Names are important."

"I'm calling them Mama Lil's Peppers."

Jonny laughed. "Howie, the Tribe may never win in our lifetimes. But by naming your peppers after Lil, at some point, luck will be coming your way."

By the harvest of 1996, Michael Brooks had moved on, so I had to go it alone. Which made it infinitely harder to get myself out the door at 5:30 a.m. to round up my crew at the Millionair Club and then drive out to Wolf Pack before dawn. But in the second week of production, I got a huge morale boost when I fell madly in love. The object of my affections was a perfectly symmetrical slicing machine called the Lettuce King which greatly sped up the slicing process. You laid the pepper on a bed of blades and with one smooth stroke, it was sliced into perfect 3/8-inch rings. I renamed the device the Bob-bitron—for Lorena Bobbitt, who was in the news back then for slicing her philandering husband's—well, you know what—off.

Besides all the hand labor, what made the pickled peppers in oil so costly to produce was the amount of vinegar used but then discarded. The vinegar represented no weight within the final product. In fact, the opposite was true since the salt in the vinegar brine pulled the water (and its weight) out of the peppers, causing even more brine to go down the Wolf Pack drains. Then in a fit of thirst in the humid cannery, I took a swig of the salty pepper brine—and it tasted downright delicious to me. The question I began to obsessively ask myself was, is there value in the brine that's going down the drain? The only millionaires I knew in Ohio were a family who made a fortune when they figured out how to market the slag waste product from making steel.

Could I do the same with that pepper brine and turn my waste into profits?

My first bad idea for using the brine was inspired by a spat I had with George. He never allowed me to take temperature readings of the jars or examine the logbooks. That was his job, not mine. But I was concerned my jars were being overcooked, making the peppers mushy. Just then George was shuffling by the pasteurization tunnel cursing to himself, so it might not have been the best time to ask him, "Can you turn down the heat in the tunnel?"

George shot back, "I'll turn the heat off, if you don't shut the fuck up.

Bingo! George gave me an idea. I'll just bottle the brine and call it *Mama Lil's Old-Fashioned Piss and Vinegar*. I'll sell it in gallon jugs and market it to health food stores with instructions to drink a cup at bedtime and by the morning, you'll piss out all your unmetabolized anger and wake up a jolly good fellow. Suffice it to say, that product idea got nowhere.

While I was obsessing on what to do with the pepper brine waste product, my poet friend Ron called me with an idea he had for a product that wasn't based on a recipe, but rather on a word he coined. In Chicago, where he'd grown up, they called hot dog relish *piccalilli*. Ron suggested, "Why not make a product called *peppalilli*? Even more fun to say than piccalilli."

I looked up piccalilli in Irma Rombauer's *Joy of Cooking*. Her recipe was far more interesting than the bland electric-green relish Chicagoans put on hot dogs. On the same page were other old-fashioned pickle recipes that used the same spices as the piccalilli: turmeric, celery seed, and mustard seed. The liquid used in all of them was apple cider vinegar.

If I could substitute pepper brine for the apple cider vinegar, I might be on to something.

Another recipe on this same page was for mustard pickles or chow-chow. (There are a hundred recipes out there that folks call chow-chow, so I'm referring only to *Joy's* version.) Rombauer described it as "a formula that meets with such enthusiastic approval that we are often tempted to abandon all other mixed pickle recipes." That's a mighty strong endorsement.

The origin of mustard pickles is East Indian, but the English made it their own by transforming the condiment into a savory relish served with salami and cheddar cheese. When these pickle recipes crossed the ocean to North America, this version—as rendered in *Joy of Cooking*—was sweetened with sugar. On the same page was its recipe for piccalilli, which called for cauliflower, beans, cucumbers, pearl onions, and green tomatoes, very similar to the vegetables in a classic Chicago giardiniera. My recipe for PeppaLilli was a mash-up of Joy's piccalilli and mustard pickle recipes, which I simplified by using goathorn peppers, sweet onions, and cucumbers, making them ideal for sandwiches.

Having set a precedent by producing both milder and hotter versions of the peppers in oil, I did the same with the PeppaLilli. I used apple cider vinegar to make the mild mustard sauce, so it had the same flavor as the classic recipe. But for the hot PeppaLilli, I used the spicy pepper brine to make the hot mustard sauce. At this stage, if I had a business plan at all, *it would be that each new product I came up with was less expensive to produce than the last one.* The hotter PeppaLilli version fit the bill perfectly since the pepper brine used to make its sauce, was free.

I asked Julie to taste the PeppaLilli, hoping it would trigger an idea for a label. Within seconds, Julie blurted, "Geese! And the hotter ones will be Honkin' Hot."

Also, from the hallowed pages of *Joy of Cooking*—in fact on the same page as the mustard pickles—was its bread-and-butter pickle recipe. As it turns out, George had been making bread-and-butter pickles for years for his own use. George's recipe was, in fact, taken straight from *Joy of Cooking*. Meaning that they were made the old-fashioned way, which entailed stewing his veggies in a kettle until they absorbed all the savory sweetness of the seasoned apple cider vinegar brine. I substituted goathorn peppers for the bell peppers his recipe called for, then named them *Bread & Butter Pickles & Peppers*. When I gave Julie Paschkis a jar to try, perhaps thinking they would be tasty on a ham-and-cheese sandwich, "Piggies!" were added to Mama Lil's menagerie of labels.

In 1996, I was at Wolf Pack making my five products six days a week for seven weeks. While there, I observed every other gourmet food entrepreneur in the region. Most I never saw again, as they had less of an idea of what they were doing than me. After one packing session, they owned a lifetime supply of Grandpa's slug butter, Uncle Billy's garlic spread, or Aunt Rosie's peach-mango chutney, that stowed in their basement, would soon resemble Reverend James's twenty-year-old peach jam I found in my basement.

But some are worth mentioning. Tom Douglas, Seattle's most eminent restaurateur over the last thirty-five years, started making his excellent line of teriyaki and barbecue sauces at Wolf Pack. I saw Tom loading cases in his truck at Wolf Pack's warehouse and I led him into the cannery to show off my pickled peppers. When Tom saw that vat dense with pepper rings, he took one step back and said, "You've been slicing peppers." As in, glad it wasn't me slicing.

The most successful line made at Wolf Pack back then, and might still be for all I know, is the Bread Dip Company. None of its tapenades or spreads used fresh ingredients, so it wasn't bound by an eight-week harvest like Mama

Lil's was. Most of its dips were excellent products, but they all originated from cans or barrels—not the field. It also had a tasteless pepper product that far outsold Mama Lil's Peppers back then, even though it was made from canned jalapeños! I can still feel my hackles going up as I'd watch George's crew open the cans and toss peppers into the mixer—and then lickety-split, by the time me and my crew had sliced a hundred pounds of peppers, an endless freight train of jars of jalapeño dip came rolling out of the steam tunnel.

If you're in this business for the money, let this be a lesson. The Bread Dip Company was smart by not using fresh produce with limited availability. Not for the glory of handmade artisan foods, but surely for the bottom line! And unlike me, it didn't have to stock up on inventory.

And then there was Ursula. As opposed to the white hairnets and aprons everyone else wore, Ursula wore a designer apron and a fancy scarf over her head. Why did she bother making her mediocre line of spreads, I wondered. Her ego, of course. Her brand was called *Ursula's*. Ursula's went bankrupt shortly thereafter, screwing George out of a bunch of money. I might add, it was due to Ursula that Mama Lil's was *not* designated as kosher-certified that year.

Even though it's costly to get that kosher symbol on your label, it denotes quality to many shoppers, so I scheduled a meeting at Wolf Pack with a rabbi who had the authority to designate my products as kosher. What I wasn't clear about from our phone call was whether the cannery itself had to become kosher-certified before any of the products made there could be kosher. After explaining to the friendly rabbi that none of the other products made at Wolf Pack ever touched my pickling gear, he said there could be exceptions to the rule. I assumed this meant some sort of gift, so I had a couple of C-notes in my wallet just in case.

On the day of the rabbi's inspection, unbeknownst to me Ursula was scheduled to make her products. She was with George's crew at the other end of the cannery dumping cans of stuff into the 100-gallon stainless steel mixer. When I pulled open the cannery's heavy sliding doors, the friendly rabbi smiled when he saw I was wearing a yarmulke atop my hairnet. But he didn't come alone. He brought a colleague—let's call him the grumpy rabbi—who wasn't so amused by what he correctly assumed was my costume. I shielded them from seeing Ursula as I took them to where my Hispanic crew, all wearing yarmulkes, were slicing peppers next to the loud vegetable washing contraption that made me have to shout to be heard.

I showed the rabbis the kosher salt and the kosher marks on the drums of vinegar and oil. "But the most important factor is: No one but me uses my pickling vats or Bobbitron,"

This flew right by the grumpy rabbi. But the friendly rabbi asked me, "The...what?"

"The bobbitron. The slicing machine we use." I demonstrated how the Bobbitron sliced peppers. "We named it after Lorena Bobbitt. Want to take a whack? It's got great action."

The friendly rabbi sliced a pepper, then laughed. "The Bobbitron. I get it. It's the pepper's briss!" I laughed at his joke. My kind of rabbi. As I watched him gleefully chop peppers, I knew I had a chance here of becoming kosher. But I'd taken my eye off the grumpy rabbi who had wandered to where Ursula's crew was stirring ingredients in the mixing tank. I caught up to him just as he asked Ursula, "What's in *there*?"

Ursula offered him a chunk and said, "It's Parmesan cheese. Have a taste." She might as well have offered him a bite of her BLT. The grumpy rabbi abruptly scurried back to our pepper slicing table and pulled the friendly rabbi away from the Bobbitron, to confer with him.

George Wolf had been observing us from the machine shop, and perhaps thinking I needed cover, came over to introduce himself to the rabbis. Speaking of not being kosher, George was a bit of a ham. "I've got a question for you rabbis." George told them. "My great grandfather is from Germany, but my cousin recently told me that I might be part Jewish too."

This was news to me. "Really George, you might be Jewish?"

"Probably not. But I'm circumcised. And since you rabbis are here today, I thought maybe you can check me out and get me certified, too." With the threat that George was about to drop his drawers, the grumpy rabbi was now heading for the exit with the friendly rabbi scampering behind him. But they had no idea how to open Wolf Pack's heavy sliding doors.

I caught up to them. "What's the hurry?"

The grumpy rabbi said, "To beat rush hour. We're taking our boys to see the Sonics play the Bulls." I slid the door open and followed the rabbis to their car.

At this point I knew that becoming kosher was a lost cause, so—why not—as the rabbi fidgeted with his key in the door, I told him, "What a coincidence! Just yesterday I was at the Seattle University gym when the Bulls were practicing there. You wouldn't believe who was standing next to me in the shower. Wanna know if Michael Jordan is circumcised?" The rabbi wasn't waiting for my answer. As their car sped away, it hit every pothole on Moonlight Drive.

So, no, Mama Lil's was not kosher certified in 1996, but I'd made headway in my fifth year of business. By then I'd read in Hall's book about the concept of line-item pricing. If I charged the same price for all five jars in my product lineup, with each one cheaper to produce than the last, then when taken as a whole, my business stood a chance of being profitable.

But who was I fooling? Myself, of course. My products were comparatively more expensive and time-consuming to make than all the others I saw being made at Wolf Pack. And considering the sheer hand labor and time involved in making these recipes, there was no economy of scale. It was just as difficult and costly to make the ten thousandth jar as the first jar. Since time is money, no commercial manufacturer would consider making these pickle recipes the old-fashioned way like I was, as there was simply no money in it.

Case in point: I was doing a trade show a few years later when a man stopped by my booth and very deliberately tasted from each of Mama Lil's jars. "I'm not sure which one I like the best," he said. "I'd love to buy some of these jars from you?"

I saw his badge. He was an executive at Unilever. I told him beseechingly, "Please don't steal my ideas. I'm a small company."

He reassured me, "Unilever makes nothing that takes longer than ten seconds to make."

The fact is the pickled peppers in oil and all the recipes I was making from *Joy of Cooking* were for folks with time on their hands. Like grandparents. I was doing a demo when an eighty-year-old woman said to me, "Bless your heart, I haven't had mustard pickles in so long."

I asked her, "Did you used to make mustard pickles?"

"Too much work. But my grandma did! They don't make grandmas like they used to."

In 1996, as well as expanding my product line, I increased my output by 60 percent to 1,600 cases. At this point, I'd never written myself a check. Sure, if cash came my way, it went into my wallet. I knew that if I was going to double my business every year, every check that came in would need to stay in the bank so I could make more jars next year. It was an organic way of growing my business without incurring debt. And even if those jars weren't selling that well and I wasn't making any money to speak of, I now had a line of five products. Not to compare my creative outburst to the few months that Keats wrote his great Odes—as heck, none of these products were even my ideas— but when I'd restock those jars on the grocery shelves after doing a demo, was I ever proud of them.

All lined up together with Julie's labels, they looked like works of art.

"Mama's in a Hurry" Pasta

Julie Paschkis

According to Julie, both her strength and weakness as an artist is that she's fast, making this fast and easy pasta recipe her perfect contribution to this book.

Serves 4 as a main course or 6 as a side dish

    1 pound dried pasta noodles
    Salt and freshly ground black pepper
    1 large bunch Swiss chard
    ½ cup Mama Lil's Peppers, oil included
    ⅔ cup crumbled feta cheese

Set a large pot of water over medium heat to boil. Add salt until the water tastes salty.

Strip the chard stems from the leaves. Stack several leaves on top of one another and slice into ribbons; repeat for all the leaves. Add the pasta to the boiling water. Set a timer for 2 minutes less than the recommended cooking time. When the timer sounds, add the chard ribbons.

When the pasta is tender, drain it (along with the chard) in a colander, and shake well. Put the pasta and chard in a warm serving bowl. Add the Mama Lil's Peppers and toss with the pasta, adding more pepper oil as desired for maximum deliciousness. Season with salt and black pepper, then sprinkle with the feta cheese. Add more Mama Lil's Peppers or feta to taste.

Substitutions:

Use spinach, kale, or broccoli florets instead of the chard.
Use goat cheese or Gorgonzola instead of feta.

TO MARKET OR NOT TO MARKET

I WAS RECENTLY WATCHING THE classic Alfred Hitchcock movie *To Catch a Thief* starring Cary Grant and Grace Kelly. Cary is posing as an advertising man, and Grace, not knowing whether he is a jewel thief or not, asks him, "Does advertising really work?" Although Cary doesn't give her a straight answer, I think Hitch's point is that people are gullible and can be subliminally influenced, which is what advertising attempts to do. Stores would ask me to buy an advertisement in the mailers they'd send to their customers, but I was making so little profit from the jars I sold that I hardly had the means to spend money on something that people just threw away.

To get the word out, I started signing up for promotional events, like the Cancer Lifeline Brewfest, held at Seattle's cavernous old train station. Along with a dozen local micro-breweries, a few gourmet food vendors were invited to promote their products as well. To commemorate my sister, Bobbi, I invited Lil to attend what I knew would be a fun event. As I drank beer and mingled, Lil and Nick's wife, Cynthia, served samples to happy beer-swilling attendees. Oy, how Lil loved telling folks that she was the real Mama Lil.

Cynthia and Lil, Cancer Lifeline
Brewfest, 1996.

It was at this festive party where I met brewers of Elysian and Pike Place Brewery who I ended up doing business with for over twenty years. I also met the the owners of two gourmet food businesses, whose approaches were diametrically opposite of each other. Cibo Naturals made cheese spreads and basil pesto that were sold in the same stores as Mama Lil's, so I was familiar with its line of products. Cibo's husband-and-wife team told me that the hundreds of demos they did in stores were what made their basil pesto—surprisingly not that well known then —go mainstream. Back then they manufactured all their products in Seattle, but since they could get steady winter crops of basil grown in Baja, Mexico, supply was not an issue for them. They wanted to make and sell as many units as possible, so all their sales were through distributors. (Cibo's pesto eventually became the Kirkland Signature pesto brand sold nationally at Costco stores.)

I also met Walt Mick, the owner of Micks Peppourri. The first thing he asked me was, "Are you going to be a retail business? Or a wholesale business? You can't really do both." Mick's business, like mine, was somewhat limited by the Yakima Valley growing season, so he only sold his jars retail directly to customers, primarily at a booth in Seattle's Pike Place Market, which is typically swarming with tourists. "By offering a spoonful of our jelly to people walking by, we get it into two hundred mouths an hour!"

I took Mick's advice and secured a booth in the popular Pike Place Market. But I soon learned why that spot was even available: location, location, location. My booth was on a slope, so I had gravity and momentum working against me. As I offered samples, one hundred mouths an hour walked right past me. After a few futile months I closed the booth. Instead, I filled up my days by doing more demos inside stores. My father called it sweat equity, as the stores were making more profits per jar for my efforts than I was. But doing these demos was the only option I had available to market and grow sales—by getting my peppers into at least twenty mouths an hour.

The problem with the hot peppers in oil was they were unique—unless you had grown up in Youngstown or Steubenville. Most people knew two things about peppers in a jar: They're roasted or cooked one way or another. And they can be hot. But my peppers in oil were sweet and savory. Spicy, yet smooth with a hint of citrus and a gentle heat. And all that amazing flavor is in the oil that lingers on the throat. To get this across, people needed to taste them. So I went the Cibo route and started filling my days doing demos in stores.

While doing these demos, I used dozens of lines to get people to stop and try them. But for some reason, my cringe-worthy groaners were the lines I enjoyed saying the most. As customers approached, I'd tell them with a sample in hand, "Mama Lil's are beyond delicious. They're beyond yum." As they walked past me, I'd call after them with the punchline, "When you get to scrumptious, you're almost there." "*The peppatunities are endless!*" was a decent pitch. But the line that seemed to work best for me was, *"A pepper for your thoughts?"* When that spin on the familiar phrase came out of my mouth, my friend Buddha Berman, bless his soul, saw a shopper stop, taste a sample, then put a jar in her cart. Buddha chuckled as he told me, "A pepper for your thoughts? That line worked." But if Buddha hadn't called my attention to it, I would've forgotten it like all the other gibberish I found myself spouting for hours on end.

At another demo I noticed a fifty-year-old man smiling at me as he watched me do my sales spiel. I almost recognized him. When the shoppers left, he stepped forward and was beaming at me when he said, "What an ingenious way of transcending a Jewish mother complex, bottle it up and *sell* it." Jeffrey Gold was my therapist when I was struggling with what I should do with my life, and now ten years later I'd become one of his therapeutic success stories.

If only *selling* were so easy. Even though I believed in my peppers, after hawking them for five hours, I was emotionally exhausted. And it was hard to tell whether it was worth the time I put into it or not, as the jars just got lost on the crowded grocery store shelves. One night when I felt forlorn about Mama Lil's prospects, I called my mom and complained about how hard it was to get the word out. She burst out with an idea. "Jane will help you sell your peppers." Jane Withers was a child actress who Lil worked for as a gofer in the 1940s. In the 1960s, Jane had a career resurgence with commercials on daytime soaps when her character, Josephine the Plumber, helped put Comet Cleanser underneath every sink in North America.

Jane called the next day. "Howie, send me some jars. I can sell anything!" I sent her two jars and in return, I received the snapshot below. Jane had oodles of confidence and probably felt these endorsements would get Mama Lil's in every pantry in the country. I displayed the framed photo at a demo, once. No one had a clue who Jane Withers was. She may have been the most bankable Hollywood star in 1938, but now Jane was as old-fashioned as mustard pickles.

Jane Withers: "I can sell anything!"

While eating a bowl of gumbo at the counter of Matt's in the Market, as was my custom after making a delivery there, I was going on about my sales woes with David Levy, a cheerful, bowtie-wearing advertising man. "I've done so many demos, but if I'm not there personally selling them, the jars just aren't moving off the shelves. No one even notices them."

Levy smiled knowingly, then explained, "According to the principles of marketing, a product needs to be seen seven times before it's even noticed. Until then, it will be invisible to people. People shop while staring at their grocery list. You've got to come up with some killer recipes so folks will have to buy your product so they can make those recipes."

I pleaded with David, "The real question is, what recipe don't they contribute to? The peppers are great thrown on everything. As it says on the jar, *The peppatunities are endless!*"

"Very cute. But when customers shop, they aren't looking for your product. They're trying to look past your product for what's on their list to make some recipe or other. Karo syrup is sold in every store in the country, but it is used for one thing: pecan pie. What's your recipe?"

"I have goats on the label. Maybe I should promote the peppers as a condiment to be served with goat cheese? Which they happen to go great with."

David urged me on, "Now you're getting somewhere. Maybe you can get the jars on the cheese counter, which makes them infinitely more visible."

So, I took David's advice and started doing demos where I served the peppers with goat cheese. A woman took a sample, then gushed as she perused the label on the jar. "These are delicious! Are they fattening?"

I boasted, "Ma'am, you can't put more fat on a fork." She set my jar down. As she walked away, I thought, *Why the heck did I say that? The fat was in the cheese* (okay, it coated the peppers, too). Blame it on my silly pepper selling costume that I'd say silly things just to get a reaction from people. But a minute later, that woman came back and bought the peppers, the goat cheese, and the crackers. Then she told me, "This will be my guilty pleasure." But I took Levy's point seriously about needing to be noticed seven times. I just had no idea how to get my jars of peppers noticed besides in-store demos and for lack of a better word, *guerrilla* marketing.

Historically, Seattle's most famous proponent of guerrilla marketing was the guitar strumming folksinger Ivar Haglund, who opened Seattle's first aquarium and fish and chips counter in 1938 on the downtown waterfront, then grew his restaurant empire for the next fifty years and became a local legend. The historian Paul Dorpat wrote that Ivar was always coming up with over-the-top publicity stunts to get his restaurants—and tartar sauce— noticed. When a freight train parked in front of his waterfront restaurant started leaking puddles of corn syrup, Ivar staged a photo op of himself wearing a bib and bowler hat while loading the gooey syrup onto his pancakes and telling people, "Eat at Ivar's. We don't skimp on the syrup." That photo not only made the front page of the *Seattle Post-Intelligencer,* but it got picked up by the newswire and "The Great Syrup Spill of 1947" was read about all around the world.

Ivar knew that guerrilla marketing, like guerrilla warfare, succeeds best in populated urban settings where you can get more bang for your buck. Places like baseball stadiums. I came home from a game in the old Kingdome one night and my friend Don Blevins asked me if that was me screaming "Julio! Julio!" all game long. I once had Julio Franco in my cab, and he was now my favorite player. Little did I know, I'd been sitting yards away from the broadcast booth and was coming in loud and clear to Mariner fans across the state. The next night, I sat right up next to the broadcast booth. Talk about target marketing! For nine innings, I screamed, "Buhner EATS Mama Lil's Peppers!" Before each pitch to Ken Griffey Jr., I'd beckon, "Junior! Come to Mama Lil!"

Ivar Haglund, Photo courtesy of the Paul Dorpat Collection.

Did my self-serving rants have any effect on Mama Lil's sales? Probably not in the short run. But I assumed I was covering one of those bases of getting noticed seven times by baseball fans across the state, even if annoyingly so. As for the rumor that a Mama Lil's label was stuck on the outfield wall between the Boeing and Microsoft logos, it was just that—a rumor. Never happened. At least, I never saw it. But what a wonderful idea. Ivar knew how to get his brand noticed, and I'm sure he wouldn't have thought twice about slapping one of his branded labels on the outfield wall.

I'd made a lot of jars in 1996 that I didn't have a market for yet, so I was in salesman mode at all times. On a trip to NYC, I loaded up one side of my briefcase with jars of peppers. On the other side, I'm afraid to say, I kept a few of my screenplays because…well, you never know. I then walked around Manhattan, passing out jars to gourmet food stores such as Dean & DeLuca, Zabar's, Murray's Cheese, Fairway, Citarella, and others. Not that it did me much good. Stores told me to find distribution in the city first, and then we'd talk. Not unlike when I'd send out my unsolicited screenplays to producers who told me to find an agent—and then we'd talk.

On this trip, I'd made a dinner date with my screenwriter friend Tony Gilroy and his wife, Susan—the Oracle of Delphi who had dared me to start a pepper business ten years before. At the last minute, Tony and Susan had to change our plans and instead I was invited to watch the first read-through of Tony's latest screenplay, the supernatural legal thriller *The Devil's*

Advocate. I brought along my lawyer friend Rick as payback for letting me crash on his couch. When we arrived at the address on lower Broadway and discovered it was Al Pacino's loft, Rick said to me, "Howard, come stay with us more often."

Tony and Susan were at a desk busily collating changes into *The Devil's Advocate* script. When Tony spotted me, he asked me, "You got one of those Mama Lil's promotional postcards? You know, the one with the goats?" I reached into my briefcase and gave him a Mama Lil's postcard. Tony placed the card in the loft's kitchenette, then got back to collating his revisions.

At the appetizer table, I tried unsuccessfully at making chitchat with some actors. My friend Rick, on the other hand, was animatedly engaged in a conversation with Craig T. Nelson, the star of the then popular TV show *Coach*. When I overheard that they both had been born in the same hospital in Spokane and had attended the same high school in Ellensburg, I cut in.

"I just drove through Ellensburg ten times on my way to Yakima."

This got Coach's attention. "Oh yeah? What were you doing in Yakima, picking apples?"

"Nope. I was picking peppers."

"What kind of peppers? I love spicy chiles."

Craig's eyes followed my hand as I reached inside my briefcase. He winced when he saw my screenplays in there, nervous that I was about to foist one of those on him. But when I pulled out the jar of Mama Lil's Kick Butt Peppers, he took it right out of my hands, twisted the lid off, grabbed a tortilla chip, scooped out a pepper, and ate it. "These are great!" Then he hooked a pepper ring onto a carrot stick and ate that. "These peppers would be great with a lot of things!"

I couldn't help myself as I let slip out, "The peppatunities are endless!"

Then a deep, familiar voice said, "Did you just say *peppatunities*?" It was Keanu Reeves. Craig handed Keanu the jar, showing him the label. Keanu read it out loud, "The peppatunities are endless. Cool." Just then the director called for the actors to come to the reading table. Keanu tried to hand the jar back to me, but I waved him off. When Keanu joined his fellow actors at the table he set the jar down in front of the empty seat next to him, then began to collate his script.

Minutes later Al Pacino entered the loft and went straight to his kitchenette. While pouring himself a glass of orange juice, Al spotted the Mama Lil's postcard on the counter, picked it up to examine it. Moments later he took his seat among the other actors. And what do you know that jar of Mama Lil's Peppers, with that same image of goats on the label, was placed next to his script. And what do you know, he reached for the jar first. Feeling that the lid had been opened, Al smelled the peppers, twisted the lid back on and slid the jar toward the center of the table.

Fifteen minutes into the reading, we got our first hint that the devil is at work when a goat is slaughtered in a voodoo ritual. When I heard the word "goat" for the second time, my eyes zoomed in on that jar, with its goats on the label, and Lil's shrill voice telling me. "How many scripts did you write? Sonny boy, you put my name on the label, we're gonna be in the movies!"

After the reading, my friend Rick was giving Keanu suggestions for his courtroom cross-examination scene. I had nothing to add to the conversation, but I had briefly met the director, Taylor Hackford, before, so when he recognized me, it was just enough of an opening that I—or was it Lil again?—started telling him, "That was quite the coincidence about the goats. I think it would be a cool device, if in the first act, when Keanu and Charlize are shopping for an apartment—that's when we see the goats on the Mama Lil's postcard. Second act: Keanu opens the refrigerator and what's inside, the Kick Butt Peppers! The goats are kicking—"

The director looked at me, absolutely stumped. "What are you talking about?"

Rick burst out laughing. "I think he's trying to sell you some peppers."

I said, "No, no, no. If the goats do a walk-on, the peppers will be free!"

Unless one counts Lil's friend Jane Withers, Tony Gilroy was my only real Hollywood contact, and I had asked him for a few too many favors over the years as I tried to get my scripts read by the right people. But when I got back home, I had one more favor to ask of Tony. "Could I send some peppers to the movie set? Who knows, maybe get a little product placement." Companies that get product placement in movies pay big bucks for this subliminal advertising. If by some slim chance the Mama Lil's goats got on a thousand silver screens across the country for even one-tenth of a movie second, it would be the equivalent of having a Mama Lil's label on the outfield wall between the Boeing and Microsoft insignias all season long. When Tony didn't say no, I sent two cases of jars and several Mama Lil's postcards to the movie set.

Meanwhile, I had a new story to tell my customers at demos. When I'd mimic Keanu saying, "The peppatunities are endless. Cool!" I'd get a chuckle, and they'd usually pick up the jar to inspect it. When I told them that those goats on the label would soon be making a walk-on appearance in a theater near you, that was the *ka-ching!* moment when the jar went into the cart.

I went to the opening night of *Devil's Advocate* and sat through it twice. Perhaps I'd told the story so many times I jinxed it. There were no Mama Lil's goats to be seen. When I asked Tony about the fate of those jars, he said he wasn't around for the shoot, but he assumed those twenty-four jars got divvied up between Coach, Keanu Reeves, and Al Pacino before the goats got around to do their walk-on appearance. But a few weeks later, I bumped into a customer who couldn't wait to tell me that she *had* seen a jar of Mama Lil's Peppers in one shot. I went back and watched *The Devil's Advocate* a third time. It's a fun movie, but still no goat sightings. Just as Hitchcock was so clever at pulling off, I'd apparently succeeded in subliminally planting the idea in her head, that she really had seen a jar of Mama Lil's.

What do you know, maybe advertising works after all.

Fresh Pappardelle Pasta, Wild Mushrooms, Goat Cheese & Mama Lil's
Matt Janke

I like to use sheets of fresh pasta, which I cut into noodles myself. Any pasta will do, but fresh is best, and a wider noodle holds the sauce better. For the wild mushrooms, use a mixture of your favorites; I prefer a combination of cremini, oyster, and shiitake.

Serves 4

2 tablespoons butter, plus more for serving, if desired
1 pound wild mushrooms (see headnote), trimmed and sliced thickly (or torn, in the case of oyster)
3 to 4 garlic cloves, peeled and sliced thinly
1 cup chicken stock, fresh or low-sodium
1½ pounds fresh pasta sheets, or fresh pasta noodles (preferably a wide noodle such as pappardelle)
1 cup Mama Lil's Peppers (Kick Butt if you like), oil included
8 ounces medium-soft, crumbly chèvre (I way prefer Laura Chenel, plain or peppered)
Salt and freshly ground black pepper
Fresh herbs, roughly chopped (such as thyme, rosemary, sage, Italian parsley)

Get a pot of pasta-cooking water going over medium-high heat. In a large saucepan over medium-high heat, melt your butter. When it foams and bubbles, toss in the mushrooms and garlic. Increase the heat and stir and toss the mushrooms continually, cooking them down a bit while being careful to not scorch the garlic. As soon as the mushrooms begin to turn color and release some liquid, add the chicken stock. Once the stock has reduced by about half, begin cooking your pasta in the pot of boiling water.

Add the Mama Lil's Peppers to the mushrooms and turn off the heat. Crumble in the chèvre, season the mushroom ragu with salt and black pepper, and add fresh herbs to taste. Cook the pasta until al dente, 2 to 4 minutes, and drain. Serve the pasta in bowls (add a little butter to them if you like), top with the ragu, and serve immediately. This dish is great with a lighter-bodied red wine such as a Nebbiolo or a Gamay Noir.

GETTING BY WITH A LITTLE HELP FROM MY FRIENDS

THANKS TO MY AMBITIOUS HAND-TO-MOUTH marketing in Seattle and Portland, in 1997 I asked Gayle Krueger to increase the number of peppers he grew for Mama Lil's by yet another 50 percent. After producing 1,600 cases in 1996, I hoped to make more than 2,400 in 1997. This wasn't that big of a gamble, as by now I was confident that the peppers became more flavorful as they aged in the jar, for at least two years anyway. What I didn't take into consideration was how the hell I would ever physically increase my output by 50 percent in the same limited production time.

The answer, I'm afraid, was by way of my friends. When I started my business, the only talent that I brought to the table—besides perhaps the gift of gab—was for friendship. If you were my friend, you were called upon at some point of need. Nick, with whom I had started the business, was in a time of need when his marriage ended. George Wolf told Nick that as long as he was working for me, Nick could live in one of the cannery's window-less second floor bedrooms, for free. This was hardly luxurious for Nick but quite convenient for me as he was there to drain the peppers, so I didn't have to drive two hours just to do that two-hour chore.

By then, George sold me his 1980 Ford three-quarter-ton van that he'd put to pasture after abusing it for two hundred thousand miles. Every inch of that maroon van had been dented, and its steering was loose, but I could squeeze a ton of goathorn peppers inside of it. On a day when I was packing jars, Nick drove the van to Krueger's to pick up the next ton of peppers. He was livid upon his return. While driving down South Uptanum Ridge into the Yakima Valley in the empty van, he was given a ticket and a breathalyzer test because the cop said he was weaving in and out of his lane. He pleaded with the cop, "Without ballast it was like steering a bronco in that wind." I paid for Nick's ticket, but a week later he found a real job and a better place to live.

I then convinced the singer-songwriter Terry Lee Hale to let me fly him in from Paris for a few weeks. Since Terry's fingers were his livelihood, I spared him from coming close to the Bobbitron blades, God forbid. But Terry made deliveries, cared for my cat when I slept at the cannery, and helped me drain the peppers. He also enjoyed hauling the peppers back from the Yakima Valley in the van. He'd grown up in Yakima and seeing the orchards reminded him of his childhood when he'd pick apples with his migrant fruitpicker grandfather. I was trying to make the most of Terry's time in Seattle—as I wasn't paying him poorly, and he wasn't slicing peppers—so I asked him to come up with a Mama Lil's theme song for me while he was driving back and forth to the farm.

"What would the song be about?" Terry asked, as if irked by my request.

"You know, the toil of it all. Slicing off stems, scooping out seeds."

When Terry brought back the next ton of peppers, he had come up with a song. And it was a good song too, called "Bruises and Stems." But it wasn't about slicing off pepper stems; it was about picking apples with his grandpa. Before he went back to Europe, Terry did save my ass big-time. A bolt fell off the Bobbitron while I was slicing peppers. I searched on the floor and in the drains for an hour and could not find it. I knew that bolt must be in a vat of peppers. I offered Terry a reward if he found the bolt when draining those peppers with me the next day.

We'd gotten through almost all four vats of pickled peppers, and I was getting more and more nervous. Biting into a Bobbitron bolt had *lawsuit* written all over it. Then Terry leaned over and plucked out that shiny chunk of metal and held it up to admire like he'd found a precious stone. My mood swung from dread to joyful celebration. Then on our drive home, the Indians beat the Yankees—the first hurdle toward getting back to the World Series. That night, Terry's last in town, the celebration moved to the Conor Byrne Pub, where he put on a fabulous show and even got up the nerve to sing "Bruises and Stems" for the first time.

Over that long Indian summer Krueger's fields kept yielding those gorgeous goathorns, and I was determined to pickle them all. Heck, the Indians were still in it, and there was nothing better for making the time go by than listening to my beloved team play. And this year I just knew they were going to win it all. But having packed as many jars in six weeks as I'd packed in eight weeks the year before, I was running on fumes. Needing an influx of energy, I convinced my friend Patrick Lango (he of the nine-pound leg of lamb) to come help me. I'm not sure what I said to convince Pat to fly from Buffalo to spend a week with me making peppers, but I was glad he said yes. He was a talented worker, and I had seven straight days of work planned for him.

When I picked up Pat at the airport at midnight, he was sniffling. When I woke him up at five a.m. to head out to the cannery, Pat was now blowing his nose. But he got out of bed, climbed into my car, then slept the whole way out to the cannery, only opening an eye to see me pull the bungee cord across the bellies of my crew I'd rounded up. But once we got inside the cannery, that Bobbitron became an extension of Pat's arm. He sliced peppers so fast my crew and I had a hard time keeping up with him. But perhaps he'd given too much of himself. The next day when he drove with me to Wapato to get more peppers, Pat was getting sicker by the hour. On Pat's fifth day, I was now feeling sick too. With both of us feeling like shit, and getting on each other's nerves, we busted our butts at the cannery and packed 220 cases of jars. I was in a hurry to get home and watch the Indians playoff game, so I was still going full bore by multitasking, catching hot jars from the steam tunnel while also hosing down the cannery floor. Pat innocently walked by me, but said to me sarcastically with raised arms, "Don't shoot."

All I can say for myself is that it wasn't a premeditated act. If he hadn't said, "Don't shoot," I never would have squeezed the hose's nozzle. Much in the same way that if I hadn't told Terry to write a song about peppers, he wouldn't have written that song about apples. But Pat did say, "Don't shoot," and I blasted him full force with that high-pressure hose. We had a scrum in the middle of the cannery floor that George put an end to before either of us landed a decent punch. Sure, I may have a talent for friendship, but in the heat of production, I'll admit I've abused that talent a time or two. Pat flew home that night. Which was too bad. We were about to have so much fun making Honkin' Hot PeppaLilli together.

After I got home from driving him to the airport, I collapsed on my couch in despair. I was guilty about the fight I initiated with a friend who had flown 2,500 miles just to help me. *I'm a schmuck.* And where would this schmuck find the strength in three hours to wake up and do it all again? I fell asleep on the couch in my work clothes. I was awoken by my phone at 5 a.m. It was Lil. "I hoped to catch you before you go to work. How's it going, sonny boy?"

"I don't know if I can do it anymore. Mom, it's making me meshuga. And I'm not making a dime. And I can't even imagine when I ever will."

After a coffee-sipping pause, my mom said, "Then you should stop."

"You think I should stop making Mama Lil's Peppers?"

"If you're not making money, why do it? You can always just drive your cab and write another of your plays. But that was frustrating for you too, wasn't it."

Then luckily another friend came to my rescue when Matt from Matt's in the Market, along with his two chefs, their wives, and a whole slew of knives, drove out to the cannery to help me on a lovely Sunday morning. We opened the large cannery doors wide to let the crisp autumn air in, and blasted *Sgt. Pepper's Lonely Hearts Club Band* all day while we sliced a thousand pounds of goathorns, onions, and cucumbers to make my last pack of PeppaLilli.

I got it done that year with a lotta help from my friends.

Twenty-four hours later, two thousand bright yellow jars were on the conveyor belt taking their slow journey through the steam tunnels. George was in the machine shop. I was standing at the end of the pasteurization tunnel, catching the hot jars and stacking them on racks.

Yards away from me, in George's bedroom, the Indians-Orioles play-off game was on his TV. I'd scope the dark tunnel with a flashlight to see where the jars were, then run back into George's room to catch a moment of the tense game where the Indians were behind in the eighth inning. Just as I stepped into the room for the tenth time, WHAM! The Indians hit the game-winning home run! I fell to my knees, raised my arms to the heavens, and let go of all my frustration from the long harvest in one long scream of utter jubilation!

But to George, who heard my scream over the whine of grinding steel, it sounded like a scream of body-ripping pain. George ran to the door. "I got 911 on the line. What happened?"

With tears streaming down my face, I told George, "Fernández just took Benítez—*deep!* The Tribe's going to the World Series, George! I'm set to win five grand!" George's jaw dropped in disbelief, and I heard him cackling all the way back to the machine shop.

Ten days later, in the tenth inning of game seven of the World Series, a soft line drive by Édgar Rentería somehow eluded Tony Fernandez's reach. The Tribe lost. I lost. I was hoping their win would not only win me $5000 but give me a shot of energy. But no such luck. As I laid on my couch in a daze, my ringing phone startled me from my torpor. It was my childhood friend Jonny Katz, whom I hadn't spoken to since the Indians lost the World Series in 1995.

"Howie, we might be fools. But we're not losers. The flip side of material loss is spiritual victory." For his wise words, Jonny received a free case of Mama Lil's Kick Butt Peppers.

In 1997, despite having been on the precipice of quitting, I increased my output at Wolf Pack by 50 percent, which seemed like a reasonable aspiration of growth for the next twelve months. But I'd been utterly dependent on my friends. What about next year? I was running out of friends.

Enter Jan Barton, a twenty-three-year-old Czech man who was traveling in Alaska when he met a fisherman friend of mine who gave him my number. Since Jan had a day to spare before he flew back to Prague, he came with me to Wolf Pack to pick up a vanload of jars. When I showed him Wallace River, teeming with spawning salmon, he wanted to walk into it and grab himself one. When I pointed to the spectacular 265-foot drop of Wallace Falls peeking out from the forested Cascade foothills, Jan asked if we could hike up to it then and there. He was penniless after his travels, so I gave him fifty bucks when I dropped him off at the airport. Two months later, I received an envelope with a fifty-dollar bill, and I knew I could trust Jan. When he agreed to help make my peppers next harvest, I asked Gayle Krueger to increase next year's yield by a third.

Being a trained engineer, Jan was a good influence on me. He looked for timesaving shortcuts and strived for more consistency in the production process. Until this point, I saw the act of adding garlic and oregano as a spiritual exercise and never allowed anyone else to do it. When Jan saw me eyeball the garlic and oregano I was mixing into the pickled peppers, he asked me how much of each went into the prep tub. I told him, "Depends on what mood I'm in." Of course, that's stupid talk. Any food manufacturer needs its products to be consistent to a fault, with no fluctuation whatsoever. From then on, whether I was in a foul mood or not, for every thirty pounds of pickled peppers, I used exactly one cup each of garlic and oregano. Until then, the peppers were always great, but their flavor may have varied slightly from batch to batch. It was the way it was because it was the way I was. But Jan put an end to that way of thinking.

Jan loved living at Wolf Pack. On days after he drained the peppers and labeled jars, he'd tend to the cannery's garden, forage for mushrooms and berries in the woods, and swim in the Skykomish River or the pools below Wallace Falls. He slept in a hammock stretched between trees on the cannery grounds. One morning, I arrived with my crew of Millionairs and found him still in his hammock, gazing upward in a state of bliss. He whispered to me in his Czech accent, "I had a *wizit!* From a deer. He stared into my eyes. Was like a *wizion*. I too will live in the country some day!" (Jan's *wizion* came true!) Most importantly for my mental health, instead of rushing home in rush-hour traffic after a long day of work, Jan got me to hike with him to the pools below Wallace Falls for an invigorating swim.

By 1998, George's grandson had moved away from Wolf Pack, and with Gold Bar being so far out in the boonies, it wasn't easy for George to find someone to replace him. Which is how George met Mike and Becky White, I guess. The Whites had dropped out of mainstream society and were hiding out in the boonies of Gold Bar. While working for George they lived in a trailer hidden behind the cannery. I should've known by their erratic behavior what dropping out and hiding entailed. The Whites and I got along well enough, but Jan and I just stayed out of their way. We were responsible for slicing, pickling, and packing the jars; the Whites ran the jars through the pasteurization tunnel and kept the production logs.

PeppaLilli Days were happy days. Jan, 1998.

By the third week, Jan and I had become so efficient at working as a team that we were packing fifty more cases per session than I had in the past. But what we most looked forward to making was PeppaLilli. We happily took turns stirring the thickening mustard sauce with a giant whisk before lowering the mixing paddles into the bubbling mustard soup. And then we'd be mesmerized by the bright vegetables being turned over by the paddles in the thickening mustard sauce, like a Jackson Pollock action painting, in action. Call it *#9 Yellow Convergence!* Our lunchtime ritual was grilling sausages, then spooning the mustard relish straight from the kettle onto our sandwiches and eating them right where we stood.

On the last pepper-slicing session of this very productive season, I went to the Millionair Club at 5:30 am to round up a crew. After ten minutes, I had lured only one Hispanic man into my station wagon. I assumed most of these men had sliced peppers for me before and were willing to hold out until a better job—or at least a better car—came along. I was approached by a man who by his looks, I assumed was a junkie, so I waved him off. But he didn't walk away.

"Vat you need?" he asked with a thick European accent. He wasn't that old, but his face was weather-worn, and his motorcycle jacket had at least a million miles on it. When I told him we'd be slicing peppers, he boasted, "I'm damn gud vif a knife. And I'll sharpen your knives so they vill cut through steel." He got in my car. When I pulled the bungee cords across his chest to close the door, he broke into a smile. "And I vill fix your doors for ya, too."

"You've worked on these old Volvos before?"

"I'm from Sweden. I was practically born in one of these Amazons. My name is Tomas." Tomas was indeed very fast at cutting stems off peppers. "Tis nuthin compared to fileting feesh," he said. During a lunch break, with a cigarette dangling from his mouth, he sharpened all my knives in the machine shop. When I took him and the Hispanic man back to Seattle, Tomas had a silly grin on his face when he told me that he was staying at the Sheraton Hotel. I couldn't imagine him staying at such a fancy hotel, but that's where I took him. When I paid him in cash, he flashed another silly smile, revealing all his nicotine-stained teeth. "Must I pay taxes on dis?"

"That's up to you."

He liked my answer. "Den vait one minute for me. I vant to fix your door." One minute later, the bellhop was wheeling out five large suitcases that Tomas crammed into my car. That night, while sipping on vodka, Tomas told me his life story. He worked as a machinist in Sweden "in the black, only in the black" until eight years ago when he got thrown out of the country for not paying taxes. Then he worked in Norway as a laborer for four years until he got thrown out for not paying taxes there either. Next he landed in Iceland where he worked on fishing boats for four more years. But—surprise—he didn't pay taxes in Iceland either, so he hopped a ferry to Nova Scotia, took a train all the way across Canada, then boarded a bus for Seattle. His life almost sounded like the Dylan song, "Tangled Up in Blue." But not nearly so romantic.

"Ever dug a ditch?" I asked Tomas.

"I dug a t'ousand ditches."

Within minutes of being dropped off at the Sheraton, Tomas's itinerant antennae found the Millionair Club. "When I saw everyone valking away from your car, I said to myself, 'Vat have ve here?'" After telling me myriad stories of his adventures as he downed the bottle, Tomas suddenly put on a malicious face and looked me straight in the eye. "Everything I've told you is a lie. I'm on the run. I kilt Olof Palme. He deserved it for raising taxes so high." I didn't believe Tomas's tall tale of being the hitman of Sweden's prime minister any more than that he was staying at the Sheraton. And I doubt he remembered he told me that tale in the morning.

But he did have the Viking killer instinct in him. When we arrived at Wolf Pack the next day, he grabbed my largest knife, and proclaimed, "Time to fix this fuckin' door!" Then like a Nordic samurai he sliced through the bungee cords holding my doors closed. While Jan and I drained peppers, Tomas sculpted the steel on my car's door. By dinnertime, no bungee cords were required anymore. I was almost sad to see them go. Those worn-out overstretched cords were symbolic to me of how I'd held Mama Lil's together during my first six years in business.

Just as Jan, Tomas, and I were heading out to dinner, we saw George Wolf's van heading down Moonlight Drive on his way to spend a long weekend in Reno. And when the Wolf is away, the rats will play. When Jan, Tomas, and I came back from dinner, Jan pointed out the bitter fumes coming from Mike White's trailer behind the cannery. Never having smelled anything quite like it, I ignored it, then drove home with Tomas.

When Tomas and I arrived the next morning and found Jan in the cannery, it was eerily quiet and none of the equipment was turned on. Jan didn't have a clue what was going on either until Mike White stomped in and with his eyes bulging and told me, "Something's wrong. The boilers won't turn on." Mike threw up his arms and stomped back out. When Mike returned minutes later, he was even more amped up as he lugged George's giant pipe wrench around the cannery. But eventually the boiler was on, and soon hot steam was flowing through the tunnels.

Over the next seven hours, Jan and I hand-packed nearly three hundred cases of vibrantly colorful Kick Butt jars while Tomas twisted the lids on them. They were all now on the conveyor belt making their half-hour passage through the tunnels. Jan, Tomas, and I were cleaning up when we noticed Mike was agitated with his wife, who was stationed at the end of the pasteurization tunnel catching the hot jars. Except these jars weren't hot. Mike reported back to me, "George must've had a tiff with the gas company. Our gas is off!" Pointing at the stacks of jars he said, "Your jars didn't get fully pasteurized. These jars got cooked to only 127 degrees."

I can't say I ever got a full explanation of what happened that day. Mike and Becky were high as a kite on crystal meth and weren't taking timely temperature readings, let alone notating them in the production logs. We didn't know when the gas had stopped flowing. Or how many jars came out of the tunnel without getting sufficiently pasteurized. Mike offered to send the jars through the tunnel a second time when the gas was back on. But I knew this would make the peppers soft and mushy, so I told him not to. I wasn't overly concerned about this snafu as Lil never pasteurized her jars at all. In fact, I was looking forward to tasting this beautiful batch of Kick Butt Peppers that got undercooked by forty degrees. By the time George got back to the cannery on Tuesday, the gas was back on, and it was never brought up again.

In those splendid nine weeks of the summer and fall of 1998, Jan and I increased the number of jars Mama Lil's made by 33 percent, to 3,300 cases. We also doubled the amount of PeppaLilli made the year before. I certainly hadn't built up a market for the PeppaLilli yet, so I assume we'd made so much of it because we had so much fun making it.

On Jan's last night in town—while Tomas stayed home sipping vodka— Jan and I celebrated at Peter Cipra's cozy Czech restaurant, Labuznik. It was because of Peter's request to get the peppers in larger jars that I'd made forty cases of quart jars specifically for restaurants. Jan exaltedly marched a case into Peter's kitchen as a gift. Peter in turn kept the Montepulciano flowing as dish upon dish of dumplings and other Czech comfort food came our way. Peter loved my story of eating nine pounds of lamb in one sitting, and thus the main course was a leg of lamb served with Mama Lil's peppers. By our third bottle of wine, Jan and I were making loud toasts.

A young businessman one table over asked us, "What are you guys celebrating anyway?"

Jan boasted, "We just canned over thirty-nine thousand jars of peppers!"

Without a glimmer of sarcasm, the man asked, "Did you make them in a day or a week?"

I assumed this pompous ass was a Microsoft executive who, with one keystroke could set in motion the production of thirty-nine thousand Encarta DVDs. He had no idea what it took to make thirty-nine thousand jars. And if I'd told him that my profits were at best a miniscule seventy cents per jar, he too would've called me a fool. And he would've been right. At this stage, I had never written myself a single check. All the money coming in stayed in the bank so I could make more jars the following year. But we had good reason to toast our glasses. We were making products that probably shouldn't even exist. Like making these jars we were performing a righteous act. You just can't put a price tag on that feeling. As for all those Encarta DVDs (talk about being old-fashioned), no one uses them anymore. But if you found a jar from 1998 in your pantry, they'll be delicious. Beyond delicious. *When you get to scrumptious, you're almost there.*

After the harvest was over, I flew to Ohio to see my parents. They were so relieved that their forty-three-year-old son had finally found himself. But then again, I didn't tell my parents I was still driving a cab a couple of nights a week to make ends meet. I brought several cases of peppers with me. One was for Lil, who loved giving away jars to her friends. The others I hoped to sell to the West Point Market in Akron. According to Lil, it was the finest grocery store in Ohio, and I knew how thrilled she would be if Mama Lil's found their way onto their shelves.

When my folks picked me up from the airport, my father wanted in on the pepper action. "There's this guy Santisi you should meet."

"I hope it's not Sam, the linebacker," I said. "I blew him out of the chemistry class window in tenth grade. Sam might still have it in for me."

"No, this is Donny Santisi. He stayed out of the grocery business. He's a trucker. But I hear he makes the peppers in oil for most of the restaurants in Youngstown and Warren."

"Dad, you're telling me a trucker makes the peppers. I find that hard to believe."

"Why? I know a cabbie who makes them too."

The office of Santisi's Trucking was exactly what one would expect—four guys sitting at cluttered desks smoking cigarettes and drinking coffee. When I walked in, one of them stood up. "I'm Donny. Let's see what you got." I pulled out a tiny sample jar and handed it to Donny. He chuckled. "You can make them in jars that small? I put them in four-gallon buckets."

"Really, you can put them in buckets that big?"

Donny plucked out a pepper ring from my jar with his pinky. "Yours are more colorful than mine." He tasted it and smiled approvingly. "They're good. Your mother taught you right."

"She taught me wrong. She doesn't pasteurize her jars."

Donny tasted another pepper ring. "I've never pasteurized a jar in my life. I make a year's supply in a month that I store in a reefer trailer. I rarely sell a bucket that's over a year old."

"You got any secrets to share with me? Besides how important it is to drain the peppers?"

"Yeah, I wash the peppers in ice water. Helps keep them fresh."

When I told my dad the meeting with Santisi went well, he was ready with his next idea. "Some guy in Warren sold all his McDonald's franchises to buy these sandwich shops called Panera Bread. Let's check them out. Maybe they'll like your peppers for their sandwiches."

I got short with my dad. "It's Donny Santisi who makes them for restaurants. Not me."

The next day, armed with the five cases of jars, Lil and I drove to Akron's West Point Market, where I had set up a sales meeting with its buyer. The store also had a popular café, and its chef walked into our meeting. When she tried the peppers, she got excited. "These would be awesome for our sandwiches and salads! Can you make them in buckets?"

"There's a guy in Youngstown who makes these same peppers in buckets."

"But I'd like to get them from you. That way we can call them Mama Lil's on the menu."

Music to my ears! And the West Point Market's owner was so impressed by his chef's response that when we came out of the meeting, he was eager to meet my mom—which sent Lil over the moon. When she later saw the large display of Mama Lil's jars the staff had quickly assembled, Lil was on her way to Mars. That night, I overheard her bragging on the phone: "Howie didn't give me grandchildren like his brother. But how many Jewish boys name their businesses after their mother? And he's doing such a good job. Someday Mama Lil's will be on grocery shelves all over the country!"

The next day I called Gayle Krueger from the airport and asked him if by chance there were any goathorn peppers in his fields. He said there were some peppers left, but his pickers had already gone back to Mexico. And besides, a freeze was forecast the following night that would wipe out the rest of the crop. The next morning, Tomas and I drove to the farm and spent four hours picking three hundred pounds of goathorns. The next day at Wolf Pack, with a couple helpers, we sliced and pickled the peppers. Twenty-four hours later, we drained the peppers.

The following night, Mama Lil's officially embarked on a new frontier when Tomas and I packed Mama Lil's first twenty buckets with thirty pounds of pickled peppers in oil in each one.

Honkin' Hot Tuna Melt

Matt Janke

Matt says, "This tuna melt was pretty much the favorite sandwich served at Lecosho and is easy to make. These tuna melts are great, as are all grilled sandwiches, with tomato soup."

Makes 4 sandwiches

1 pound fresh albacore tuna (or canned solid white albacore, thoroughly drained)
8 to 10 ounces Mama Lil's PeppaLilli Mustard Pickle Relish, chopped in a food processor
1 cup mayonnaise
¼ cup Mama Lil's Peppers with the oil (or substitute sambal or chili sauce)
Butter or oil for grilling
8 slices good grilling bread, such as sourdough or potato loaf
4 good slices Gruyère cheese, preferably cave-aged

At Lecosho, we would sear the tuna in a pan on the stove over medium heat for about 2 minutes on each side, or until the internal temperature reached 140°F on an instant-read thermometer. (But you can grill or cook it however you prefer.) Then flake the tuna and chill it.

In a large bowl, combine your tuna and Mama Lil's PeppaLilli, without overmixing or mushing it up. In a small bowl, make your spicy mayo by thoroughly mixing mayonnaise and Mama Lil's.

Butter the bread on the side it will be grilled. Then assemble sandwiches. Spread spicy mayo on one side of each slice of bread and top with the tuna-pickle mixture, followed by a slice of cheese and a second slice of bread. Grill the sandwiches in a lightly buttered frying pan over medium-low heat for 3 minutes on each side, or until golden. (Weight them with the pan's lid.)

PAY TO PLAY

LIKE EVERY OTHER FOOL I MET AT Wolf Pack trying to start a business based on a family recipe, I aspired to have Mama Lil's Peppers make it on the national stage. And seeing the jars of peppers on the shelves of that fancy Ohio supermarket gave me confidence that just maybe I could accomplish this. When a small local distributor invited Mama Lil's to be part of its lineup at the 1999 Winter Fancy Food Show at Moscone Center in San Francisco, I jumped at the opportunity.

To cut down on my expenses, I was crashing on my cousin Frank's rooming-house couch. Frank was a gypsy-like jazz musician who, wherever he went carried a duct tape covered saxophone case on his shoulder. Frank was eager to check out the food show, and I gave him an extra badge labeled "Buyer," which I'd acquired so folks would pay more attention to me when I was exploring the show. When Frank came back with three full shopping bags, he told me, "You gave me the magic badge!"

Behind our long booth I was standing elbow to elbow with a dozen other vendors sampling their products. Chef Myron Becker, a short nebbish-like hippie, was next to me, peddling his line of Japanese cooking sauces inspired by his time as a cook on a Navy ship off Japan. After an hour of listening to me cast out my cringeworthy lines at everyone walking by—"You gotta mama, I gotta mama, my mama is Mama Lil!"—Myron had reached his limit.

"Shut the fuck up!" Myron berated me. "You're devoting too much time to the wrong people. While the *right* people—*the buyers*—are passing you by! Buyers are the only people here whose badges you should be focusing on. And buyers don't give a fuck who your mama is."

I told Myron, "Some people who say they're buyers aren't really buyers."

"Know your buyers," Myron warned. "Some are worth kissing ass for. Most will get from you whatever they can and will lure you in with *free fill.*"

"What's free fill?"

With a look of disgust Myron informed me, "Free fill is pay to play. The stores get the first case of your products for free. Getting products in stores for the first time is easy as you're giving them away. But once a store gets your product for free, odds are they'll never order again. And free fill would be the death knell for a crop-driven business like yours." Even though it was relatively easy for Myron to replenish his products, he'd had it with paying to attend food shows only to be asked to give away his product for free.

Frank learned that on the last day of the show, vendors gave away all their unwanted products for free. Now Frank was remarkably fit, even though he possessed the Lev gene for gluttony. On the last day Frank showed up with three large duffel bags. Within an hour those bags were stuffed to the hilt with a couple hundred pounds of every kind of gourmet food imaginable.

That's when we both noticed a homeless man in a tattered overcoat enter the hall through an emergency exit door. He was rubbing his eyes in disbelief. This was no fashion show. This was no computer show. This was no fooling around. This was a full-on food fest! The man ran a comb through his hair in a vain attempt to look presentable. Then in a moment of pure inspiration, Frank draped the buyer's badge around the man's neck, placed a shopping bag in his hand, and sent him on his merry way. Transformed, the man joined the throng of buyers in the aisles of commerce.

Like I'd told Myron, "Some people who say they're buyers are not really buyers."

Mama Lil's had a successful first national trade show. The Mildly Spicy Peppers in Oil were voted the best product in the whole aisle we were set up in. (But then again, there were one hundred aisles in the show, so there were a hundred winners of that award.) As a result, Mama Lil's did get placed in a few grocery stores, and I managed to talk their buyers out of free fill in exchange for doing lots of demos. Frank volunteered to help with those. Being a musician, he was a natural performer. And he claimed that he could quote all my bad lines by heart.

When Frank and I walked out of Moscone Center at the end of the show, he looked like Santa lugging his three bulging duffel bags. A homeless man propped up against a parking meter got a whole smoked turkey laid into his lap. The next poor man Frank encountered was astonished when he found himself holding a ten-pound hunk of ham wrapped in fancy red foil . When I boarded the BART on my way home, Frank was in a jolly mood and down to one duffel bag that he planned on making last until next year's food show.

"Substantial" Fish al Limon & Mama Lil's

Myron Becker

For the fish, use a fillet (at least ¾ inches thick) from a firm, white-fleshed saltwater fish. You could use king salmon or even walleye pike—but lingcod, halibut, black sea bass, striped bass, haddock, grouper, or a light-colored tuna would be preferable. Here in the Northeast, we'd use cod or haddock. Lightly season the fish with coarse sea salt and black pepper (y'all know freshly ground is bettah).

Rub the top side of the fillet with **1 tablespoon of olive oil** mixed with maybe **1 tablespoon of mayo**. Lightly dredge the fish in **all-purpose flour** that's been mixed with some **panko breadcrumbs**. Squeeze at least 3 tablespoons of juice from a **fresh lemon** into a small bowl or cup. Then scoop 3 heaping tablespoons of **Mama Lil's Kick Butt Peppas** outa the jar and put them in a separate small bowl. Gather a half-dozen nice, ripe sweet **cherry** or **pear tomatoes** and set them aside.

Set up a heavy sauté pan or skillet over medium heat with **3 tablespoons of clarified butter or ghee**—or regular butter if you don't have time to clarify it. (Although you can easily do that—just use Google or YouTube, of course! What you want is a fat that can tolerate a pretty high heat. You can use peanut oil or bacon fat, but don't use extra-virgin olive oil.) Get your grease good 'n' hot and fry the fish, presentation-side down, until it turns nice and golden. Then carefully flip the fillet to cook the other side. The fish is done when the internal temperature reaches 140°F, which usually takes 5 minutes per inch of thickness.

Add all your lemon juice to the pan and deftly turn the fish in it as the juice reduces, trying not to break the fillet apart. Remove the fish from the pan and drain it on a paper towel if you want (or are oleophobic). Slide the fillet onto a warm plate.

Add the **tomatoes** to the still-hot pan; cook, tossing them, for about 30 seconds. Then add the Mama Lil's to the pan and stir to combine until heated through. Nap the fillet with this scrumptious mixture, then garnish with some **chopped fresh scallions** or cilantro or parsley (or all three), plus another spritz of fresh lemon juice (to counter the rich oil from the Mama Lil's peppers).

Serve with pride and a crisp white wine.

PUTREFACTIVE ANAEROBES OF C. BUTRICUM

AFTER FINISHING THE THANKLESS JOB of following up on the food show's sales leads—many of them no doubt coming by way of that homeless man with a buyer's badge—I went to see my folks in Ohio again. This time I brought along six of those 30 pound buckets of Pickled Peppers in Oil that Tomas and I made, for the West Point Market. When I pushed the buckets up to the busy airport check-in counter, the confused ticketing agent looked incredulously at the buckets.

"What's in the buckets?"

"The most delicious peppers on the planet." I charmingly said, in full salesman mode.

"Are they? You don't think you're bringing them on the plane, do you?"

"Why not? I upgraded to a first-class seat. I'll just put them in front of me."

"That's totally against FAA regulations."

"I'll pay to put them in baggage then. "

"That's not going to fly either. "

As I then reverted into begging mode with the ticketing agent, I was holding up the lengthening ticketing line. A man behind me tapped me on my shoulder.

"Excuse me. Are those really *buckets* of Mama Lil's Peppers?"

"Unfortunately, they are," I said ruefully.

As the ticketing agent was watching on, the man went over to his suitcase, and presto, he pulled out a jar of Mama Lil's Peppers. "If I'd known I could buy these peppers in a bucket, I would've brought my brother one of those." Then what do you know, some other guy in line flaunted a jar of Mama Lil's Peppers in a plastic baggie that he pulled from his suitcase. "My family wouldn't let me in the door without at least one jar of Kick Butt Peppers!"

The ticketing agent's jaw dropped. "Okay. You can check in the buckets. This one time. But you're totally responsible for them. And we are not insuring them!" We put the buckets in garbage bags, slapped luggage tags on them, and off they went down the conveyor belt. In my seven years as a salesman for Mama Lil's Peppers, persuading that ticketing agent to let me take those buckets on the plane may have been my greatest victory yet. And I have my loyal wingmen customers to thank for that.

It was a short-lived victory. At 5:30 a.m., I was standing at the baggage carousel at the Pittsburgh airport, wondering how the hell my buckets would come down the steep chute without tipping over. One of those fans of Mama Lil's saw me when he grabbed his suitcase and shook my hand. "My brother is picking me up from the airport because he knows I'm bringing this jar for him." That's when I smelled the distinct garlicky aroma of Mama Lil's wafting in the air. I feared the lid on his jar had come loose due to cabin pressure on the airplane. It had happened to me before and ruined my favorite sweater.

When the baggage carousel finally stopped, I was the only person remaining there. But where were my buckets? I ran up the luggage chute to look for them, but they weren't there. When I came down the luggage ramp, I was tapped on my shoulder.

It was an FAA agent. "By chance, are you looking for some buckets?"

"Phew. I was starting to worry. I'm glad they didn't send them down that luggage chute."

The agent was not amused. "Follow me." He stopped abruptly. "What is in that oil?!"

I was almost bragging when I told him, "Peppers, oregano, and lots of garlic. Why?"

"Why?! Because that oil leaked onto almost every suitcase on your flight."

When we got to the FAA office, the agent showed me where he had stashed the buckets behind the counter. Two people were filling out claim forms, no doubt for their damaged luggage on my flight. The agent told me, "Wait right here Mr. Lev. I got some forms for you to fill out."

Which is when I heard a familiar shrill voice calling my name. Lil poked her head into the FAA office. "There you are! I got a parking spot right out front. Let's go."

"I can't. Some buckets tipped over. I'm waiting to fill out some claim forms."

Lil quickly surveyed the situation and spotted my buckets behind the counter. "What good could come out of filling out forms? We gotta go!" She walked out, then reappeared with a luggage cart, demanding I put the buckets on it. Being a law-abiding citizen, I hesitated, but when she hoisted one of the heavy buckets onto the cart, I had no choice but to load the rest of them onto it. Then she pushed that cart right out of the airport to her car where the trunk was wide open, like it was a planned getaway. As I loaded the buckets into the trunk, I luckily spotted the two loose lids and snapped them onto the buckets.

My father was asleep in the passenger seat, so I hopped in the car and drove off. In the rearview mirror, I thought I saw the FAA agent looking for us, but I didn't stop to find out. In the back seat, Lil nervously kept turning her head to glance behind us. When we crossed the state line into Ohio fifteen minutes later, my mom let out a sigh of relief. "I think you're safe now."

And my dad once called me a scofflaw? The pepper doesn't fall far from the bush. Lil probably thought we were getting away with it. But those buckets had my labels and my luggage tags on them. The next day, when we delivered the buckets to the West Point Market, I told the chef, "If I ever bring a bucket on a plane again, I'll get arrested."

"Next time," the chef told me, "we'll order enough buckets so you can ship them on a pallet." Good to hear. In this business, shipping pallet-size amounts was a sign of success. When I returned home, I was feeling even more hopeful about my prospects for the foodservice angle of the business, where I could supply restaurants and other institutions with bulk quantities. When I listened to my voicemail there were several orders waiting for me for jars and buckets. No doubt about it—Mama Lil's was experiencing a surge of sales that boded well for the future.

But the last message was the gravelly voice of George Wolf. He usually led with some sort of joke, but this time he was blunt. "Come out to the cannery as soon as you can." When I arrived at Wolf Pack on that cold, wet evening, George wearily showed me a jar of Kick Butt Peppers. Its lid was bulging, as if it were about to explode.

I asked George, "Is that what happens when a lid doesn't seal?"

The lines on George's forehead deepened when he told me, "Howard, this is a bigger problem than unsealed jars. And I fear it's not the only jar with this bigger problem. You know how you'd tell me to turn down the heat in the tunnel? Well, this is what can happen when jars get underpasteurized!" George then opened that jar with the bulging lid. A volcano of spoiled peppers and oil came bubbling out, emitting such a putrid smell that I ran outside with a case of dry heaves. I'm not sure if it was from the stench or my impending sense of doom.

When I came back in, I asked George, "Is that the smell of botulism?"

"No, you're smelling the putrefactive anaerobes of *C. butyricum*. C-bot isn't as putrid so it's more dangerous. You couldn't get those spoiled peppers close to your mouth."

"Whatever it is, it's never happened to me. Or my mother's jars!"

"Well, your mom probably sterilizes her jars before she packs them. We assume our jars arrive sterile. When we pasteurize the filled jars, we doubly sterilize them. Because your peppers got under pasteurized, the jars never got sterilized."

After checking the codes on the spoiled jars, we found that they were all packed on the same day when George was in Reno and Mike and Becky were high on crystal meth. But this debacle was on me, too, because I had given Mike the okay not to pasteurize the jars a second time. Why? Because I feared the peppers would get overcooked and ruin their texture—which seemed too high a price to pay. In hindsight, that gamble was a major and costly fuckup. But God damn it, you've got to be kind. Or at least be fair. And George Wolf was a kind and fair man. We split my losses down the middle.

Let this be a lesson to the home canners out there. Lil, who knew absolutely zilch about chemistry, sterilized her jars and lids in boiling water before she packed them. So even though she didn't pasteurize her filled jars, she started out with sterile ones. And regardless of whether she knew it or not, her peppers had a very low pH, so nothing would grow in its acidic environment. If you make this recipe at home—and you adequately pickle your peppers and have sterile jars and lids—go ahead and experiment with NOT pasteurizing the jars. As for me, to this day that putrid odor of spoilage is so deeply embedded in my psyche that whenever I fear something is about to go very wrong, my olfactory nerve recalls that horrific smell. I pasteurize all my jars.

But it was my responsibility to go through the thousands of jars and cull the ones with bulging lids. It took me four days (and four one-hundred-mile round trips in the rain) to inspect every jar we'd made. Unsurprisingly, all the bulging lids came from that one run when the steam mysteriously turned off in the pasteurization tunnel and Mike and Betty White were too zonked on crystal meth to notice.

Losing 250 cases of Kick Butt jars meant that before next year's harvest, I'd most likely run out of my most popular product. I was beyond devastated—my "little business that could" had derailed. I wanted to walk away from this wreck that so easily could've been avoided. That time felt as dark to me as the train tunnel I'd gotten stuck in when I was a teenager, with no light in sight. Not able to face the darkness, I joined it by crawling into bed with my cat Marion and going into hibernation.

Chicken & Chickpea Salad

Danny Conkling

Danny, a Culinary Institute trained chef, fine-tuned his technique and knowledge of French cuisine at Daniel's in NYC before moving to Seattle. I met Danny at the dog park during the pandemic when, with a short-handed staff he somehow kept the fine Pioneer Square Café, London Plane, up in the air. And then, like the fate of many restaurants by the end of the pandemic, he closed, bringing it down for a soft landing just as his first child was born. He's presently private cheffing and making his daughter the best baby food in the world.

Ingredients

1 qt cooked chickpeas

1 cup of Mama Lils Mildly Spicy Peppers, including the oil

2 cups of cooked chicken meat, ideally leftover meat from the night before. Chopped or shredded into bite sized pieces.

4 scallions sliced thin

1/2cup chopped parsley

1/2 chopped cilantro

3-4 tbsp lemon juice

1 tbsp each toasted and blended coriander seed and fennel seed

1 fennel bulb, shaved thin. Save this till last or shave it directly into the salad bowl

Salt and pepper

To make the salad

Combine all ingredients in a large mixing bowl. Season with the lemon juice, salt & pepper.

Serve immediately. Or mix it in the morning and hold on to it for lunch or a picnic.

Because of the lemon juice, the slight acidity in the peppers and Mama Lil's oil this salad keeps very well.

I CAN'T GO ON. OH, GO ON.

IT WAS EARLY FEBRUARY WHEN the phone woke me out of my stupor. I was dreading the call from Gayle Krueger who'd be asking me how many peppers he should grow for the harvest of 1999. I had no idea, so I told him I needed more time to assess my situation. The Whites were still working for George, so I felt that Wolf Pack was not a good option to pack the peppers. But if not there, where? I talked to everybody I knew in the business, looking for leads for where else I could pack my peppers, but I came up empty. Now was probably the time to quit and I knew it.

When I called my mom to talk it over, she was still flying high from having seen her name on display at the West Point Market. I didn't tell her about the spoiled jars, knowing it would've broken her heart. She was as proud of Mama Lil's jars as if they were her grandchildren. I did mention that I needed to find a new cannery. I could hear her turn the page of the *Youngstown Vindicator* when she told me, "Sonny boy, I know you. You'll find a way."

It might have been the next day when I received a flyer in the mail for the Columbia River Kitchen, a state-sponsored incubator kitchen located in a business park in East Wenatchee, Washington. I drove across the mountains to check it out. It was no cannery, that's for sure. It was used mainly to bake cookies or make soup for charity benefits. And its location couldn't be more inconvenient, as it was a two-hour drive to the pepper fields and a three-hour drive from Seattle. (But in a pinch, a five-minute walk from the Wenatchee airport.) As for how I'd pasteurize the jars, they had a brazing oven, normally used to make soup, that I'd use to boil the water to cook my jars. In that regard, this was a step backwards from Wolf Pack cannery.

On the positive side, this kitchen had an ice machine, so I could wash the peppers in ice water, which Donny Santisi claimed increased the shelf life of his buckets of peppers in oil. It also had a commercial dishwasher that we could sterilize the jars in before we packed them like Lil did. But the deciding factor was that the price was right. Linda, who ran the facility and its accompanying business park, was knowledgeable about government programs that existed to help start up small businesses. Other companies who rented space in the building took advantage of a new program called Back to Work.

The government would reimburse half the salaries of my employees—if they were hired off the unemployment rolls. This benefit alone would save me thousands of dollars in labor costs—money I could use to make yet more jars.

But making my peppers in Wenatchee also meant I'd be taking on the responsibility for every single aspect of production, including keeping accurate production logs. Seven years into Mama Lil's, I couldn't get away with faking it anymore. It was time for me to grow up and at least pretend that I knew what the hell I was doing. To do this, I had to become certified as a licensed canner by taking a one-week course called "Acidified Foods in Glass-Enclosed Containers," taught by the primary food-processing authority in the state, Dr. Dick Dougherty. Dr. Dougherty apparently was a thorn in George Wolf's side, as George had mentioned his name to me on many occasions. "I may have only a master's degree in food science, but I got over forty years of experience canning every fuckin' food under the sun."

The class began at 7 a.m. in Olympia, so it was a bleak sixty-mile drive in wintry, morning rush-hour traffic. Admittedly I never seemed to get my thinking cap on straight all day. Of the twenty of us taking the class, most of whom were Hispanic with English as their second language, I was one of two students who failed the test. When I failed a second time, I was on Dr. Dougherty's radar. Tellingly, I kept missing the same questions. The first was about the temperature needed to cook the jars. Dr. Dougherty implied that all pickled vegetables should err on the side of safety by being cooked to a core internal temperature of at least 175 degrees Fahrenheit. I knew from my experience at Wolf Pack that this was much hotter than necessary, but whatever. On the third try, I answered it their way and I passed the test.

The other question I kept missing was how many people should keep the production logbooks. The answer was—only one. If multiple people kept the logs, confusion could easily occur. I should have known the answer to this question not only from my experience at Wolf Pack, but also from caring for my sister when she was dying. She got pain medication twice a day, and I had to keep accurate medication logs. On a day my mother and I overlapped our shifts, one of us—and I won't say who—mistakenly gave Bobbi a second dose of her pain meds.

I told the doctor about our fuck up. He didn't want Lil to feel guilty about overdosing her own daughter, so an ambulance was called. Bobbi seemed fine, so getting her stomach pumped was a drastic measure. But that was an instance of a fortuitous fuckup. When Bobbi got out of her room for the first time in months, that ambulance gave her a magic carpet ride through her beloved Cambridge neighborhood, and Bobbi was in heaven. (Or perhaps on the right dosage.) When we arrived at the hospital, we turned around and took the long way home.

After Dr. Dougherty congratulated me for passing the test, I proudly showed him some jars of Mama Lil's Peppers, which he complimented me on as a good-looking product. But when I mentioned that I made my jars at Wolf Pack for the last four years, he looked at me with suspicion. "I know George Wolf, and well. Is that where you're packing this year?"

"Nope. I'll be making my jars at the Columbia River Kitchen."

"Really? That's an incubator kitchen. It's hardly a cannery."

I confidently told the state's foremost expert on canning, "I intend to turn it into one." Then that day I called Gayle Krueger and asked him to double his yield of goathorns for Mama Lil's.

But I was not feeling confident about the upcoming harvest. I badly needed a right-hand man. I tried to recruit Jan Barton, but he was unavailable. Luckily, my singer-songwriter friend Terry Lee Hale hooked me up with his former drummer, Chris Adams. Chris was a wiry, energetic man who took on part-time jobs so he could indulge his love of sailing. If I covered motel expenses, Chris said he would be willing to give Mama Lil's two months of his life.

As for the rest of my crew, that was a crapshoot. Chris and I would go down to the labor office to try and choose our employees. Chris joked that it felt like the old days when he'd hang out at the musicians' union, hoping to get hired for a gig. For me, it was only somewhat easier than choosing people off the street. After my experience with the Whites at Wolf Pack, I thought I could recognize who the speed freaks were. But sometimes I was flat-out wrong. On one day they'd be working with manic energy and then burn out quick, and not show up the next day.

But by our second week, Chris and I settled on a steady crew of eight workers. Perhaps because we allowed everyone to take turns choosing music (be it oldies, country, mariachi, or Chris's hard-core rock), the morale was good. Using two Bobbitrons, we were soon plowing through a ton of peppers in an eight-hour day. But we weren't taking the seeds out. Because of the spoilage from last year, I was anxious to get these Kick Butt pint jars made, especially since the peppers were spiciest when the weather was hottest at the beginning of the harvest.

On packing days, Chris oversaw seasoning the peppers, stuffing them into jars then filling them with oil. Being a drummer, he set the perfect tempo as our packing days were filled with crescendos of me pulling three hot racks of 24 jars each coming out of the boiling water, then dropping three more racks back into it. After those jars were cooled down in the walk-in, they were taken to a room where we labeled and date-coded them with a price gun.

Meanwhile, Krueger's fields were right on target to double his yield over last year. Everything was going swimmingly at the Columbia River Kitchen as its namesake river flowed below us. When Linda, who ran the business park, poked her head in the door and saw how many pallets of jars we'd managed to make in just a few weeks, she was so proud that we were able to pull this off in her little kitchen that could.

It was during that harvest I came up with the perfect addition to Mama Lil's product line. When I was visiting my family in Ohio the year before, Jonny Katz's mom Ellie gave me a jar of peppers she had bought at a farm stand. It used the same Hungarian hot peppers as Mama Lil's, but they were packed in a sugar-sweetened vinegar brine. This product had no vinegar waste product and no expensive oil, and the peppers were good. I called the number on the jar. When the seventy-year-old farmer's wife shared the recipe with me, I told her, "You sweetheart!"

I think that's how I came up with the name Sweet Hot Peppas. But maybe it was because when I was modifying their recipe, my girlfriend at the time (who was both sweet and hot) flew into the Wenatchee airport to offer a helping hand. After my crew went home, we experimented with other ways of sweetening the Ohio farmer's pepper recipe besides using sugar. We agreed that maple syrup and fennel seed imbued the peppers with the perfect licorice-laden sweetness. That night in my motel room, we giggled nonstop as we wrote the romance copy of the Sweet Hot Peppas label: "Endear hors d'oeuvres, entice omelets, seduce sandwiches. Undress your favorite salad with the sweet hot brine!" The next day we made our first hundred cases of Sweet Hot Peppas, and when my girlfriend flew home that night, she had several jars in her backpack.

Seduce sandwiches, endear hors d'oeuvres!

When I told Julie Paschkis my one idea for the Sweet Hot label—that a heart symbol would replace the o in the word *hot*—she burst out, "Bunnies! Kissing bunnies." (This was years before POM Wonderful used the same heart symbol to replace the "o" on its pomegranate juice label. Luckily for POM, I'm not a litigious type.)

On the fifth week of the harvest, we switched to making the Mildly Spicy Peppers in Oil, which was far more laborious than making the Kick Butts since we had to scoop out the seeds. During these prep sessions, I'd show off how fast I was with a butter knife. But every single one of my crew, including Chris, hated this job, and some threatened to quit. I knew my crew was disgruntled when I left that morning to get our next ton of peppers. But upon my return five hours later, I noticed the crew had de-seeded and sliced more peppers than I ever anticipated. But the crew were no longer using butter knives to scoop the seeds out. They were using a coring tool that had a pointed tip and serrated edges designed for coring apples. With one push and twist of the wrist, it could dig out the stem and the seed core in one motion, and in so doing, turn a two-step process into one.

But stubborn me, I felt betrayed. While everyone else used their apple corers, I joined the prep line and continued to use my butter knife to prove my Paul Bunyanesque point. My protest lasted five minutes. That apple corer was not only the right tool for the job, but it represented the biggest leap forward in pepper production since I was introduced to the Bobbitron.

I also learned something else when working with my crew. These goathorns are very tasty peppers when fresh and when prepping them, inevitably everyone, including myself, would nibble on the peppers as they worked. After a while I noticed that each one of my crew preferred one color over another. I asked a young Hispanic man, "Why do you only eat the orange ones?"

He said, "Yellows aren't sweet. Reds are too sweet. Orange is perfect."

He was right. Each color did taste slightly different. At the yellow stage, the pepper's flavor is grassy with just a hint of sweetness. As the goathorns progress from orange to red, they become higher in sugar content until they can become sweeter than a bell pepper. And the mix of goathorns at every stage of ripening—besides looking so beautiful in the jar—is what accounts for the hot peppers in oil having such a complex yet balanced flavor.

Chris and I were working seven days a week. On days when the peppers were draining, we drove over Stevens Pass to Wolf Pack to make jars of PeppaLilli and Bread & Butter Pickles & Peppers. I didn't like being around the Whites while I was there, but I liked George, and I'd become very adept at using his steam jacketed kettle, despite its stiff crank.

It's worth noting that most products made at Wolf Pack weren't nearly as sensitive to heat as my peppers in oil were, as their primary ingredients originated from cans that had *already* been pasteurized. George cooked most of those products to 180 degrees. For my pickled peppers, with their very low pH, he went down to a 167-degree core internal temperature, which he said was an adequate seven degrees on the side of safety. I thought seven degrees was too adequate.

George had shown me a technical paper on this subject that he claimed to have worked on for years and even presented

Chris Adams, Wolf Pack, 1999.

for scientific review to the Oregon processing authorities—but not to Washington's. His theory was that the lower the pH of a product within a jar, the less heat is needed to kill whatever microbes could live in that acidic environment. According to George, if the pH was below 3.43, a core internal temperature of 160 degrees would safely preserve the peppers. If the product had a higher pH of say, 3.6, the jars needed to be cooked to 168 degrees, and so forth upward. (As a comparison: George tested an unpasteurized jar made by Lil. Its pH was 3.41. My jars that spoiled had a low 3.49 pH but were cooked to a mere 127 degrees.)

I felt confident about my pickling protocol at the Columbia River kitchen for two reasons. We were sterilizing the jars in the dishwasher right before filling them, just like my mother did. I also made a stronger pickling brine to achieve a low 3.41 pH, like my mother's peppers. Because I was keeping such a close eye on the jars I was pasteurizing, I also felt confident that bringing them up to a 162-degree center temperature, or two degrees on the side of safety, would ensure the peppers highest quality. In addition to all the jars we were packing and pasteurizing, Chris and I made 200 four-gallon buckets of peppers in oil that I stored in the very crowded walk-in refrigerator.

Towards the end of an industrious afternoon of pasteurization, Linda, who ran the business park, poked her head in the door and shouted over the blaring mariachi music, "You're about to get a visit from someone who just landed at the airport."

"From whom?" I asked, hoping it was my girlfriend flying back to lend a hand.

"You'll find out soon enough," Linda said as she pulled the door shut behind her.

Ten minutes later, without the warning of a knock, that door was thrown open, and Dr. Dick Dougherty marched in the kitchen like the new sheriff had arrived in town. He set down his large briefcase on the table next to my production logbook, then sternly told me, "I'm here to do an audit. Show me what's going on around here." Why should I be nervous about this surprise attack out of right field? I kept pristine production logs. What concerned me most were the four-gallon buckets that I was storing in the walk-in refrigerator. So first, I showed Dick those buckets. But he had no problem with them if they were kept refrigerated at 36 degrees.

So far, so good.

Minutes later, Karen, his deputy at the Health Department, arrived, setting her own large briefcase next to Dougherty's on the table. I'd never met her before, but I recalled George Wolf mentioning her name, usually about giving him grief when she was inspecting Wolf Pack. The three of us moved into the kitchen where they watched me pasteurize jars. I waited for the basin of water to start boiling, then dropped the three racks of 24 jars each into it. I had been pasteurizing the jars to 162 degrees, or according to George, two degrees on the side of safety. But this time, I waited a minute longer until they hit 167 degrees, then pulled them out.

Dr. Dougherty asked me, "What's the center temperature of those jars?"

I pulled the thermometer out of the jar and showed it to him, "Exactly 167 degrees."

"WHAT?!" he screamed. "Why only 167 degrees?"

"That's all they need. That's seven degrees on the side of safety."

"Show me your production logs, now," he demanded.

I hesitantly handed him my logbook. He reviewed my tidy columns, then scowled at me. "You pasteurized these jars to only 162 degrees. Not 167 degrees like you just told me. These should've been cooked to 175 degrees. Where are these jars?" I walked them over to the next room. He was aghast when he saw nearly twenty-four pallets of 100 cases each shrink-wrapped in plastic. "You cooked all these jars to 162 degrees?!"

I meekly nodded yes. Then I showed him the graph George Wolf had given me, stating that at 3.43 pH, 160 degrees would kill the spores living in that acidic environment. Dougherty crumpled up the piece of paper, tossed it on the floor. "Bullshit! What George Wolf deems as science is not acknowledged by my processing authority. Get me a pH meter."

Dick stuck the pH meter's probe into a jar of Kick-Butt Peppers. The numerical display started out at 4.2 then dropped to 3.6, then 3.55, and was still dropping when he pulled the probe out. "I'm getting a higher pH reading than you."

"Dr. Dougherty, the pH meter was still going down."

He looked at me like I was an object of shame. "It was not. We got a problem here, Lev. You got garlic and olive oil in your jars, right? C-bot just loves to live in garlic and olive oil. To adequately process these jars, they must be pasteurized to 175 degrees, as you were told in class. You've got to make sure you absolutely kill that C-bot before that C-bot kills someone. This is a serious business. And I'm going to make sure you take it seriously."

Then his assistant, Karen, opened her large briefcase and pulled out an ominous roll of large yellow stickers. Then she proceeded to slap those stickers on each side of all 24 pallets. They read:

EMBARGO! AUTHORITY OF THE STATE OF WA DEPT. OF AGRICULTURE.

I was ordered by Dr. Dougherty to move all those pallets into an empty room that was then locked up, with only Dick and Linda possessing the keys. Minutes later, with my jars in jail, the sheriff and his deputy strode out the door. When the door shut behind them, Chris, who'd been watching all of this from the wings, whistled, before chiming in, "Hot Diggity Dougherty!"

Now dear reader, you must be wondering—considering what had happened at Wolf Pack the year before when those Kick Butt jars spoiled—why-oh-why would I have thought it so important to tread the line so closely between safety and perfection? And to tell you the truth, I'm asking myself the same question as I write this. It might be best answered by a psychiatrist.

What I will say is that it certainly wasn't because I was out to make more profits. To the contrary—it was only because I was striving for my product's perfection. The less one cooks the peppers, the firmer they are, and the better they hold up over the long run. I trusted George's expertise. I knew that, as opposed to those 250 cases that spoiled last year, I pasteurized these jars perfectly. And safely. And yet, because of my actions, I was now in a heap of trouble.

I gave Chris the keys to my Volvo so he could take the weekend off to go sailing. I drove the van to get another ton of peppers. I was in a daze the whole way there, like I'd entered a tunnel that had no way out. On the way back to Wenatchee, with a ton of peppers in my van, I stopped at a rest stop to take in the view over the Yakima Valley, where the desert sky was lighting up with stars. Then I did what anyone who'd been a teenager in the 1960s would do: I smoked some weed and asked the stars what I should do. Not that they had an answer, except to say, *You're in a heap of trouble.* On the way back to my van, I spotted a pay phone and called to tell my mommy what had happened.

"You sterilize the jars first, right?" Lil asked. "That's all I do. And my jars never spoil."

"Yes, I sterilized them. I'm not concerned about those jars. That's over with. But I don't know what to do about all the jars from here on out. Maybe I *should* cook them to 175 degrees?"

Lil chuckled, "Or maybe just *tell* them you are?"

"What did you say, Mom?"

"Sonny boy, you're doing a good job. I trust you'll do the right thing."

By the time I arrived back in Wenatchee that Sunday night, I'd made up my mind. To be on the safe side, from here on out, I increased the strength of the pickling brine to lower the pH to 3.41. And since this happened more than twenty years ago, I'll confess that I started keeping two sets of logbooks. One recorded the real core internal temperature of 165 degrees (three degrees hotter than before); the other book said the jars were cooked to 175 degrees.

In the end I bought every goathorn in Krueger's field, over thirty tons in all, doubling my output over last year. Before we were done, we packed 1,500 more cases of Mildly Spicy pint jars.

All the new pallets of Mildly Spicy Peppers that were not embargoed, were shipped to a warehouse in Seattle. The nineteen pallets of Kick Butt Peppers and five pallets of the Mildly Spicy that were embargoed were locked up in a room at the business park in East Wenatchee. Being embargoed was embarrassing and it would be hard to spin it otherwise. Much like the spoilage I experienced last year, the embargo was a touchy subject that I kept mum about, as the last thing I wanted was to have rumors about Mama Lil's spreading around.

Like after every harvest, Mama Lil's was in debt but pepper rich, which compelled me to do demos nearly every day, so the checks kept coming in. But due to the previous year's spoilage and now the embargo, it was nerve wracking that I had run out of my most popular product, the Kick Butt Peppers. One memorable demo I did back then was in the wealthy neighborhood of Mercer Island on the day before Thanksgiving, the second busiest shopping day of the year. There were two Kick Butt jars from last year still on the shelf, so I left them there, not wanting to lose their shelf space. Then I built a display of my other five products on a small table and started peddling peppers.

A middle-aged schlump with a pasty face and baggy, ill-fitting clothes came forward after observing shoppers tasting the peppers, then inevitably buying a jar. He picked up a jar and examined it. "People like your product. Are they made locally?"

"Peppers are grown in the Yakima Valley. They're packed in Gold Bar and Wenatchee."

"Gold Bar and Wenatchee? That's inconvenient." He then sampled the peppers, but his face registered no impression of them. Then he told me, "I have property in North Bend, on the direct route between Seattle and Yakima. Maybe we could build a cannery there?"

I had no idea why this odd man was taking an interest in Mama Lil's. I wasn't sure he even liked them. I told him, "No thanks. We make all our products during a two-month harvest period. What will I do with my cannery the rest of the year?" But he took my card and walked into the checkout line with one item, a jar of Honkin Hot PeppaLilli. When he reached into his pocket and pulled out a $100 bill to pay for it, my business card fell onto the floor.

A week later, I was watching the Portland Trail Blazers vs. Seattle Super-sonics basketball game on TV when the camera focused on a man in a front-row seat standing up to cheer. When the announcer exclaimed, "Paul Allen liked Rasheed's dunk," I recognized that he was the same man who offered to build Mama Lil's a cannery. *You idiot! Couldn't I have shown just a bit more interest in this man who offered to build me a cannery? Or at least picked up my own card and given it back to the cofounder of Microsoft, one of the world's richest men?*

In early December, just before winter's first big snowstorm was expected to land in the Cascade Mountains, I drove back to the Columbia River Kitchen to clear out all my pickling gear I'd left behind. Snow flurries were coming down when I arrived, so I needed to be quick. The parking lot was empty but for one car. Luckily my keycode still got me inside the building. I waved hello to José, the janitor, who was buffing the hallway floors. I'd once given José a jar, and we'd been friends since. After moving my pickling vats, bob-bitrons, and various other accessories into my van, I walked back in the building to check if I'd left anything behind.

And wouldn't you know it, José was now buffing the floor in the room where my embargoed jars had been locked up. I poked my head in and looked wistfully at my twenty-four pallets. One of them was a partial pallet of about seventy cases of Kick Butt Peppers. On top of that partial pallet was a case that was folded shut. It had nine jars of Kick Butt Peppers in it. I gave José a jar, which he happily accepted, as he buffed his way out the door. Then, perhaps because I didn't want to drive back over here anytime too soon, I put ten cases of Kick Butt Peppers on my hand truck and wheeled them through the snow. Then as I started loading the cases in my van, someone shouted. "Señor!" I instinctively raised my arms, fearing I'd been caught. But it was just José. He didn't know what those embargo stickers meant, did he? Jose then pointed at the snow that was quickly accumulating, then demonstratively told me, "Mas nieve. Necessario, mas balasto."

"Que?" I asked. Then repeated back to him, "Balasto?"

He walked over and picked up a case of peppers. "Mas chiles. Mas balasto."

"Oh, ballast! I get it." Now I'm not saying it was José's idea, but he did help me load that partial pallet of sixty more cases into my van. And I'm not saying I bribed José for his silence, but he did put one of those cases of Kick Butt Peppers in the trunk of his car. And it was a good thing I had *mas balasto* in my van, as the snow kept coming as I climbed up and down Stevens Pass and into Gold Bar, where it was raining hard, and the Wallace River was flooding over its banks.

I ran into George while unloading my pickling gear at his warehouse. George was someone I could talk to about the embargo. When I told him what happened George just laughed at me. "Welcome to the club. Those cocksuckers like to flaunt their authority. They'll drop the embargo once they think you've learned your lesson. Hey, I learned *my* lesson and fired all those drug addicts I had working for me." That's when George noticed the seventy cases of peppers inside my van. "Are those some of the embargoed jars?"

"No, that's just ballast." I told him before making a shushing gesture. George put his hands over his eyes, and started walking away, mimicking Sergeant Schultz from *Hogan's Heroes*: "I see nussing. I see nussing."

I didn't want to make it too hard on the authorities if they came looking for those seventy cases of embargoed jars, so I put most of them in my basement pepper cellar. I figured I'd leave the other ten cases in my Volvo wagon delivery car. It doesn't snow in Seattle often, but you just never know when you can use "mas balasto."

Honkin' Hot PeppaLilli

Howard Lev

Mama Lil's doesn't currently make the Honkin' Hot PeppaLilli, which is why I'm offering the recipe here. One of the reasons I loved this recipe was that it uses the waste product brine drained off the pickled peppers to make the mustard sauce. Several chefs have told me they tried to duplicate this relish, but they couldn't do it. The reason they couldn't do it was because they didn't have this relish's secret sauce, the pepper brine. I loved making this chunky relish. And I love eating it, especially on hot sausage or barbeque beef sandwiches. You can vary the proportions of the veggies as well as the amount of heat added, through the proportions of hot mustard flour, or habanero powder. (I suggest acquiring a three-gallon ceramic crock for pickling purposes, but large nonreactive metal pots or gallon jars work. Whatever you do, don't pickle peppers in the tub overnight.)

Makes about 5 quarts or 10 pint jars

To make the PeppaLilli vegetables:

2 quarts diced pickling cucumbers (about 3 pounds)

1 quart diced sweet onions, such as Walla Walla (about 1½ pounds)

⅔ cup salt

Mix the diced vegetables and salt in a pickling crock or large bowl. Let sit for at least 3 hours, stirring occasionally. After the veggies are brined, rinse them thoroughly with water until the taste of salt is gone. Transfer to a colander to drain in the sink for 3 hours.

To make the pickled peppers:

1½ quarts (3/8-inch thick) sliced goathorn peppers or similar chile peppers (about 2 pounds)

2 cups distilled vinegar

2 cups water

¼ cup salt

Place the pepper rings in a pickling crock. In a large bowl or pot, combine the vinegar, water, and salt and stir until the salt is dissolved, then pour this brine over the peppers. Put a weight on top of the peppers to keep them submerged (perhaps a plate topped with a vinegar bottle filled with water). Let the peppers pickle for 12 hours. Then drain off the brine. But be sure to save it for later.

To make the mustard sauce:

1¼ cups unbleached flour

⅓ cup hot dry mustard powder

2 tablespoons turmeric (this amount might be on the heavy side, but I hear turmeric is good for arthritis)

¾ teaspoon habanero powder (or some other hot chile powder)

Place the flour, dry mustard, turmeric, and habanero powder in a large mixing bowl. Whisk in 1¼ cups of the reserved pepper brine, or however much it takes to make a thick, smooth sauce about the consistency of bottled mustard.

To bring it all together:

Place 1½ quarts of pepper brine in a large cooking pot. (If there's not enough brine, add apple cider vinegar to make a total of 1½ quarts. This will give you more of the traditional chow-chow flavor, which is typically made with just apple cider vinegar as the liquid component.) Bring the vinegar brine right up to a boil on high heat, then lower the heat as you whisk in—

1½ cups brown sugar

1 tablespoon celery seed

2 teaspoons honey

Bring the sweetened brine to a simmer, then slowly add the mustard sauce, whisking constantly; the flour will begin to thicken. Keep simmering until the sauce is smooth, then add the well-drained vegetables and pickled peppers to the pot. You will need to increase the heat to bring the mixture just below boiling. Keep stirring for about 10 minutes as the veggies cook in the sauce.

While the mixture is still very hot (at least 170°F), ladle the Honkin' Hot PeppaLilli into sterilized jars, using a large-mouthed canning funnel. Twist on sterile lids until they're snug. If you're using two-piece canning lids, after placing the center piece on each jar, screw the ring on tight without torquing. (Consult standard recipe instructions—like *Joy of Cooking's* "The Foods We Keep" section—for how to set up for canning pickles.)

Let the jars cool. Before storing them, check to make sure that all the lids are sealed, and the centers of the lids are pulled in. If there are a few that haven't, keep them in your fridge and they'll be fine for months.

A PEPPER FOR YOUR THOUGHTS?

I CALLED THE WASHINGTON STATE Department of Agriculture daily to ask when the embargo would be lifted, but they kept telling me the same thing: "We're still testing the peppers. " But the week before Christmas is the busiest time of the year for grocery stores, so I wanted to be out there, even if I was still prohibited from selling the popular Kick Butt Peppers.

One of my favorite stores to do demos was a half hour drive from my house but it had a dedicated demo station, so I could build a large display of jars to attract the holiday shoppers. When I got there, I sold the store a couple cases of each of my products, except of course for some of the cases of embargoed Kick Butts, which I left in my car. I hoped the store would have a supply from last year's on the shelf, but it was empty and had lost its space on the shelf. Man, I needed this embargo to be over soon.

Once again, the store was swarming with people, and they were buying jars like mad. A customer came up to me and asked, "Hey, where are the Kick Butt Peppers?"

I told him, "We're temporarily out. Buy the Mildly Spicy Peppers instead. They're almost as hot as the Kick Butts this year."

He pleaded, "My six-year-old daughter loves to look at the label and shout, 'Kick butt!' Then she laughs her head off. I'd buy a whole case from you if I could."

I was about to go back to my car to grab more cases anyway, so I told him, "Follow me."

In what may have looked like an illicit transaction and certainly felt like one, while standing in the freezing rain in the parking lot, I sold that fan of Mama Lil's a case of Kick Butt jars and a XX Mama Lil's logo t shirt. He put the shirt on right over his coat then proudly held up a case and told me, "All my pals are getting Kick Butts for Christmas!" As he turned to walk away, I saw a piece of the yellow embargo sticker with the letters "ARGO" dangling off the case. I was almost able to rip it off. In hindsight it was probably a good thing he got *that* case.

Perhaps emboldened by the man singing the Kick Butt Peppers' praises, I felt an internal tug-of-war while loading cases on my hand truck. And wouldn't you know it my lower risk-taking self, won out, yet again. Along with seven cases of my other products, I grabbed two cases of the embargoed Kick Butt jars and checked them in to the store. I then set up a large display at my demo table and got back to passing out samples. Those new Kick Butt Peppers were delicious, and I was on a roll, selling jars to seemingly everybody in the store. A woman walked past me and just for the sport of it, I cast out my line, "A pepper for *your* thoughts?"

She bit on it and turned around. When she saw me, she smiled. "It's Howard, right?" I did recognize her, but from where I wasn't sure. She quickly reminded me. "I'm Karen from the Department of Agriculture. We met a couple of months ago at the Columbia River Kitchen in Wenatchee." Holy shit! It was Hot Diggity Dougherty's deputy, the woman who had slapped the embargo labels on my pallets. I must have looked as guilty as hell, because I *was* guilty as hell.

"Oh…Karen! Hi. This is a nice store…um…what are you doing here?"

"It's my neighborhood store," she said. Phew. At least she wasn't here hunting me down. "I've wanted to try them." She took a sample. "They are good. So, I guess the embargo is over?"

Uh oh. Maybe she was onto me. I didn't know what to say, but I had to say something. "Uh…no, not yet. Luckily, I have some Kick Butt jars left from last year."

She picked up the jar of Kick Butt Peppers. If she would have looked, the evidence of this year's date-code sticker was on the bottom of the jar. But she kept sampling my products. "I don't know which one I like the best—they're all good. But my husband likes real spicy food." And before I knew it, she plopped that embargoed jar in her cart, where I could plainly see the 1999 date-code sticker.

Grabbing one of the Mildly Spicy jars, I blithely insisted, "You sampled out of this jar."

Now Karen was bewildered. "The peppers I tasted are spicy. And getting spicier."

"Last year's Mildly Spicy have a creeping heat." I said, exchanging the jars in her cart.

"You know what?" she said decisively, "I'll take one of each." She took the jar of Kick Butt Peppers right out of my hand. But with Houdini-like grace, I flicked off that date-code sticker before it went into her cart. As she disappeared down the aisle, I swept the embargoed Kick Butt jars back into the box. That was too close for comfort. But what should I do with the case of Kick Butts I'd already sold the store? The easiest thing: which was remove the date-codes from all the jars. When I left the store I filled their shelves with Kick Butt Peppers, so I didn't have to return to the scene of the crime too soon.

Luckily, it was only two weeks later, right before I went to the 2000 Winter Fancy Food Show in San Francisco, that I received a letter from the Washington State Department of Agriculture notifying me that the embargo had been lifted. As it turned out, the lab's pH readings matched mine, exactly. I'd been acquitted and my jars had officially been let out of jail. And was I ever relieved the embargo was over before *I* got thrown in jail for selling those jars.

It's worth noting that while writing this chapter, I scoured my pepper cellar to see if I still had some of the embargoed Kick Butt jars left. I assumed that my son Elijah, who preferred the vintage peppers, had eaten them all. But I found three jars from the embargo. Would they even be safe? I cracked open a jar. Not only did it pass the smell test, but I used the whole jar in a pasta dish. I gave a jar to my neighbor, who polished his off in no time. The peppers were soft, of course, as they were twenty years old! But they'd been pickled and pasteurized to perfection and their flavor was extraordinary. How many times had I told customers over the years, *The peppas only get betta in the jar!* Well, to quote Reverend Franklin James, *It's the Lord's truth.*

The difference between the economy in 1999 and when the recession hit in 2000 is perhaps best exemplified by the parties that Jelly Belly threw for the Winter Fancy Food Show. In 1999, Jelly Belly rented the entire top floor of San Francisco's famous Transamerica Pyramid for its over-the-top party that anybody with a show badge could attend. My cousin Frank Lev was in heaven as there were tables upon tables of the best spreads of gourmet food that he piled onto his plate then scarfed down. Two bands were playing, and when my cousin Frank wasn't jamming with them on his saxophone, he was on the dance floor swinging a woman over his shoulders.

The Jelly Belly party of 2000 required more than a food show badge to enter. You needed an invitation. But Frank and I managed to sneak in anyway. Within seconds, Frank was stuffing food into his coat pockets as he was being chased around the appetizer table by a security guard. I was biting into a lamb chop when I was nabbed and led to the door. Frank lamented afterwards, "That was kinda fun. But I think the glory days of this food show might be over." But those Kick-Butt Peppers, and all my other products, did quite well at the show and it gave me some momentum. I was determined to get these jars of peppers into yet more buyers' mouths.

Which is why two months later, I exhibited at the Natural Foods Expo West in Anaheim, California, where I shared a booth with David Lee, whose company Field Roast was starting to take off. But that was hardly the right show for Mama Lil's Peppers. The convention floor was inundated with supplement companies whose booths were hosted by muscle-bound body builders. Mama Lil's Peppers are a healthy food (the goathorn peppers are loaded with vitamin C, especially if they haven't been pasteurized), but it's not considered a *health-food*. The buyers at this show were not searching for new gourmet condiments. They were looking for products like Field Roast, a vegan, high protein, "grain meat" product. Luckily for me, the vice president of a California natural foods distributor stopped by the booth to chat with David, and upon trying my six products, showed interest in all of them.

A week later, my fax machine cranked out the largest order I'd ever had—for four full pallets of all six of Mama Lil's products. The invoice I mailed to them was for over $20,000, my largest invoice ever. And was I ever looking forward to that check. When the check finally arrived, it was in a thick envelope, so it certainly looked like a fat check. But that check was stapled to ten pages of paperwork, all of them filled with subtraction problems. Without notifying me, the distributor had taken the liberty to give all these new stores that ordered Mama Lil's, the dreaded *free fill*. The check wasn't for $20,000. It was for less than $2,000! That check was a punch in the nose that I did not see coming. And I was aiming for a fight.

A friend who worked as a salesman for a line of South African hot sauces happened to walk into my basement office while I was on the phone giving the distributor's VP a piece of my mind: "How dare a big business like you *steal* from a little business…" *Click*.

When the VP hung up, my friend scoffed at me. "This racket always involves *pay to play* at the start. You were lucky to even have that distributor in Southern California." He was probably right. To this day, Mama Lil's has done much less business than it should in Southern California. So be it. I saved thousands of dollars by not attending that food show again.

ML's Vegan Quiche Bites

David Lee

The Field Roast Plant-Based Meat and Cheese Company was founded by David in Seattle in 1998, though he worked on this product for six years before bringing it out. The company, which now makes many varieties of 100 percent vegan products, has grown phenomenally since then. These classic, appetizer-size mini-quiches of David's are compelling because of their combination of textures, flavors, colors, and a hint of heat from Mama Lil's.

These quiches, like every baked good, are best when freshly baked—but they can be made ahead, covered loosely with foil, and reheated in a 300°F oven.

Makes about 30 quiche bites.

2 Field Roast Italian Sausages (or another brand of vegan sausage)

Oil or butter for greasing

Thawed dough for 2 (9-inch) pie crusts, homemade or store-bought

½ cup Mama Lil's Peppers in Oil, drained (save the oil to use later)

1¼ cups JUST Egg substitute (or another brand of plant-based egg substitute)

2 tablespoons finely chopped Italian parsley

1 teaspoon salt

Freshly ground black pepper to taste

1 tablespoon Mama Lil's pepper oil

Preheat the oven to 425°F. Lightly grease thirty cups of a mini-muffin tin (with 1½-inch wells) with oil. Set the muffin tin on a cookie sheet.

Peel the vegan sausages, then thinly slice them into thirty rounds.

Unfold the crust dough and use a rolling pin to press out the fold lines and evenly flatten the edges. Using a metal pastry cutter or the mouth of a drinking glass, cut out thirty 2½-inch rounds from the dough. (You may need to reroll the dough scraps.)

Place one dough round inside each cup and press it gently into the bottom and up the sides of the cup. Add a sausage slice to each cup. Place one Mama Lil's Peppers on top of each sausage.

In a small bowl, whisk together the egg substitute, parsley, salt, and black pepper with the oil from Mama Lil's peppers. Pour mixture into each cup, filling to just below the top.

Bake 20 minutes, or until egg has set, and top is puffy and golden.

Cool slightly before serving.

WHERE LUCK COMES FROM

IN 2000, WHEN SEATTLE-AREA FARMERS' MARKETS started allowing local food manufacturers to sell their value-added products there, my quandary of how to sell more jars directly to consumers, was solved. Not only would I charge full retail price for the jars so my profit margins would increase, but I was getting the peppers into at least fifty mouths an hour as they strolled the market. If Mama Lil's were to expand outside of Seattle, I hoped it wouldn't necessarily be the retail jars but rather the buckets of peppers I was selling to restaurants, or what is known as the foodservice side of the business, where I was told no customers asked for free fill.

On my way to the 2000 Summer Fancy Food Show in New York City, I stopped off in Ohio to visit my aging parents. As my mother spun her meat grinder making eggplant salata, I was at the kitchen table confessing to my dad about my trials and tribulations in the food business. When my phone rang, it was from an unrecognizable number, so I answered it in another room.

Little did I know this call would change the course of Mama Lil's. And my life.

A woman named Betsy, who ran the test kitchen for Panera Bread, asked if she could talk to the director of sales. Panera's name vaguely rang a bell from when my dad mentioned it a year ago, so I had enough wits about me to tell her an innocuous white lie. "Our sales director stepped out of the office, but I'm the owner. Maybe I can be of help?"

"Good. So, you've heard of Panera Bread?"

"Kinda."

"Well, we make gourmet sandwiches featuring our bread. Some of our executives just got back from doing a bread tour in Seattle where they were looking for upcoming trends, which Seattle is known for. Like coffee, good bread—and what's that music my son listens to? Well, maybe your peppers are setting a trend too. Scott, our head of product development, kept seeing jars of Mama Lil's Peppers at all the bakeries he visited in Seattle."

I imagined Scott walking into Macrina Bakery where Pearl Jam's hit "Last Kiss" was playing for the third time he'd heard that day. I told her as nonchalantly as I possibly could, "Yep, Starbucks, Pearl Jam, and Mama Lil's. We're all local trendsetters here."

"Can you make your peppers in foodservice buckets by chance?"

"We can. And I'm glad you called. Our pepper harvest begins in two months."

"Great! We have a very deliberate decision-making process, but you might consider making some buckets for us. I think we'll be wanting to do a sandwich test with your peppers at some point soon. But for the time being, could you send a case of jars to our test kitchen?"

"I can't do *that*." I told her. Not that I was playing hard to get, but I was tired of *freebies*.

She seemed shocked by my dismissal. "But this could be big for Mama Lil's."

"I realize that. But I can't just give you a case. I'd *sell* you one, though." She chuckled and told me to send her an invoice. As I hung up the phone, my first thought was one of my favorite lines of poetry: "The world's fullness is not made but found." It was from a love poem by Richard Wilbur, but maybe it applied to business, too. When I considered the amount of time I'd spent hustling Mama Lil's at food shows this stroke of luck fell out of the sky like a ten-pound ham onto a homeless man's lap. When I walked back into the kitchen, Lil was still cranking out eggplant salata and Harry was starting to dig in. In a state of disbelief, I told them, "I just got off the phone with Panera Bread. They might be interested in using Mama Lil's on its sandwiches."

My dad jumped up and boasted, "Didn't I tell you about Panera?"

My mom said, "Come see us more often. We bring you luck!"

At the Summer Fancy Food Show in 2000, Mama Lil's kept getting lucky. On the first day of the show, a dapper middle-aged man by the name of Jay Stein stopped by my booth. As the second-generation owner of a chain of women's clothing stores called Stein Mart, he was very selective about the two dozen products he displayed in the small gift section of his stores. Jay came by my booth three times with Steinmart employees to taste my products. On the last day of the show, he returned once more, shook my hand, and then told me that his favorite product at the whole show was Mama Lil's Honkin' Hot PeppaLilli. He wanted it, along with the Kick-Butt Peppers in Oil and the Sweet Hot Peppas, in all one hundred of his stores!

Unfortunately, the jar size Stein Mart wanted was smaller than the formerly embargoed jars that I had pallets of. But still, this boded well for Mama Lil's, as the jars I'd be making for them would be competing with only a few other products for shoppers' attention. And since I'd be shipping directly to each store, there'd be no middlemen—meaning, I'd have decent profit margins on these sales. And best of all, there was no talk of free fill. Stein Mart's stores were in thirty states, including one in Youngstown, Ohio. And if Lil happened to walk into it and discover jars of Mama Lil's there, wouldn't that be wonderful?

Between Panera Bread and Stein Mart, an extraordinary opportunity for growth in both sectors of my business—foodservice buckets and retail jars—

had fallen into my lap. But I faced a serious dilemma: I'd established Mama Lil's as a solid brand, but I still had no production facility of my own to make the products. After my issues with the embargo, the Columbia River Kitchen told me Mama Lil's was no longer a fit for them. At Wolf Pack, where I was booked to the max, I'd be able to produce the jars for my current customers and the Honkin' Hot PeppaLilli for the Stein Mart stores. But where was I going to make all the other jars of Peppers in Oil and Sweet Hot Peppas for Stein Mart? And I had no clue whatsoever where I'd be making buckets for Panera.

I *most definitely* should have had Paul Allen build me that cannery.

Then in late July, six weeks out from the harvest, I was put in touch with a man who owned a fresh pasta company called Noodles. Bill Thompson, a good-natured fellow with a sardonic Bronx-bred wit, had been a computer geek until at the age of fifty, he decided to pursue his passion for pasta. His business had done well for years, but now for some reason he needed help paying his facility's rent. For a reasonable price, I could make my buckets there in the evening using his Hispanic crew, who wanted the overtime. This facility was only a mile from my house, and best of all, it had a walk-in refrigerator to store the finished buckets.

But making all those half pint jars of Kick Butts and Sweet Hots for the Stein Mart stores was a whole other ball of wax. Should I even take it on? But when the first Stein Mart purchase orders for $15,000 appeared on my fax machine in early August, and then days later a $25,000 line of credit on my house came through, I badly wanted to take it on. But how and where will I be making those jars. It was beyond me.

With the harvest weeks away I happened to be exhibiting at a local food show where I met a Canadian husband and wife who made their own brand of pickled vegetables at their small cannery a few miles across the border. They were already done making their products for the year, so they'd have the time to make jars of Kick Butt Peppers and the Sweet Hot Peppas for Stein Mart for me. Or so said Jane, the matronly sixty-year-old woman who bragged about her husband's experience with canning vegetables. All I'd need to do was come up a few times to teach them how to make my products, and then they'd handle it no problem.

I decided to give the Canadians a shot. Having my jars in a hundred Stein Mart stores where they would be competing with only a few products for shoppers' attention was just too good an opportunity to pass up. Initially, I rented a refrigerated truck and personally hauled the peppers from Yakima across the border to Canada where I worked alongside the Canadians to show them the intricacies of making my products, which primarily meant draining the peppers well—an instruction I emphasized over and over to them. I wasn't concerned about the Sweet Hot Peppas. If they used high-quality maple syrup, they'd be fine. Since this was Canada, the maple syrup capital of the world, no problem there either.

After two weeks of teaching them how to make my jars, I felt confident they knew what they were doing, and from there on we shipped the fresh peppers from the Yakima Valley directly to their facility in Canada. I wouldn't need to go up there again until I picked up all my pallets of jars at the end of the harvest. With that taken care of, I could focus on making the four-gallon buckets—prospectively for Panera—at Noodles every night of the week. Four days a week, I was at Wolf Pack making Honkin' Hot PeppaLilli for the Stein Mart orders. This gave me three days a week to fetch peppers and cucumbers from the farm in Wapato, make deliveries, and squeeze in a few farmers' markets. Luckily for me the Indians were in a pennant race, and I was feeding off their energy as I was making peppers, morning, noon, and night.

While I was draining the peppers at Noodles one night Bill walked in with a cardboard box filled with files. I'd never seen him there at night before and he wasn't cracking sarcastic jokes as he normally would. As he shuffled past me, he muttered out of the side of his mouth, "You can keep working here, but I went bankrupt."

"Bankrupt?!" I exclaimed. "What happened? You make such great pasta."

Bill was glum with regret, "I tried to grow too fast. I trusted the wrong people because I needed to trust them. Not because they were trustworthy. Let it be a lesson to you."

That was a lesson I wish I'd heeded right then and there. But greed's booming voice drowns out the wise whisper that cautions, "Be ye all, patient." Just ask Sam Bankman-Fried. When his cryptocurrency exchange collapsed, his first excuse was, "I tried to grow too fast." All I knew was that both Stein Mart and Panera wanted my products, and this was my opportunity to grow. Was it irrational exuberance on my part? Perhaps. Due to the peppers' limited growing season, I was prone to thinking this way. Because, if not now, when?

By late September, Krueger had harvested fifty tons of goathorns. The Canadians were on target to reach the quantity of jars I *assumed* Stein Mart would order over a year's time. At Wolf Pack I'd made one thousand cases of Honkin' Hot PeppaLilli, or half of what I'd assumed Stein Mart would order. At Noodles we had already made 1,700 four-gallon buckets and were on target to reach 2,500 buckets, the quantity I *assumed* Panera would need.

Then, as fate would have it, the Cleveland Indians lost three games in a row that eliminated them from making the postseason. Was it an omen? How could I make the peppers—or make all those long drives to get them—without listening to ball games? Turns out it *was* an omen. The very next day, an early frost in the Yakima Valley wiped out Krueger's entire pepper crop. Not only was my baseball season over, but the pepper season was over too.

But was that early frost ever a blessing in disguise, for me anyway. When I reached out to Betsy at Panera, asking when they might want some of the

Buckets of peppers inside the walk-in fridge at Noodles.

buckets I'd made for them, she said, "I'm sorry if you misinterpreted me. We're interested in your peppers, but we have no plans for them, yet." Why did I make so many buckets? Had I heard Betsy wrong? Or just wishful thinking? No doubt the latter. I should've made them 170 buckets, not 1,700.

The year before, I had sold a grand total of 200 of the four-gallon buckets of pickled hot goathorn peppers in oil. Now I was the proud owner of 1,700 buckets—with no buyer in sight. Donny Santisi gave his buckets a one-year shelf life so I could only hope that those twenty pallets of buckets—that I was storing in the walk-in refrigerators of three different food businesses around town—had more life in them than that.

Thankfully, the Stein Mart orders finally started appearing on my fax machine. But I was only given a week to box them up and ship them out. I drove to Canada to inspect the jars, pay them off, and arrange to ship the cases down to Seattle. When I walked into their facility, all twenty-five pallets they made for Mama Lil's were shrink-wrapped and stacked on top of each other. The way they were arranged, I could check only three jars from three pallets, and the peppers tasted fine. When I handed Jane the check for $60,000, she and her husband noticeably sighed with relief. I was surprised by their reaction. Hadn't they trusted me?

All those pallets of jars—along with the twelve pallets of Honkin' Hot PeppaLilli I made at Wolf Pack—were shipped to a warehouse where with the help of a couple of Millionairs, I packed up two hundred boxes with three cases in each that were shipped to one hundred Stein Mart stores. I never opened any of the cases made by the Canadians as they were taped shut and I was in a hurry to get them shipped. It was only after the three UPS trucks picked up those two hundred boxes that I got around to inspecting the remaining twenty pallets of jars made by the Canadians. My heart sank. The oil seemed thin and cloudy. I tasted them. And spit them out. "FUCK!" I opened more cases and inspected the jars in them. The jars I'd tasted at their facility were from the first two pallets they made, when I was closely watching over them. But after that, they'd committed the cardinal sin of *not draining the vinegar out of the peppers well enough!*

Then, as I went through the Sweet Hot Peppas, I saw that the vinegar they were packed in had a dark tinge to it, with flaky particles floating around. When I tasted the peppers, it wasn't maple syrup I was tasting. But what was it? I frantically called the Canadians and asked Jane's husband if they'd altered the recipe . He hemmed and hawed before confessing, "We had to switch to Aunt Jemima. Our supplier ran out of maple syrup."

"What do you mean you ran out of maple syrup?! That's a maple leaf on the Canadian flag, eh? I want to talk to Aunt Jemima, I mean…Jane…"

"Jane died of a brain aneurysm last week. Jane is no more. Our cannery's no more."

There wasn't much for me to say after hearing that. Even in the worst of situations, *God damn it, you've got to be kind.* When he hung up, I realized that I'd already fallen into the same trap as Bill did when he tried to grow his pasta business too fast. I trusted people because I needed to trust them, not because they were trustworthy. So now I was the owner of 1,700 four-gallon buckets of peppers in oil that didn't have a home. And fifteen pallets of jars made by the Canadians that didn't deserve a home. Not surprisingly, Stein Mart's next two orders were only for the Honkin' Hot PeppaLilli. When those thousand cases I made for them were gone, I never heard from Stein Mart again.

The best thing Mama Lil's Peppers had going for it in eight years of business was its reputation for consistently high quality. But I didn't want these inferior jars made by the Canadians to tarnish Mama Lil's reputation in the Pacific Northwest, so I donated sixteen pallets of those jars to a food bank. If Mama Lil's ever made a profit, I could use the loss as a tax-write-off. Luckily, at Wolf Pack I had made jars of all my retail products for my local customers. And I still had ample inventory of my formerly embargoed pint jars, which were aging beautifully.

I did save twenty of those Canadian cases, which I took to a farmers' market and sold real cheap. A homeless man appeared at my booth and was making a running commentary as he used toothpicks to taste from the jars. "This one is not bad…but this one here is my favorite." He held up the jar of Aunt Jemima-flavored Sweet Hot Peppas and proclaimed, "And I get them for free." What do you know? There was a market for those jars. And a growing market at that.

Getting lucky in business does happen from time to time, and it's a blessing when it does. But as I reflect on the stumbling path of my business, it's how I responded when I was *unlucky* where the real growth spurts occurred. Having gotten rid of all those bad jars the Canadians made for Stein Mart, I could now focus on my other problem—the hundreds of buckets that, on a hunch, I'd made for Panera Bread. Up against a wall, I elevated my sales calls into higher gear. I would be cruising in my car looking for restaurants just like when I was cabdriver cruising for fares.

I was driving up Fremont Avenue on a sunny afternoon when I noticed a sign for Brad's Swingside Café. It claimed to be "Seattle's Best Little Italian Restaurant." It was closed until dinner, but since the door was open, I walked in, bucket in hand. A diminutive and garrulous man who I assumed was Brad was at a table tasting wine with a wine salesman. Brad squinted at me for a second as if trying to place me, then poured me a glass of wine while I waited.

Decorating the Swingside's walls were images of Catholic symbolism mixed with photos of jazz musicians from the 60s, as well as several legendary Pittsburgh Pirates ballplayers. When the wine purveyor left, I told Brad, "Pirates? I grew up in Youngstown, where you had the choice to root for the Pirates or the Indians. The Tribe's been breaking my heart my whole life."

Brad chuckled. "Hah! A fan's fate, the formative years... Don't I know you from somewhere?" But I had no memory of him. I then snapped off the lid from the bucket and Brad waved in Mama Lil's aroma to his nose and said, "I'll buy this bucket."

A month later I brought my friend Jeffrey—he of the magic mushrooms and salt-scarred bathtub—into the Swingside to dine on Brad's fabulous Italian fare. When we peeked into the kitchen, Brad was juggling four frying pans of pasta bubbling in sauce. Jeffrey instantly recognized him. "Brad's the guy who told us to pickle the peppers in the bathtub!"

Brad laughed as he handed me a plate of Puttanesca pasta. "Aha. That's why I couldn't remember you. I scrubbed that event clean from my memory."

Jeffrey chortled, "My tub still remembers that memory."

During this time of vigilant door knocking, I landed several new accounts at restaurants, brewpubs, and pizzerias that I was personally delivering to. I loved this aspect of my business. Besides bringing out my refined cab-driving instincts, I delivered to chefs who loved feeding people, including me. After dropping off a bucket at Salumi, a chicken sandwich with Mama Lil's on it was waiting for me on my way out the door. After squeezing a bucket into Serafina's crowded walk-in refrigerator, I'd always pause for a glass of wine with an appetizer of goat cheese smothered in Mama Lil's. At Bizzarro, its chef back then, Mike Easton would slow me down from my hustle with a glass of wine and a plate of his pasta Bolognese.

I mention a few of these many wonderful Seattle restaurants who used Mama Lil's—many of which no longer exist—because nothing helped spread the good word of my brand more than being listed as an ingredient on their menus. And vice versa. Bob Brenlin, the owner of three popular Seattle neighborhood brewpubs, said that by listing Mama Lil's as an ingredient on his menus, he was telling his customers that he used high-quality local ingredients.

By this time, I'd become friendly with many chefs and restaurant owners whom I did business with. But admittedly, not all of them. I was delivering a bucket of peppers to an Italian restaurant owned by an ambitious up-and-coming Pacific Northwest chef. When the sous chef, who had ordered the bucket, handed me the check, the owner, who was scowling as he deboned a duck, asked me, "What am I supposed to do with all the oil that's left in the bucket?"

"That oil is so flavorful that you can use it in infinite ways. For instance, you can make a fabulous aioli for that duck."

He sneered at me, "Maybe I'll use the oil to make my own peppers."

"Where are you going to get the peppers in the offseason?" I asked him.

"I'll just get them from my produce distributor," he said dismissively.

"I don't think so. These goathorn peppers are grown especially for Mama Lil's. We have only two months to harvest, pickle, and pack all our goathorns for the entire year."

As I started to walk out, he called out to me, "You work only two months a year?"

Just before the door closed behind me, I told him, "Pal, you don't think talking with you isn't work?" That was the last time I walked through that door.

I started selling the four-gallon buckets to grocery stores in Seattle and Portland that had self-serve olive bars in their deli sections. I instantly saw the potential to increase my foodservice bucket sales, in part because shoppers could sample the peppers directly from their crocks on toothpicks, and without me needing to be there coaxing them. Sure enough, these peppers, which were sold under Mama Lil's brand name, were selling quite well.

While making bucket deliveries I met Joshua Smith, a nineteen-year-old wild man who lorded over the cheese section and olive bar at a fancy grocery store in West Seattle. Josh was all too happy to support Mama Lil's by pairing the peppers with cheeses and charcuterie he demoed. But after making a delivery there one day, Josh showed me a new product in his olive bars that he said might be competition for Mama Lil's. They were called Peppadews. I'd tasted them before and was not impressed. "My competition?" I said disdainfully. "They're more like maraschino cherries than peppers."

"Exactly," Josh replied. "They taste like candy. And they sell like candy." And true enough, in time the Peppadews replaced Mama Lil's in a few local olive bars. Pissing me off!

Since I'd been successful selling my peppers to some Seattle pizzerias as a pizza topping, my next attempt to build my bucket business was by exhibiting at a pizza show in Las Vegas. While trying to nab customers as they walked by to taste my peppers, I overheard some pompous sixty-year-old man in a leisure suit and cowboy hat bragging to another man as they stopped to try my peppers. "You know why there are so many pizzerias? Not because people love pizza so much, but because there's so much money in pizza. That's why I own fifty of them." In other words, the same reason, in reverse, was why there was but one person making spicy pickled peppers in oil.

If you were an attendee (as opposed to being an exhibitor), the pizza show was fun. It had a party atmosphere, with competitive dough-twirling contests to entertain you. Across the aisle from me was the Buffalo Wild Wings tent with scantily clad go-go girls pouring Bloody Marys from a hose. Folks stumbling out of that tent sure weren't buying my peppers. The fact is, hardly anyone at the show was looking for unique Kick Butt pizza toppings—they were there for tax write-offs and the fun like everyone else in Vegas.

As the show was winding down, a man in chef's whites strode past, paying no attention to me. I tried anyway. "I don't make the pizza and sandwiches: I just make them awesome!"

He took a sample without stopping and kept walking. A moment later, he was back.

"What did I just taste?"

I pulled the lid off the bucket. He took in the aroma. "What's the cost per ounce?"

"Per ounce? I have no idea," I said. "This four-gallon bucket has thirty pounds of peppers in oil and costs $150. I guess that's $5 a pound."

He quickly plugged some numbers into his calculator, then frowned. "Vegas chefs have tight condiment budgets. Your per ounce price is too high for us."

Then I launched into the sales spiel I've heard myself say a thousand times, usually to no avail. "Most of the weight in condiments is water. But by pickling the peppers, I take the water out of them, so the oil goes *into* the peppers. Bite into another pepper ring." The chef did as I said. "That flavorful oil is now coating the taste buds on the back of your throat, enhancing the other flavors passing through. That's why the peppers are so great on sandwiches and pizza."

The chef leaned forward as if to let me in on a secret. "Listen, it's all about pricing. Chefs here price condiments based on one-ounce portion sizes. Here's a wild card to use with chefs and distributors. Tell them what you told me. Then tell them a portion size should be a *half*-ounce." In exchange for that excellent advice, he happily took away two jars in his briefcase. I'd never thought about pricing in those terms before, but if someone dealt me the right hand, who knows, that wild card could come in handy someday.

So no, I didn't sell many peppers at the pizza show. But I was learning things, nevertheless. Also while in Vegas I placed my yearly bet on the Cleveland Indians to win the World Series. Someday, they were going to win big for me.

Pickle Pie
"New England Bar Pizza"
Joshua Smith

This delicious pie is a simple, fun interpretation of a New England classic. Please note that this dough takes two days to prepare; this extra fermentation time means more flavor and better texture. You can also use a digital kitchen scale to weigh the ingredients if you want to be super precise.

Makes 2 (10-inch) pizzas

Pizza Dough

2½ cups (300 grams) all-purpose flour, plus more for rolling

1 cup (250 grams) water

1 scant teaspoon (3 grams) active dry yeast

1½ teaspoons (7 grams) fine sea salt

6 tablespoons (3 ounces) extra-virgin olive oil

Pizza Topping

½ cup (4 ounces) ricotta cheese, divided

1½ cups (6 ounces) shredded mozzarella cheese, divided

¼ cup Mama Lil's Bread & Butter Pickles & Peppers, divided

Garnish

¼ cup Mama Lil's Peppers in Oil, drained well (oil reserved), coarsely chopped, divided

Tajín seasoning

In a 7-quart bowl of a Kitchen Aid stand mixer fitted with a dough hook, add the flour and water. (If you don't have a stand mixer, you can use a large bowl and a sturdy spoon.) Mix on low speed for 2 minutes until the water and flour have fully combined. Cover the dough with a damp towel to prevent it from drying out, and let it sit for 30 minutes at room temperature. (It's okay if this stretches to more than an hour.)

After 30 minutes, add the yeast and mix (or stir well, if mixing by hand) on low speed for 1 minute. Add the salt and mix (or stir) on low speed for 1 minute.

Oil a large stainless-steel bowl with 1 tablespoon (½ ounce) of the olive oil. Transfer the dough to the bowl, turn it once to coat with oil, and let it sit, covered, in a warm place for 30 minutes.

Then fold the dough as follows: Keeping the dough in the bowl, reach down into the bowl and pick up one side of the mound with both hands. Lift it up a little way, then fold it to the center of the mound and press it down gently. Repeat this action with the opposite side of the dough mass, then move to the far side of the dough and finally to the side nearest you. The dough mound will now look a bit like the back of an envelope. Flip the dough over—that's one fold.

Repeat this process every 30 minutes until the dough has been folded four times, for a total of 2 hours (the dough will simply rest for the final 30 minutes). Each time you complete the folding process, the dough will become more and more stretchy and filled with air pockets. This is exactly what you are striving for.

Remove the dough from the bowl, then oil the bowl with 4 tablespoons (2 ounces) of olive oil. Put the dough back into the bowl, cover, and place it in the fridge overnight.

On the second day, divide the dough into two equal balls. Oil two 10-inch pie pans with the remaining 1 tablespoon (½ ounce) of olive oil, and place one dough ball on each pan. Cover with plastic wrap and place the pans in the fridge overnight.

When you're ready to make the pizzas, preheat the oven to 500°F.

Stretching method for the dough:

Lightly flour the cutting board or your countertop with flour; dust your hands as well. Pat each dough ball into a thick, even disk. Begin stretching the dough by holding one edge of the disk in the air with both hands (the circle will be hanging vertically, perpendicular to the work surface), then letting the weight of the dough stretch and pull it downward. Rotate the circle of dough, letting it stretch evenly into a larger and larger circle. Eventually, you'll have a form that looks like a pizza crust, with the dough a bit thicker around the edges; each crust should be about 9 inches in diameter. Set the crust onto one of the 10-inch pie pans, then pull it gently to the edges of the pan. (Note that a perfectly symmetrical circle is not required!) Set this first crust aside and repeat with the second.

To finish the pizzas, use a spatula to spread the ricotta (divided evenly between the two pizzas) all the way to the edge of both crusts. Sprinkle with mozzarella, making sure the cheese reaches the edges of the pan (this will caramelize and become lacy, crispy deliciousness).

Sprinkle the Mama Lil's Bread & Butter Pickles & Peppers evenly across the pies.

Place the pizzas on the center rack of the oven and bake for about 8 minutes, or until the cheeses are bubbling and the outer edges are turning brown or even a bit charred.

Remove the pizzas from the oven and top each one with 1/8 cup of Mama Lil's Peppers in Oil. Sprinkle with the Tajín seasoning and enjoy.

HAPPY BIRTHDAY MAMA LIL

AT THIS STAGE OF MY LIFE, I'M AFRAID to say I was also still gambling by writing spec screenplays in my spare time. They certainly weren't paying off either, but it sure was hard to let that dream go.

Around this time, I'd befriended a sweet, avuncular seventy-five-year-old man named Stewart Stern. Stewart had achieved early fame as the screenwriter for the James Dean film Rebel Without a Cause and the Joanne Woodward drama, *Rachel, Rachel*, directed by Paul Newman. Stewart liked my peppers, so I gave him a case of jars. In return Stewart was generous with his time when he read my latest script, *Mississippi Muse*. He was lukewarm about it at best. "Mississippi Masala, Mississippi Mermaid, Mississippi Burning. So, you need a new title." Then he soberly told me, "When you write a play that no one produces, it's like designing a house that no one builds. Nothing exists. Considering you knew nothing about your business when you began—*abracadabra*—you made the peppers appear from nothing. How magical is that?"

In late October of 2000, Stewart invited me to a political event in Seattle where he said there was a chance that I'd get to meet his friend Paul Newman, perhaps the most celebrated food entrepreneur of our day. Stewart was chaperoning Paul around town as he stumped for Democratic candidates, and he told me to be at the side door of the Labor Temple after the event. I was waiting in the rain when Stewart's car pulled up and I saw Paul being escorted into it. They had forgotten about me. As their car started to pull away, I knocked on the passenger window. It stopped and when the window rolled down, Paul Newman's famous blue eyes were looking at me with trepidation. Then Stewart leaned over from the driver's seat. "Paul, this is my friend Howard. He makes peppers." I handed Paul a jar of Mama Lil's Peppers. Considering that Paul's face was on every single label of his salad dressings, tomato sauce, candy bars, and cat food, I shouldn't have been surprised when he said with a grin, "You sure don't look like Mama Lil."

When I told him, "Unfortunately for Lil, I do," I got a chuckle from him, that turned into a warm Cool Hand Luke smile. "I bet you've made your mama proud. Is Mama Lil still alive?"

"She sure is. But she might drop dead of jealousy when I tell her I met you!"

On my way to the next Summer Fancy Food Show in New York City, I stopped in Ohio for Lil's eightieth birthday. When I entered my mom's kitchen, I spotted her oiled-up countertop grinder, so I knew she'd made salata. I lifted the lid of the large pot on the stove, and yep, there was my favorite food in the world, her chicken and dumplings.

Lil was dozing on the couch in the next room over. When I woke her, she was happy to see me, but she was tired. I figured it was because she had gotten up at 4 a.m. to roast eggplant in the basement. The next day was her birthday, and I weeded with her in the garden, helped her cage her tomatoes, and staked her Hungarian goathorn pepper plants. Then we went shopping.

Walking the grocery aisles, Lil asked, "Why aren't Mama Lil's here?"

I gave her a side hug as we strolled and said, "Mom, my business hit a rough patch last year. But I have a good feeling about the upcoming show. Who knows, maybe Giant Eagle will find me there." On the drive home, Lil was having a hard time keeping a smile on her face and told me if anything were to happen to her, not to let her fate be the same as her Aunt Pearl, who after a stroke spent her last two miserable years debilitated in a nursing home.

For her birthday dinner, Harry grilled steaks. Lil brightened up when she asked if I had brought her the case of peppers she requested for her birthday. In my haste, I'd forgotten the jars and felt guilty. The next morning, my mom still looked sad. But Harry was in better spirits, mimicking my bad lines he'd heard me say at food shows: "I got a mama, you got a mama, my mama's Mama Lil. Like fine wine, these peppas only get betta with age."

My mom shook her weary head. "This Mama Lil isn't getting better with age." As she walked me to my car, she handed me a small gift box. "I meant to send them for your birthday." Inside the box was a pair of very fine black leather gloves. Having forgotten the case of peppers for her birthday, I felt even more guilty accepting her gift. And the gloves were too nice, as knowing me, I'd lose one of them.

Fancy Food Show, 2001.

At the 2001 Winter Fancy Food Show six months prior, I'd succeeded in getting Mama Lil's retail jars into every Whole Foods store in the southern region of California. Since each region made its own buying decisions, my next goal was getting Mama Lil's into all the Whole Foods on the East Coast—even though after the distributor's cut and transportation costs, I could expect no profits to speak of. Worth noting: It was only because of the greater profits per jar I was making at farmers' markets that I could afford to even think that being in all the Whole Foods stores in the country was a worthwhile ambition.

On the NYC Summer Fancy Food Show's first day, I could feel the buzz about Mama Lil's as food-loving folks, one after another, were finding their way to my booth. Gourmet magazine wanted to do an article about Mama Lil's. An editor from Better Homes & Gardens wanted to feature the Peppa-Lilli in her grandmother's potato salad recipe. As for sales, by the second day of the show, grocery buyers from two more regions of Whole Foods stores and all the A&P stores wanted Mama Lil's on their shelves with the caveat that I do lots of demos. I was so busy I barely escaped from my booth, except to take a leak, as I didn't want to miss out in case the Giant Eagle's buyer happened by.

I was scurrying the crowded aisles of the convention floor on my way to the restroom when I came across—what do you know—the Peppadew booth. By then, I'd lost a few crocks in supermarket olive bars to them, so Peppadews had become firmly lodged in my brain as Mama Lil's nemesis. The friendly salesman didn't know much about its production process, but when he handed me a sales brochure, he mentioned its products were made in South Africa but that the company's owner was French.

I read the Peppadew brochure when I got back to my booth. It led one to believe, without explicitly saying it, that the Peppadews were a naturally sweet pepper. Horseshit! As far as I could tell, this pepper—or whatever this shiny red thing was—had none of its own natural sweetness. And its crimson color was very similar to maraschino cherries, which are dyed red. There was also a Peppadew origin story where a South African farmer tripped in his field, hit his head on a rock, and when he opened his eyes, he was staring at the very first Peppadew plant. No doubt being grown in horseshit! Sure, I had an axe to grind with the Peppadews; I'd lost a lot of business to them. And they were sold in almost every store in the country, including Giant Eagle.

It was midway through the last day of the show when my brother called. While Lil was rotating the mattress on the bed I'd slept in, she'd developed a severe headache. When it hadn't subsided after two hours, she went to the hospital, where it was discovered that she'd had a brain aneurysm. Within a few hours, they had to decide whether she should have brain surgery, or not.

Having yodeled Lil's name so many times at the show, I had been guiltily haunted by my last image of her, tearfully saying goodbye as she gave me that fine pair of black leather gloves. Her demise shouldn't have come as a total surprise to me. Lil had grown old and *oy*, she'd eaten too many tenderloin steaks in her life. But the news of her condition slammed me in waves that just kept coming. Falling to my knees behind my booth, I started sobbing uncontrollably. I finally pulled it together to cancel my flight to Seattle and make a reservation for Pittsburgh. I packed up my booth on a pallet in record time. Since it was the last day of the show, I had my suitcase with me and saved a case of peppers to take to Lil's hospital room to cheer her up—that is, if she ever opened her eyes again. More tears. I was just about to collect my things and leave my booth when a stout woman with a badge and a clipboard blocked my exit.

"I'm the head of security. You're not allowed to close your booth before the show ends."

"But this is an emergency. My mom is about to go into—" more tears.

But this woman wasn't fazed by my sorrow. "Hire someone to keep your booth open. Attendees pay a lot of money to be here. Booths must stay open until the closing bell rings. Those are the rules. You are no exception. If you leave, you'll never exhibit at this show again." As she stood there, arms folded, blocking my path out of the booth, she reminded me of the mean concentration camp commandant in the Lina Wertmüller film, Seven Beauties. But the last thing I wanted was to be appeasing my Frau Kommandant with sweetness. I had a flight to catch! I grabbed my suitcase, lowered my shoulder, broke past her, and dashed for the escalator.

The second I stepped out of Javits Center, there was a colossal clap of thunder, and a vicious rainstorm was unleashed. I jumped into the safety of a cab. We had just gotten onto the freeway when I realized that I'd left the case of peppers for my mom on top of my pallet. When I got to the airport, due to the storm all flights had been cancelled until tomorrow, so I took a cab right back to Javits Center. The show had just ended by then, and it was a madhouse of people bustling about. I was rolling my suitcase weaving in the aisles around people when I ran right smack into someone walking in the opposite direction. To lessen the impact, we had no choice but to embrace. When we pulled apart, BOO! It was Frau Kommandant!

I pushed past her and broke into a trot. She was jabbering into her walkie talkie following me all the way to my booth. Without breaking stride, I snared the case of peppers off my pallet then bolted out of the convention center for what felt like my second touchdown of the day. You'd think all that running around would've settled my grieving soul, but just like the rain my sorrow seemed boundless. I sobbed myself to sleep on my friend's couch and I was sobbing on my way back to the airport in the morning. I had no idea until then how much I loved Mama Lil.

At the airport check-in I tried my best to be calm. I was still nervous about the buckets that had spilled their oil in baggage a year ago and didn't want to alert anyone about the case of Mama Lil's I had with me. But no one said a word about the case at check-in. By the time I reached the boarding area, my emotions had subsided enough that like many of the other hard-working fancy food-show folks I recognized sitting among me—many of them buyers who'd walked by my booth at the show—I was reviewing my sales leads. In the boarding line minutes later, I had the box of jars tucked under my arm when a ticketing agent told me that they didn't want me to board the plane with the box. Mind you, these were jars, not buckets with lids that could snap off. And this was July of 2001—pre-9/11—when you could still take glass jars of food products on the plane, as many fans of Mama Lil's did.

"But I have to bring these jars," I begged the airline employee. "They're for my mom."

The woman could see I was tearing up. "Sir, you can take the jars. We don't want you to take the box. I'll help you with this." Although this made absolutely no sense to me, the ticketing agent helped me stuff twelve jars from that box into my luggage and carry-on, and then I boarded the plane, and put my suitcase and carry-on in the overhead above my first-class seat. Then I ordered a much neede Bloody Mary.

As I sat there waiting for my cocktail, I spotted outside the plane's door just a few feet away, my empty cardboard box. I flashed on a horrific image of me walking through the airport with jar after jar falling out of my carry-on, shattering on the concourse's floor. In the blink of an eye, I got up, reached out the plane's door, grabbed the empty box, and shoved it under the seat. The pilot was announcing to get ready for takeoff when the first-class steward handed me my Bloody Mary. Which is when he saw the empty pepper box under the seat. "You were told NOT to take the box!" he sternly barked. Then pointing to the exit, he shouted. "Get off my plane! Now."

I looked at him bewildered. "Why? I can't get off the plane. I'm going to see my mom." The steward sneered at me, then walked into the cockpit.

Seconds later, the pilot's voice was on the intercom. "There'll be a slight delay in takeoff." The cockpit door opened, and the pilot walked out, followed by the steward who was pointing at me. "It's that man! He took the box."

The pilot asked me, "Why'd you take the box?"

I was doing all I could to fight back my tears. "To bring the jars to my mama."

When the plane's door reopened, and a policeman walked in, I wouldn't have been surprised if Frau Kommandant was right behind him. "Follow me off the plane," the cop ordered.

"I can't get off this plane, I've got to get to Pittsburgh," I sputtered. When the policeman reached for his handcuffs, I stood up, grabbed my carry-on overflowing with jars, and followed him to the exit door. Before I stepped out, I glanced back down the aisle and saw all those grocery buyers staring at me. They knew the man from Mama Lil's was south of sane, *but what did he do to get thrown off the plane?* I had no idea myself. I was led into a departure area where a space had been cordoned off. I was greeted by the airport's head of security, backed up by three security agents and three cops. The head of security sat me down on a chair, aimed a light at my face.

I pleaded with the seven men. "I take full responsibility of that bucket that spilled."

The head of security asked, "What bucket? Why did you take the box on the plane?"

"To put the jars in. I didn't want jars to fall out and spill more oil like the buckets did."

The head of security threw up his arms. "What bucket? What oil? What jars??"

I was doing all I could to hold back my deluge. "The jars I was taking to my mama!" I reached into my carry-on and put a jar in his hands. "I named my business after my mama." Outside the window, my plane was leaving the terminal. "And now I may never see Mama Lil alive again!"

The head of security looked at the jar in his hand. "Your mama is Mama Lil?"

Having said it a hundred times at the show, I said it again. "You gotta mama, I gotta mama, my mama is Mama Lil"— then the dam broke, and I started sobbing my eyes out.

A cop cried out, "Mama Mia!" and he started sobbing. Now, we all know yawning is contagious, but tears are too, I guess. When the head of security turned and saw all six of his posse crying in a wailful chorus of "Mama Mia," he walked over to the ticketing agent and told her, "Get this man on the next flight to Pittsburgh. And he can take that damn box with him."

When I arrived at the hospital's ICU, Lil had just come out of surgery. She was in a coma with her arms strapped to the bed with gauze bandages wrapped around her head. I set up the jars, so they'd be in her line of sight in case she regained consciousness. And then I sat with her.

Ten hours later, when Lil opened an eye, she hardly noticed the jars of Mama Lil's Peppers. When she saw me, she tried to talk. But when she couldn't, she just shook her head in despair. Fighting back my tears, I worked up a smile for her and whispered, "I'm sorry it took me so long to get here." Then holding back my tears, I proudly showed her one of the jars. "They loved Mama Lil's in the Big Apple." For a moment, I saw her lips curl into a smile, but it dissipated into a look of horror. She stared at me, shaking her head in disbelief at this terrible nightmare she'd awoken to. I could read her terrified eyes—*Why am I still alive?*

Bolognese á la Mama Lil's

Mike Easton

Mike is a premier craftsman of fresh pasta and innovative sauces, which he served at his Seattle restaurants, Il Corvo and Il Nido, and in Waitsburg in eastern WA where his Bar Bacetto was nominated for a James Beard award as best new restaurant in the country.

This recipe makes four dinner-size portions of pasta, but you'll have a fair bit leftover. A good thing, because it freezes well.

Makes 6 cups sauce

2 dried bay leaves

3 whole cloves

2 teaspoons fennel seeds

1½ teaspoons crushed red pepper flakes

¼ teaspoon black peppercorns, plus more freshly ground

1 tablespoon olive oil

3 ounces chicken livers, rinsed, finely chopped

½ large yellow onion, finely chopped

About 8 fresh thyme sprigs

¼ cup Mama Lil's Kick Butt Peppers in Oil

5 garlic cloves, finely chopped

1½ teaspoons kosher salt, plus more

1 (14-ounce) can whole tomatoes

⅓ cup red wine

1¼ pounds ground beef chuck (20 percent fat)

1 pound ground pork shoulder

1½ cups whole milk

2 tablespoons red wine vinegar

1¼ pounds fresh pappardelle noodles, or 12 ounces dried pasta

4 tablespoons (½ stick) unsalted butter, at room temperature

3 ounces Parmesan cheese, finely grated (about ¾ cup)

To make the sauce:

Toast the bay leaves, cloves, fennel seeds, red pepper flakes, and whole peppercorns in a dry small skillet over medium heat, tossing often, until fragrant, about 2 minutes. Let cool; transfer to a spice mill (or mortar and pestle) and finely grind.

Preheat the oven to 250°F. Heat the olive oil in a heavy, medium-size pot or Dutch oven over medium-high heat. Add the livers and stir to coat with the oil; season with pinches of salt and black pepper. Cook, stirring occasionally, until the livers are deeply browned (they will look almost burned), 5 to 8 minutes.

Add the onion, thyme, and Mama Lil's Peppers; stir to coat. Taste and adjust the seasoning with salt and black pepper and cook, stirring as needed, until the onion is golden brown and soft, 5 to 8 minutes. Add the garlic (adding garlic after the onion has been going for a while will keep it from burning) and stir to coat. Cook, stirring often, until the garlic is soft, about 2 minutes. Stir in the spice mixture and 1½ teaspoons of salt (this will toast the spices one more time, deepening their flavor).

Add the tomatoes and wine, stirring and scraping up any browned bits. Mix in the beef and pork (the mixture will be fairly stiff but will soften and loosen as it cooks). Add the milk and mix well; everything should be evenly coated. Cover the pot and braise in the oven for 6 to 8 hours. (Resist the urge to check on it. It's fine! We promise!)

Remove the pan from the oven. As the sauce cooks, it will firm up (looking somewhat like meatloaf); stir it to loosen. Pluck out the thyme sprigs and, using an immersion blender, purée the sauce until mostly smooth. Add the vinegar; taste and season with more salt and black pepper as needed.

To make the pasta:

Cook the pasta noodles in a large pot of boiling salted water, stirring occasionally, until al dente. Drain, reserving 1½ cups of the pasta cooking liquid. Toss the pasta and butter in a very large skillet set over medium heat. Ladle in 1½ to 2 cups sauce—enough to coat the pasta well—and cook, adding pasta cooking liquid as needed, until the sauce is thick and glossy; taste and adjust the seasoning as desired. Serve topped with Parmesan cheese.

Do ahead: The sauce can be made up to 5 days ahead. After cooking, let the sauce cool; cover tightly and chill, or freeze for up to 1 month.

STAYIN' ALIVE

AFTER STAYING WITH MY MOM for a few days, I had to get back to Seattle to prepare for the harvest of 2001. I'd get reports from my dad about Lil. "She can talk now. But the other day she nailed Abe Malkoff with a slice of cantaloupe."

Luckily, I was able to convince my Czech friend, Jan Barton, to come help me again. I even convinced Tomas, the ultimate pepper slicer, to ride his motorcycle to Wolf Pack cannery to slice the stems off the peppers. And since it's best to have one comedian on the crew during those eight-hour slicing sessions, I persuaded my cherub-faced Moldovan friend Leonid to come work for me. Leonid, a self-employed computer geek, was not at all talented with a knife, but he sure took pleasure in manning the Bobbitron—just as we took pleasure in his endless chuksha (Russian hillbilly) jokes that he told in his thick eastern European accent. This one hit home:

> Chuksha goes to university and tells his teacher, "Chuksha wants to be writer."
> Teacher asks, "Chuksha, have you read Tolstoy?" Chuksha says no.
> Teacher asks, "Chuksha, have you read Dostoevsky?" Chuksha says no.
> Teacher gets exasperated. "Chuksha, have you at least read Chekhov?"
> Now Chuksha is exasperated. "Chuksha wants to be a writer. Not a reader."

Just after we arrived at the cannery on September 11, terrorists flew the airplanes into the Twin Towers and the Pentagon. George Wolf put on his Korean War medals and asked my crew to recite the Pledge of Allegiance with him. Leonid, Tomas, and Jan had never heard it before, but they mouthed along until Leonid ignited a chain of restrained snickering.

The following day, after being interviewed for *Gourmet* magazine by a woman in New York City still shell-shocked from the Towers falling, I drove to Krueger's farm to get the next load of peppers. My friend Jean Sherrard came along to take photographs of the Yakima River for a Then & Now book he was working on about Washington state. During the ride, I was telling him the bizarre story about getting kicked off the plane when on the radio we heard the news that the terrorists used box cutters as weapons. Jean's eyes widened with a look of revelation.

"That's why they didn't want the box on the plane. Intelligence picked up chatter about box cutters and focused on the word *box,* not *cutter.* Hah! They thought you were a terrorist!"

Gourmet magazine, 2002. Photo by Rick Dahms

Jean was still snapping photographs when we arrived at Krueger's farm-stand to load up the peppers. A tractor zipped past us and set down a pallet of my sacks of peppers onto the scale. I could see through the burlap that the peppers were green. Green peppers are unripe and don't look or taste good yet, and I knew all too well that Salerno Turci's Peppers went out of business because of green peppers! Now, like everyone else after the terrorist attack, I was a bit unhinged. But seeing these green peppers really got me riled up. Was I channeling my bedridden, melon-mashing mama when I screamed at the ten pickers, "The peppers are green!" Then I reached into a bin of baby watermelons and heaved one at the tractor. Bullseye! Melon fragments splattered onto the pickers. I turned to Jean, "Tell me you got that *shot* on film?"

Stunned by my tantrum, Jean hadn't moved.

I then warned him, "Then make sure you get this one on film!" I reached into the bin and nailed the tractor with a second melon. The pickers had no idea what I was so upset about. And Jean was so aghast he still hadn't raised his camera. So, I nailed the tractor with a third melon.

Prompting Jean to proclaim, "You *are* a terrorist!" The pickers then burst out laughing at me, and humiliated, I put the fourth melon down. But all the world's craziness aside, it was another long Indian summer that yielded a bountiful pepper harvest that stretched almost until Halloween. And after the debacles of the spoiled jars at Wolf Pack in 1998, the embargo at the Columbia River Kitchen in 1999, and the fiasco of the peppers made by the Canadian cannery, in 2001, I regained my pride in all 48,000 jars we made.

When production was over, I went to Ohio to visit my ailing, bedridden mother in the nursing home. To quote Dylan Thomas, Lil did not go gentle into that good night. She was experiencing many ministrokes by then, her moods swinging wildly from extreme joy to furious anger as she raged, raged against the dying of the light. At one point, the nurses had no choice but to place her geriatric chair in the middle of the common room so she couldn't grab an object—like a slice of melon—and heave it at someone's head.

On my visits back east to see her, I would kill two birds with one stone by taking her car to the Beltway region and doing demos at the A&P and Whole Foods stores. Even without the aid of Google Maps I could find the stores more easily than I could find where my jars were hiding within them. There were simply too many jars of too many products on too many shelves. If *I* couldn't locate the jars of Mama Lil's, how would a customer ever find them again?

After doing fifteen demos in four days, I drove straight through the night to Lil's nursing home in Youngstown. As I walked down its quiet, dark halls at midnight, I came upon the common room. I saw Lil's silhouette in her geriatric chair. She was leaning over making repetitive reaching motions with her arm. As I got closer, I could see her frustration as she repeated that futile reaching gesture. She wasn't aware I was even there, so I stuck out my arm just out of her line of sight. Lil snatched my forearm like a starved animal making a kill. She tightly held onto my wrist as her gaze moved up my arm. When she saw my face, she erupted into an ecstatic smile, and looked up to the heavens to joyfully proclaim, "My son! My son! I picked my son!"

I had no idea what this meant. "Mom, what were you just doing?"

Her eyes were clear and shining ecstatically. "I was in my garden. Trying to pick a tomato. I couldn't reach it. Then I picked—you! But you weren't a tomato. You were a ...pepper? I could just eat you up." Then meekly, she asked, "Can you get me a knife?" It broke my heart to hear this. Was my mom asking me to help put her out of her misery?

I nervously asked her, "What do you want a knife for, Mom?"

She smiled sheepishly, lest I consider her a fool. "To slice the pepper. For my salata." My mom *did* want to eat me up! She'd been intubated for months, so her hallucination was a rational desire. I gave her a pretend knife. She pretended to slice a pepper. Long live the imagination!

On one visit, I found myself apologizing to her for not giving her any grandchildren. She looked at me like I was the one who was meshuga then said. "You're too old to be a dad." Another time when I visited her, she seemed halfway lucid, so I asked her for the umpteenth time how she made chicken and dumplings. "Easy-peasy sonny boy. Roll 'em up, toss 'em in the pot."

Three months later, I visited Lil again. Her bed had been lowered almost to the floor in case she fell out. I lay down beside her and whispered, "Hey, Mama Lil."

She opened her weary blue eyes, then smiled lovingly. "Good to see you, sonny boy."

Lil died the next day. While sitting shiva for a couple of days, I scouted around the house for old photos and mementos. Not surprisingly, a box of the things she wanted me to inherit was already prepared. As a kid, I misread the care she put into the things she treasured—always polishing bowls and silverware—as a form of materialism. But I had it all wrong. By the care she put into these *things*, Lil was tending to the *spirits* that lived within them.

The last thing I remembered to pack in my suitcase was the only object of hers I had ever really wanted: that countertop meat grinder she inherited from her mother. Lil put a lot of care into preserving those few pieces of eighty-year-old worn steel. It had once made the trip to Seattle in 1992, the year I started Mama Lil's, when she taught me how to make the peppers in oil and her Romanian eggplant salata. I was taking the grinder back to its new home. It was my turn to spin its crank.

Lil's Romanian Eggplant Salata

Lil just called this Romanian eggplant dish *salata*. It's a smoky, flavorful spread that can be served with crackers and bread or scooped with vegetables. It really is magical in the way the flavors of the raw peppers and smoky eggplant meld when they're shoved through a grinder together. If you don't have a countertop grinder, get one at a secondhand store. Or you can run the roasted eggplant and fresh peppers through a Cuisinart and hope for the best. If you do use a Cuisinart, try not to process the vegetables too finely, or they'll come out mushy.

This recipe calls for equal parts, weight-wise, of roasted eggplant and fresh peppers. For one eggplant, that usually means one large bell pepper or three goathorn peppers. You can alter the spicy heat from one to five stars by using a combination of sweet bells and Hungarian goathorns. Lil made hers with just bells, whereas I use goathorns, so it's quite spicy.

Makes approximately 6 cups

  4 large globe eggplants
  4 large bell peppers, mixed colors, or Hungarian goathorn peppers, or a mix (see headnote)
  Oil from Mama Lil's Peppers in Oil, or olive oil
  1 small red onion, chopped

Preheat the broiler.

Char the whole, fresh eggplants right on top of your gas burners or directly on an outdoor grill to get a nice, smoky flavor that permeates the "meat" of the eggplant. Keep turning them on the flame until the skins are thoroughly blackened, about 10 minutes. Then finish roasting them at 400°F on a baking sheet in the broiler, turning them occasionally, until thoroughly cooked, about 30 minutes.

When the eggplants are completely soft, remove them from the broiler, let them cool for a bit, and then scrape off the charred skin with a spoon or the back of a knife. Refrigerate the deskinned, mushy eggplants for at least a half hour to firm up the flesh a bit, which will make it easier to feed them into the grinder.

While the eggplant is chilling, remove the stems and seeds from the peppers and quarter them.

Place a mixing bowl under the grinder's chute to catch the salata. Slowly feed the chilled, roasted eggplant and fresh peppers together into the grinder's mouth and turn the crank. The salata should be the consistency of a relish. Sprinkle in the chopped red onion for texture. Add salt and oil to taste and mix thoroughly. Lil drizzled olive oil over her finished salata—but mixing in some spicy oil from a jar of Mama Lil's Peppers is even better.

Lil ate salata on challah. But she also just scooped it up with sliced tomatoes or cucumbers.

Making salata with Lil's grinder.

PART TWO

The Juggler

BE CAREFUL WHAT YOU WISH FOR

WHEN THE BOXES OF LIL'S STUFF ARRIVED at my house a week later—the fine china, cut glass, heirloom silverware—I packed them away. More than twenty years later, they haven't moved. The only piece I ever used was a long-stemmed crystal candy dish whose base broke off from the stem. I hated to throw it out, so I plunged its sharp stem into my garden, where its bowl collected rainwater. For the last eight years of my cat Marion's life (including the three years after she went blind), she would climb out her cat door when it rained, whisker her way around my house and descend twenty steps into the garden to drink the rainwater from Lil's cut-glass bowl.

I'd ask my cat, "Why would you go through so much trouble for a drink of water?" Then it dawned on me. Since I hadn't given Lil any grandchildren to spoil, she would send cat toys as Chanukah gifts to Marion. I think Marion knew this broken candy bowl was Lil's last gift to her. And she was honored to drink from it. What a wonderful thought. And I think it's true.

I always got anxious before the start of the pepper season, but for the harvest of 2002, even more so. I had asked Gayle Krueger to again increase his yield by planting two more rows for me, and true to form, I still hadn't found a right-hand man yet to help me out.

By the time I drove over the mountains to scout the pepper fields that were weeks away from ripening, the rest of Yakima Valley's abundant harvest was going full bore. In the peach orchards, men were climbing up and down ladders. On the other side of the road, women were kneeling amid the tomato fields. As I drove on, the sweet smell of Concord grapes was thick in the air. Further up the road, lush hop vines were being pulled down off their trellises. As I approached an intersection, a fully loaded hop truck turned right in front of me, and soon stray hop flowers came dancing through my open windows. My senses were so intoxicated with their sweet and bitter smell that I got completely lost. Then I made another wrong turn. And whoa! The piercingly sweet fragrance of mint that went on for miles!

When I finally found my way to Krueger's, I got excited as I drove past the rows of goathorns just beginning to show color. I stopped and picked a dozen yellow peppers and even found an orange one. While paying for them at the farmstand, I spotted a middle-aged, red-headed woman squeezing an eggplant. And so, I bought some eggplant too.

Thirty miles after crossing the high desert, I was coming down Manastash Ridge into the sprawling green alfalfa fields of the Kittitas valley as the sun fought through the clouds above the jagged Cascades. The sky was pulsed with brilliant rays of light. I was sobbing uncontrollably again and found myself talking out loud to Lil. "Mom, did I ever describe to you this view on my way home from the farms? And if you're here—like it feels you are—let's chase this sunset together."

Lil was still alive in my thoughts when I got home that night, so I got to it. After washing the peppers, I roasted the eggplant on top of my stove. I've always associated the smell of charred eggplant with Lil, and I was crying again as I peeled off its blackened skin. But my tears were now warm as they trailed down my face. On that cathartic drive across the mountains, had I mourned my mother so thoroughly that I set her spirit free? Was that what it means to become an angel? Was that miracle the source of my joy? It sure felt that way.

The next morning, I took out Lil's meat grinder, cinched it to my countertop, and started pushing the roasted eggplant and fresh peppers through it while spinning its crank. It almost felt like Lil was watching over my shoulder. Was I not making this ancestral dish properly? Or was her lingering soul just longing to eat salata one last time?

When my phone started ringing, my first thought was that it was Lil calling me. But I had food prep gloves on and didn't want to peel them off to answer it. I let it go to voicemail. Then five minutes later I sat down and scooped some salata into my mouth with sliced tomatoes and cucumbers, like Lil would eat it. It was as delicious as Lil's. Then I listened to my voicemail.

A familiar woman's voice came on. "Blast from the past. Howard, this is Betsy from Panera Bread. Remember I told you that we take our time? Well, we finally came up with something. Call me back."

As I put the phone down, I was excited. And nervous. Was this another trap? After all, I still had four hundred of those four-gallon buckets left from what I'd made for Panera two years ago. Fearing more trouble, I didn't really want to call her back. Until I heard Lil's shrill voice egging me on: *What are you scared of? Success? Want me to dial her number for you?*

I dialed.

Betsy was exuding excitement from the second she got on the phone. "We've been trying Mama Lil's Peppers on a steak sandwich. Everyone in the test kitchen loves this sandwich." My first thought: Those formerly embargoed jars I sent them were now three years old. Of course, they loved those peppers. They were pickled and packed to perfection and got better as they aged! My second thought: It's a steak sandwich. Lil must be behind this. She's probably savoring that sandwich as she smiles down at me now.

Betsy explained Panera's process of doing a series of tests before it put a new sandwich on its national menu. Typically, it started with a five-café test at its St. Louis outlets near its corporate offices. "If that test succeeds," she continued, "we'll do a regional test of twenty-five to thirty-five cafés. If the regional test succeeds, we'll probably run one more regional test before we take that sandwich national—in all 350 of our cafés."

I repeated back to her, "So first, a five-café test? If successful, then a regional test. Or two? Then, that sandwich could go…national? How long would that take?"

"You know us. We're slow and deliberate. Could be four months, six months. Maybe longer. After this five-store test, we'll certainly know more."

I told Betsy about the four-gallon buckets I still had left from two years ago. Could I use them? No. Panera preferred a smaller two-gallon bucket that would be easier for its staff to lift. Then, acknowledging the elephant in the room, Betsy asked me cautiously, "So, supply won't be an issue for you, will it?"

I hesitated, for good reason. When she asked me whether supply would be an issue, was she talking about the regional tests or about providing for all their cafes nationally? Even with Krueger's increased yield in the upcoming harvest, at best there would be enough for one or two of the twenty-five café tests—not nearly enough for all 350 of its cafés. But she also said it could take longer than six months before management decided, which gave me some leeway to come up with a plan to make that unimaginable number of buckets. But I was hesitating too long, and I heard Lil's shrill voice screaming into my mind's ear: *Opportunity is knocking!*

"No. Supply won't be an issue. We have tons of peppers growing."

Betsy let out a sigh of relief. "That's good to hear."

Sit down with me here at the table as I play cards with the big guys. By letting Betsy think I held the better hand at this crucial moment in the game, I was bluffing, kind of. When I told her that supply wouldn't be an issue, was she hearing that I could supply all 350 of its cafés? Because there was no way in the world that I could pull that off. Or was she asking if I could make enough buckets for two tests involving twenty-five cafes? Which I knew I could probably pull off. It was an open question that was left unclear, intentionally perhaps, by both of us. The fact was, Betsy was the dealer and didn't know how to play her hand either. She couldn't commit to how many peppers would be needed until after the tests were run—by which time the harvest would be over. From my side, I didn't want to get stuck with so many buckets again, and besides, I had no real idea how many Hungarian goathorns Krueger's fields would even yield this year. Or where I'd even be making those buckets of peppers, for that matter.

Before we got off the phone, Betsy enthusiastically said to me, "We love this sandwich! And we want to get the sandwich test going ASAP. The sooner you can make some buckets for us, the better. If we can get forty buckets, it should get us through the first five-café test."

That night I called Gayle Krueger to see if he could have his pickers selectively harvest eight hundred pounds of colorful goathorn peppers. Because I'd seen the fields of mostly green and yellow peppers just a few days before, I knew it would not be easy picking. The next morning Tomas and I drove to Krueger's, and when I spotted the sacks of peppers on the scale, they were miraculously filled with yellow and orange beauties.

Maybe my humiliating melon tantrum had gotten my point across after all!

Tomas and I took the sacks to Wolf Pack, where at 3 p.m., with the help of two of George's crew, we proceeded to destem, deseed, slice, and pickle four hundred pounds of peppers late into the night. We slept at the cannery, and the next day we sliced the remaining four hundred pounds. The most laborious part of the job, as always, was removing the seeds. I was thinking ahead when I made two buckets from peppers that we didn't take the seed cores out of in case I could talk Panera into taking a hotter version with some seeds left in. These would be infinitely easier for me to make, especially considering how many buckets I might be making.

If Panera could have seen Tomas and I in action, they probably would've quit Mama Lil's right then and there. Tomas was not a junkie, but he sure looked like one. I was so bedraggled and exhausted that I didn't look much better. But who knows what Panera knew about Mama Lil's. Maybe the beautiful label on the jar fooled management into thinking Mama Lil's was a legitimate enterprise as opposed to a one-man show. And I wasn't about to tell Panera otherwise. But as for those forty buckets of colorful goathorns we'd just packed—they looked good, smelled good, and in a month, I knew they'd be tasting good too.

When I went down to my office the next morning, two Panera purchase orders were waiting on my fax machine. One was for twenty buckets to be shipped out tomorrow. The other was for twenty more buckets to be shipped two weeks later. Panera had taken its time making up its mind about using Mama Lil's, but now it was full speed ahead.

I was scheduled to begin packing a year's supply of retail jars at Wolf Pack, so I asked George whether I could I make the buckets for Panera there. But he told me he was in the pasteurization business, so I should find somewhere else with ample refrigeration. Since Noodles had gone out of business, that very convenient facility near my house wasn't available either.

It wasn't going to be easy to keep up my bluff with Panera for much longer.

Two days later, Betsy was acting as an intermediary on a call between the buyer and me. The conversation quickly turned to the sensitive subject of pricing. At this stage, for the twenty buckets I had shipped to Panera to initiate its five-store test, I charged the same price that I charged a restaurant in Seattle when I personally delivered one bucket—$70. I gave them no volume discount. Which it turns out was a smart move, as it gave me some negotiating room.

In the background, I could hear Betsy tapping on a calculator as she talked to me. "I'm calculating the cost of a one-ounce portion size…Your price is too high. Can you do better?"

I knew I *could* do better. But then I recalled the advice, that "wild card" that the Las Vegas chef had given me. I told her, "My customers tell me that due to the pepper's depth of flavor, a *half-ounce* portion size is more than sufficient on a sandwich."

"Interesting. I'll share that info about portion sizes with our chef."

But I hadn't finished playing my hand. "I could lower the price of a bucket from \$70 to \$57. *If* you took the peppers with some seeds left in. Most of the seeds are flushed out in water anyway. These peppers will be slightly spicier, but not that much spicier. It's a better deal."

Betsy said, "I think I got it. Some seeds left in, the peppers are much cheaper. I'll mention it to our buyer. Overnight me samples."

Normally, when I sold buckets in quantity to distributors, I charged \$60 per bucket for the seedless peppers. And \$57 if some seeds were left in—a \$3 difference in price. But at \$70 per bucket with no volume discount, my offer to Panera was a \$13 difference in price. My logic was that I wanted it to be cost-prohibitive to Panera to take the seedless peppers because frankly, I didn't want to have to hire so many people to scoop all those damn seeds out.

Betsy called back two days later. "The test kitchen wants the peppers without any seeds."

That caught me by surprise. "Are you sure? Considering the price?"

"Too many seeds for our customers. We'll pay the higher price."

I pulled the phone away in case she heard me shout, "Blackjack!" By trying to persuade her to take the peppers with some seeds left in them, I had inadvertently turned my mediocre hand into a great one. Sure, I'd be hiring a larger crew. But at the volume price of \$70 per bucket, for the first time since I started producing Mama Lil's Peppers, I could make some real money here—even if it lasted but the length of one sandwich test. That is, if only I had a place to make those buckets.

Enter Jerry Mascio, stage right. Jerry was born in Sulmona, Italy, in the Abruzzo region where the hot peppers in oil recipe theoretically originated. After Jerry's family moved to Seattle, his mother Flora started making raviolis for her friends in the Garlic Gulch neighborhood (Seattle's former version of Little Italy), where in 1973 Mascio's Pasta was born. In 1994, the Mascios sold their pasta business, and Jerry began making polenta under the brand name of San Gennaro.

When I first walked into his polenta production facility, Jerry—a deceptively capable man with a weak chin and slumped shoulders—was changing the oil on a jacked-up car. Sliding out from under it, he peeled off his oily gloves, stepped out of his overalls, and slipped into a white lab coat. When I gave him a jar of my peppers, his face lit up. "My daughter brings them home from the Husky Deli. I love these things!"

Jerry then gave me a tour of this building where he had set up shop. It had a large walk-in refrigerator and a loading dock to ship out pallets from. In the main production area, chubs of polenta were shooting out of large stainless-steel mixing tanks into tubs of ice water. In another corner, Paul Gilroy, a middle-aged man with a limp and an ever-present sly smile, leased space from Jerry for his mayonnaise making business. Outside the building, Paul showed me the two-thousand-gallon storage tanks of vinegar and expeller-pressed canola oil—two of the ingredients for making mayonnaise and Mama Lil's—that I could buy directly from him instead of schlepping it here. This alone would save me a thousand dollars in chiropractic bills!

On my very first day there to do a trial run, I was moving a pallet of my gear through his cluttered production space when I bumped into a tall box, and twenty fourteen-foot fluorescent lightbulbs came crashing down at Jerry's feet. I assumed he'd have thrown me out on the spot, but Jerry said, "You're so lucky I like your peppers." Luckily for me, Jerry was an intuitive engineer who allowed me to pick his brain. One thing I hadn't figured out when making buckets was how to press the peppers into the oil without creating an oily mess. Jerry handed me the perfect tool for the job: a stainless-steel, wire-mesh fryer basket that fit perfectly within the circumference of the bucket. Twenty years later, we still use fryer baskets for that task.

By now I owned four Bobbitrons, two of which I kept at Wolf Pack, where I spent most of my days making jars. The others I kept at San Gennaro Foods, where six nights a week I made buckets with a rotating group of friends. There was no stopping us. That is, until a day after the Cleveland Indians were eliminated from making the playoffs, Gayle Krueger informed me that he'd picked his fields clean. It wasn't even October yet, but the pepper season was over too. I had hoped to produce more than the 1,200 buckets I'd made so far for Panera, but I assumed those buckets would supply the next two rounds of regional tests anyway. At this stage, I was just hoping Panera could give me an idea how many peppers they'd need for the next harvest.

But that was a long way away. My inventory of three hundred four-gallon buckets—the ones I'd made for Panera two years before—would supply all my other foodservice accounts. And the buckets I had just made for Panera for the sandwich tests, were basically presold with checks coming in soon. I could put my feet up, and for the first time in three months, relax.

Polpettone (Italian Meatloaf)

Jerry Mascio

No one I know enjoyed feeding the masses more than Jerry. I once watched Jerry make a giant polpettone in the Boeing Employees Union kitchen for a Sons of Italy banquet. Its oven was large enough that he could fit a 2-foot-wide by 10-inch-thick meatloaf (or a meat roll, really). It took four hands to roll up that meatloaf that fed over fifty people. I stored pallets of buckets of Mama Lil's in Jerry's polenta facility's walk-in at the time, so since he got the peppers for free, he didn't skimp on them in his layer of eggs. This recipe has been modified to serve six.

This polpettone consists of three layers that are rolled up into a log: meat, eggs, and greens. In Italian, *polpettone* means *big meatball*. This recipe, then, is basically one big spicy meatball.

Serves 6

Polpetonne

    1 pound hot Italian sausages (about 4)
    1½ pounds lean ground beef
    ½ cup freshly grated Parmesan cheese, or pecorino
    2 slices bread, soaked in milk, with excess moisture squeezed out
    ½ teaspoon oregano
    1 egg
    2 pinches salt
    2 dashes freshly ground black pepper
    3 ounces ketchup

Filling

    1 pound spinach (or other similar greens)
    1 small onion, diced
    5 eggs, whisked
    12 ounces Mama Lil's Peppers in Oil, drained, oil reserved

    Oil for greasing

Preheat the oven to 350°F.

Remove the casings from the Italian sausages and break the meat into pieces. In a large bowl, add the sausage and beef. Add the Parmesan cheese, the soaked bread, oregano, egg, salt, and black pepper. Using your hands, knead and mix the meat mixture thoroughly until everything is well combined and evenly distributed.

Cut a 15 by 15-inch square of parchment paper. Evenly spread the meat mixture over the paper to form a flat square slightly smaller than the paper, leaving at least a 1½-inch border on all sides.

In a large skillet over medium-high heat, sauté the spinach and onion in the Mama Lil's oil until the spinach is wilted but still bright green and the onions translucent, about 4 minutes. Remove from the heat and set aside.

Lightly oil a rimmed baking sheet that is sized to fit on top of the meat layer. Add the whisked eggs and the Mama Lil's Peppers and stir to combine. Bake the eggs and peppers for about 4 minutes, or until they start to set.

Using a spatula to loosen the edges, carefully slide the baked eggs and peppers on top of the meat layer. Evenly layer the spinach mixture on top of the eggs.

With the help of the parchment paper, carefully roll the meat, egg, and spinach layers to form a log. Pull back the paper and drizzle the ketchup on top of the log. Then finish rolling up the paper, pinching the ends of the polpettone to make sure they're well sealed on all sides. Twist the ends of the parchment paper like a Tootsie Roll.

Transfer the polpettone to a baking sheet and bake for 30 minutes. When the internal temperature reaches 155°F on an instant-read thermometer, it's done.

Remove the polpettone from the oven and let it rest for 15 minutes. Then slice and serve.

"THE SQUIRREL'S GRANARY IS FULL. THE HARVEST IS DONE."

WITH THE HARVEST OVER, I BADLY needed a vacation, but decided to go see my lonesome father first. With Lil gone, he seemed to have become even more emotionally invested in my business, so he sure was stoked about that sandwich test Panera was doing with his son's peppers. And when he bragged to friends, he happily shared credit with Lil for helping engineer my potential success.

When I got back to Seattle in the late fall of 2002, I was literally making a reservation to go to Hawaii when I saw a call was coming in from a St. Louis area code. It was Betsy, from Panera, and she was bubbling with excitement. "I got good news. The steak sandwich with Mama Lil's passed the five-store test with flying colors."

"Wow. That *is* good news!"

"In fact, our customers liked that sandwich so much, we put the peppers on our vegetarian sandwich, too."

"Bow wow wow! That's even better news!"

Before I could get another word out, Betsy blurted, "And I have some *great* news! We're skipping the regional test, and we're taking these sandwiches national—into all 350 of our cafés!" Unless Betsy could hear my gulp, I was dead silent. I had no idea what to say to her. She then asked, "This *is* great news, Howard, isn't it?".

"Yes, it's great news…but *when* are the sandwiches going national?"

"We hope to have our new menu out within six weeks. That will give us time to properly promote the new sandwiches."

Right, but not enough time for me to make the peppers for those sandwiches. "I thought there was going to be two or three more regional tests," I said, sinking with dread.

Betsy asked with trepidation, "Howard, you'll have enough buckets of peppers for us, won't you? We're planning a big rollout. With major advertising."

I didn't want to reveal my weak hand quite yet, so I bluffed by enthusiastically flinging out a line aimed at a far-off future. "For next year's harvest, we'll be growing hundreds of tons of peppers in the Yakima Valley—"

Betsy stopped me. "Howard, how many buckets does Mama Lil's have for us now, from this year's harvest?"

I turned my cards over. "After sending you 240 buckets, I now have 960 buckets left. Until next September when—"

"What?! You're telling me..." her fingers tapped at her calculator, "you have enough peppers"...*tap tap tap*..."to last us thirteen and one-half days. And you can't make more peppers for ten more months?" When I didn't contradict her, Betsy said, "Aren't *we* in a pickle?"

I gave her the courtesy of a chuckle, then apologized about the confusion around the regional versus the national tests. I was ready to raise the white flag and confess that there was no way in the world that I could supply them, but instead, I found myself telling her, "Can you give me a few days to make some calls and talk it over with my...staff?"

But I didn't have any staff. And I didn't know who to call. At a produce warehouse, I found a similar pepper called a hot banana, which was grown in Florida year-round. These peppers were picked green and not at all sweet. Seeing no other options, I bought a box of them. I made samples with these green peppers in my own kitchen using extra garlic and oregano to make up for their lack of flavor. Panera was lukewarm about those samples. To stay in the game, I stalled by asking Betsy for yet more time. But I had no other ideas and no other contacts. The growing season in California starts and ends before Yakima Valley's, so there'd be no goathorns there. Farmers in Turkey grew similar peppers, but they were picked green as well. No one in the world grew these colorful goathorn peppers in the off-season without a contract.

Then I had a vague memory of meeting two amiable brothers who had introduced themselves to me at the National Fiery Foods and Barbecue Show in Albuquerque a few years back. They owned a pickled pepper company in California and even gave me a sample of their peppers, which were quite good but completely different from mine. When they left my booth, one of them gave me a card and told me, "If you ever need anything, let us know."

I emptied my shoebox of business cards and eventually found their card. It was Bruno's Pepper Company, based in Lodi, California. At 7 a.m. the next morning I called them. Chris Bruno remembered Mama Lil's. "Right, you use Hungarian goathorn peppers?"

"Yeah, by any chance, do you have any available?"

"I think we do have some goathorns out there in the yard somewhere. But I don't even know how old they are. You'll have to come down to Lodi to check them out for yourself."

I flew to Sacramento the next day, then drove fifty miles south to Lodi, an agricultural town in California's Central Valley. According to Bruno's Pepper Company's faded sign out front, their business was started in 1954. The Bruno brothers were as friendly as I remembered them. Scattered on their property were dozens of wooden pickling cauldrons on stilts. Chris explained that the

California Department of Agriculture insisted they use preservatives such as sodium nitrate and sodium benzoate in their pickling brine that enabled their different varieties of peppers to be stored outside—and not refrigerated— in these cauldrons, sometimes for years.

Chris jumped like a monkey from one pickling cauldron to the next, reading their name tags. The last cauldron had an illegible tag. "These might be the goathorns in here. Wow. They're five years old!" Chris chuckled. "They should be pickled by now." Using a giant pipe wrench, he managed to pry the lid off the cauldron. Then he scooped some of these faded and flimsy red goathorns into a jar. I tried one, and surprisingly it wasn't bad.

Until the aftertaste came on, which I knew was the flavor of the preservatives. An acquired taste, for sure.

For their own retail jars, Chris told me they drained the preservative-laden brine so thoroughly that they're listed on their label "as a *trace* of sulfites or nitrates." Chris also showed me some peppers that were grown year-round in either California or Mexico. One of them was a small, mild yellow wax pepper. The other was a red jalapeño, also known as a Fresno pepper. Chris told me, "Both of these peppers are almost always available. And I'm told, if the hot peppers and mild peppers are together in the bucket long enough, there should be a heat transfer between them. The hot ones become less hot. The mild ones become hotter."

"A heat transfer between the hot and mild peppers actually happens?" I asked skeptically.

Chris giggled, "Some people claim it does."

I flew back to Seattle that night with twelve sample jars of different varieties of Bruno's pickled peppers. I rinsed them well to get as much of the preservatives out, then drained them overnight. I then packed two jars of each of twelve combinations: one each for Panera and one each for me. My instincts told me that whatever jar I labeled #2, Panera would most likely choose. I put #2 on a combination of mild yellow wax peppers and hot red Fresnos. Not that they tasted any better than the other samples, but since they were readily available, if Panera had to choose one, that would be the best alternative. I also packed a jar of the five-year old Hungarian goathorn peppers. I put #12 on that jar, knowing that there was a very limited supply of those and since it was the highest number, I figured it would be the last one they'd choose.

I felt conflicted about sending Panera any of these jars as none of them were even close to being the real Mama Lil's Peppers. I was hoping they'd respect me for trying. From my point of view, the best outcome for all parties was that Panera delayed those sandwiches until the next harvest so that all the peppers could be grown in the Yakima Valley.

A couple of days later, I got a call from a St. Louis area code. The man's name was Scott, who oversaw product development at Panera. He was the executive who had spotted Mama Lil's in Seattle and seemed to have taken a proprietary interest in my peppers' success. I told him, "I'm sorry about the misunderstanding I had with Betsy. We had a very limited supply of the real Mama Lil's Peppers. Those jars I sent to Panera are a stopgap measure until the next harvest."

"To the contrary," Scott said, "I think I prefer the flavor of some of these jars you sent."

Taken by surprise again. "Really? Those peppers aren't the real Mama Lil's by a long shot. Of the samples I sent you, which one did you like the best?"

"You sent me quite a few jars, so, it was confusing. I think I preferred... #12."

My surprise turned into shock. "Are you sure that's not jar #2 you prefer?"

"Yep, it's definitely #12. I have #2 in my hands. They're not bad, either. They're both kind of like a gourmet version of the pepperoncini that used to be on that sandwich."

"Scott, those goathorn peppers in jar #12 have been sitting in preservative-laden brine for five years. I'm supposing you stopped using pepperoncini—because of the preservatives, right?"

"May have been one of the reasons. Can you drain the preservatives out of it somehow?"

Now, if my strategy was to try to get Panera to delay the sandwiches until the next harvest, I misplayed my hand when I all too convincingly told Scott, "Look, once we get into the peppers in jar #2, we'll rinse them so thoroughly there will only be a *trace* of nitrates in them."

"Hmm. If it's a trace, that should be acceptable. I like these peppers."

I was not at all a fan of them—but you've got to play the hand dealt to you, right? I told him, "I can make those peppers for you. But I still have one thousand buckets of the real Mama Lil's Peppers made from Yakima Valley goathorns—these were for the sandwich tests. I'd like to send them to the cafés where the testing was done. Why give them something different?"

"Glad you brought that up. That's an important point. We train our employees to report if they ever see any product fluctuation. If you're starting out with two different sources of peppers, make sure the same cafés always see the same peppers. Or they could get rejected."

Now that I had Scott's confidence—but zero confidence in the product he wanted—I changed my tack to steer him toward the outcome that I wanted. "You know, it would be my preference if you delayed the sandwich until the next harvest. By then we'll have enough goathorns to supply every café with the real Mama Lil's Peppers—the ones that passed the sandwich test with flying colors."

"Too late for that," Scott said. "We'll start with the peppers in jar #12. When those are gone, we'll switch to the ones in jar #2. For our Midwest cafés, keep sending the peppers made for the sandwich test. By next year, will all the peppers be from the same source?"

"Absolutely. A year from now, all your cafés will be using the real Mama Lil's Peppers."

"Sounds like a plan. Our buyer will call you tomorrow to talk pricing."

Then, just like that, Scott was off the phone. And I never talked to him again.

As I lay sleepless in bed that night, I tried to play out what tomorrow's phone call with the buyer would be like. I'd been warned about buyers, that's for sure. And even though I'd been given the okay by Scott to proceed with this plan of using two sources, with one of them having preservatives, should I even mention this to the buyer? Holding my cards close to my vest seemed the best way to play the game. But what I did want to get across to the buyer was the reality of our growing season. And the best scenario in the future was to use only Hungarian goathorn peppers grown in the Yakima Valley.

It was going to be a tricky conversation.

When the buyer called the next day, she was young and much friendlier than I expected. The first thing she said was, "I love these two sandwiches. What kind of peppers are they?"

"I'm so glad you asked," I said. "They're Hungarian goathorn peppers. And they don't exist unless we contract to grow them. We need to know eight months in advance of the two-month harvest, how many buckets we'll need to pack. This of course represents a big risk—"

The buyer cut me off. "It represents a risk for Panera as well. For this reason, I'll write up a contract that guarantees Panera an uninterrupted supply of the Hungarian goathorn peppers from Mama Lil's. It will be based on our estimate of how many buckets we'll need for those two sandwiches over the course of a year. I'll fax you the contract tomorrow so we can get going."

I hesitantly asked, "Will the…price be in the contract?"

"Pricing will be in the contract. Run it by your lawyer, and if it's satisfactory, overnight me a signed contract. Everyone here is excited about these sandwiches and raring to go."

I had expected there to be some sort of negotiation. Instead, the buyer filled my hand with winning cards. When I descended into my basement office the next morning, the contract was on my fax machine. Perusing it, I had to sit down in my chair in case I fell over. It said that Panera was obligated to buy 28,860 buckets. If I read it correctly, there was no time limit. Panera had to buy all those buckets, however long it took until they expired.

And there was the price: $70 a bucket.

Below it was the figure Panera would be on the hook to Mama Lil's for: $2,020,200!

As I stared at this astronomical number, I had no idea how or where I'd ever make that many buckets. But having the figure of two million dollars waved in front of me was like sticking my nose in it. I took a deep whiff and wanted it. Badly. I also realized the gambit I made—when I gave Panera cost-prohibitive pricing for the seedless peppers to make sure it would take the ones with seeds left in—had backfired to the tune of $400,000 more profit within that $2,020,200 of sales.

Maybe I wasn't such a foolish gambler after all.

I had my friend Mark Wittow review the contract. It took him a minute to confirm it had been written very favorably for Mama Lil's. And that it clearly stated that Panera was committed to buy 28,860 buckets regardless of how long it took to use them. I'd known Mark since the first grade and he'd given me gobs of pro bono legal advice over the years, perhaps as payback for that autographed copy of *God Bless You, Mr. Rosewater* that I gave him fifty years ago. And that day, Mark gave me his best advice yet.

"Sign it. And get it back to Panera before they change their mind."

At this stage in my business, all I was ever trying to do was eke out enough of a living so I wouldn't have to drive a cab any longer. The best year Mama Lil's ever had was $200,000 in sales. Not that I ever paid myself any of that money—it just went back into the kitty to make more peppers the next year. As far as I could tell, the most profits I'd ever made for a year's work was $33,000. But if I could somehow pull this off, I might be able to pay myself— big time! I could practically hear Lil bragging to some cousin about how she'd pulled a string or two for her son. But there were too many unknown factors that I had no control over. I knew from experience that if I wasn't careful, those strings would get wrapped around my neck. Tightly.

Panera Bread had big plans for the rollout, including radio and print advertising for the two sandwiches that featured Mama Lil's Peppers. Since its advertising firm's headquarters was in Seattle, Panera asked me to deliver some jars there so they could assemble and photograph the sandwiches. As I sat in my car outside the firm's office, I was in a quandary. I had brought jars made from both the real Mama Lil's Peppers and Bruno's peppers, but I hadn't decided which jar to give them. I mean, how many commercials showed fast-food sandwiches that in no way looked like the real sandwich you're about to bite into? I'm an ethical guy. Truth in advertising, right? Not knowing what to do, I flipped a coin.

I walked into the firm's office and gave them a jar made from Bruno's peppers. By the time I got back home, I realized that I should've flipped that coin at least three times! Or at least given them one jar of each. Not only did the real Mama Lil's taste better, but they were also vibrantly red, orange, and yellow. The ones from Bruno's were drab in comparison. I woke up in the middle of the night still fretting, so I drove back to the advertising firm first thing that morning with a jar of the real Mama Lil's. The woman at the front desk said, "I'm happy to take the jar. But the photo shoot was yesterday. Panera already has the artwork."

On a positive note, even though most of the peppers I'd be receiving from Bruno's weren't the right ones—mild yellow wax peppers that I'd be mixing with hot red Fresnos—at least they'd be consistently wrong. Another advantage of using Bruno's peppers over the real Mama Lil's was that I wouldn't need to build up an inventory. I could buy its barrels of preservative-laden pickled peppers when I needed them—like most manufacturers of tapenade olive spreads, giardiniera, or muffaletta spreads did. Because of this—or at least until the next harvest anyway—I needed to increase the line of credit on my home to only $50,000 instead of quadrupling that if I had to make all the buckets at one time with Hungarian goathorn peppers.

I must admit that I only tried the product we made from Bruno's peppers once—and never again, whereas I ate my perfectly pickled peppers in oil at least twice a day. But at this stage, striving for perfection was beside the point. The point now was to somehow make nearly 29,000 buckets with Mama Lil's labels on them so I could arrive at the $2,020,200 destination!

And soon enough, full truckloads of black pickling barrels of Bruno's peppers were being delivered to San Gennaro Foods. When San Gennaro's regular crew knocked off, I'd arrive with whatever posse of helpers I could round up. The pallets of buckets we made with Bruno's pickled peppers got shipped out the next day from San Gennaro Foods to seven Panera distributors. The eighth distributor was in the Midwest region, which included St. Louis where Panera's corporate offices were. All those cafés got buckets of "the most delicious peppers on the planet" that were also warehoused in the walk-in refrigerator at San Gennaro Foods.

My biggest expense in using Bruno's peppers was shipping truckloads of pickling barrels 787 miles from Lodi, California, up to Seattle. Each pallet of four barrels weighed (literally) a ton. After a month, Chris Bruno connected me with Raffi Santikian, whom he referred to as a trustworthy copacker who could make my buckets at his processing facility on the grounds of his Fresno farm. This would cut my shipping costs by 70 percent. Now, the last time I had hired someone else to make my product for me was that Canadian cannery and, boy, did they ever fuck up. But there was a big difference: I wouldn't be hiring Raffi to make the real Mama Lil's. He'd be making a mediocre product that couldn't be made any better, or worse.

When I flew down to Fresno to meet Raffi, I was instantly charmed by this jolly, mustachioed man with a Zorba-like personality. Raffi was part of the Armenian diaspora, many of them farmers who had settled in California's San Joaquin Valley. His house stood yards away from his production facility, and it was all surrounded by hundreds of rows of grapevines, the leaves of which he used to make thousands upon thousands of cases of Greek-style dolmas (which his Hispanic crew called "burritos") that he shipped all over the world.

When Raffi gave me a fair price for packing the buckets and said he'd even handle shipping them to Panera for me, it was too good to be true. Yet, it was true. I'd be making great profit margins from those buckets without having to make them myself. And I didn't have to pay for all those buckets at one time of the year, making the enterprise much less stressful. But the peppers being pickled by the Brunos and packed by Raffi weren't close to being the real Mama Lil's Peppers, and I hated that.

Every newbie gourmet food producer I'd met had dreams of grandeur about how their products—of which they all had over-inflated opinions—would win an award at some food show, they'd be discovered, and soon then they'd be making gobs of money and be able to quit their day jobs. Then this dream really happened for Mama Lil's.

I would be making real money. But not from the real Mama Lil's Peppers.

And with Raffi's crew making most of the buckets for me, my primary job in the whole enterprise was arranging shipping and then sending out these big invoices. Initially I felt giddy about what was happening for Mama Lil's Peppers. But at the same time, my potential success made me feel anxious. And conflicted. I identified so strongly with my peppers that I was embarrassed about these buckets we were sending to 80% of the Panera Cafes. Perhaps I was suffering from what is popularly known as impostor syndrome. As I was certainly selling Panera impostor Mama Lil's Peppers.

But when I received my first check from the Panera distributor for $98,980—half the amount my business had sold all last year—I was giddy again. And when I walked that check into the bank, maybe feeling a little guilty too. Like I knew I was depositing counterfeit money. But when the teller handed me the receipt with that astronomical figure printed on it, I got giddy again, like I'd won big time at the casino. Thanks in part to that wild card that the Vegas chef gave me at the pizza show, for the first time, Mama Lil's would have excellent profit margins, and a contract to guarantee sales into the future.

I suppose I could learn to live with conflict like that.

Sicilian Style Steamed Mussels with Acqua Pazza, Fregola Sarda, Mama Lil's

Dylan Giordan

I first met Dylan when he was Serafina's sous chef. He's now the head chef at the Pink Door, serving wonderful Italian food for forty years in Seattle's Pike Place Market.

Serves 4

Ingredients:

2 cups leeks, quarter moon, julienned, rinsed

2 cups fennel, diced

2 cups red bell pepper, julienne

2 cups diced tomato

2 each bay leaves, fresh

2 tablespoons chopped garlic

2 tablespoons orange zest, chopped

½ cup orange Juice

1 cup white wine

1 cup chopped basil, mint and parsley, mixed

2 cups Fish/prawn broth

½ cup Campari

1 pinch of saffron

1 pinch red chili flake

4 lbs mussels

3 cups Fregola sarda, cooked

2 Tablespoons Mama Lil's pickled goathorn peppers, chopped

Finishing olive oil, such as Laudemio Frescobaldi or Trampetti

Salt and Pepper to taste.

Method:

In a non-reactive pot, sweat the leeks and fennel on low heat with the bay, chili flake, some evoo and a little salt.

When the mixture is softened and aromatic, add the garlic. When the garlic is cooked and aromatic, add the tomato, bell peppers, and a little salt.

Cook for 5 minutes and add the wine and reduce. When the wine has reduced a little, add the zest, juice, and half of the herbs.

Simmer for a few more minutes and add the fish stock, saffron, Campari and simmer for 10 minutes. Add the mussels, cover and steam until opened, 10 minutes. Check for seasoning.

Add the fregola and Mama Lil's peppers and mix well. Transfer to 4 warmed bowls.

Garnish with the remaining herbs, and a healthy drizzle of really nice olive oil.

(Note: If you like your food on the spicier side, double up on the Mama Lil's goathorn peppers. Also Fregola Sarda is a Sardinian pasta resembling Israeli cous cous, that is toasted.)

DO YOU WANT TO KNOW A SECRET?

I'D BARKED AT FOOD SHOWS THOUSANDS OF TIMES, "Mama Lil's doesn't make your sandwiches, we just make them awesome!" But at this point, the peppers I was supplying to most of the Panera cafés were not in the least bit awesome. When I went to Fresno to check on Raffi's production, I ordered a steak sandwich from a nearby Panera café with the impostor peppers on it. There was certainly no craving for the next bite. But when I ate the same sandwich at a café in Illinois where I shipped Panera the real Mama Lil's, it really was an awesome sandwich.

For eight months, I supplied Panera this way with more than 80 percent of its cafes getting the impostor peppers. And I didn't hear a word from anybody, bad or good. I was getting away with it so far, with bigger and bigger checks appearing in my mailbox weekly. But it felt like I was keeping a secret that I couldn't talk about. Of course, Paul Gilroy, the mayonnaise man, who had seen me make buckets from Bruno's peppers at San Gennaro, just looked at me with that sly grin of his and tell me, "Pal, you're pulling this off with smoke and mirrors."

I wanted desperately to move beyond the smoke and mirrors, so, for 2003's harvest the Bruno brothers had a trustworthy farmer in the northern San Joaquin Valley plant the real Hungarian goathorn peppers, with a prospective yield of two hundred tons, or enough to provide half of the Panera cafés. Even though cafes would be getting peppers with a trace of preservatives in them, at least they would all be made with the same variety of goathorn peppers. As a backup, Raffi had his friend, Arman, who primarily raised livestock but was trying to get into farming, grow three acres of goathorns at his farm outside Fresno. Being a novice, there was some uncertainty about the seeds Arman ordered, so I sent him some of our own seeds.

Meanwhile, in the Yakima Valley, Gayle Krueger and his neighbor Leonard Calhoun would each grow an estimated one hundred tons of goathorns for Mama Lil's. A year from now, it was my hope that every bucket I made for Panera would be preservative-free and grown and produced in the Yakima Valley. I had a plan in place to make this transition, but when San Gennaro's polenta business outgrew its own building and no longer had room for me, I had no idea where to produce the buckets.

Damn, I *really* should've had Paul Allen build that cannery for Mama Lil's.

Luckily, Bill Thompson, formerly of Noodles Pasta, became the operations manager of an outfit called Real Foods, which made a hundred different varieties of salads. For a reasonable price, Real Foods would allow me to make my buckets at night at its facility in Seattle and use its crew members who wanted the overtime. When Jan, my friend from Prague, agreed to come back to help me, I knew there was a chance I'd be able to pull off my largest pepper harvest ever, where we'd be making buckets at Real Foods, and fifty miles away making jars at Wolf Pack.

With four Bobbitrons now in action, we were cranking out those buckets of peppers in oil like never before, though not without issues. Real Foods, with its low ceilings and claustrophobic production space, always had dozens of projects going on simultaneously. When you added all the fifty-five-gallon pickling barrels that had to be put somewhere, that somewhere was always in somebody's way. Another problem was that Real Foods didn't have the refrigeration space available to store the buckets. And they did not want the responsibility of shipping them for me.

Fortunately, I worked it out with Calhoun to store and ship buckets from his refrigerated warehouse in Wapato. Three times a week, I'd drop off six pallets of finished buckets at Calhoun's warehouse and within no time, Miggy, its ever-smiling yard boss, had me loaded up with six tons of freshly picked peppers to take back to Real Foods. Miggy also loaded the pallets of buckets going out to Panera, for which I tipped him $20 and two jars of peppers for each load. He would open a jar on the spot, then tell me, "Señor, Mama Lil's are *so goo-ood!*" This accelerated rhythm of producing buckets at Real Foods and then shipping them out from Calhoun's warehouse was going as smoothly as I could possibly hope. Halfway into the harvest I was on target to meet my goal of supplying 70% of the Panera cafés with the real Mama Lil's Peppers.

Then let me count the ways my luck went south on me—if not necessarily in biblical proportions, certainly in biblical imagery. Just by the sound of Chris Bruno's resigned voice on the phone, I knew I was in trouble, with a capital T that rhymes with B and stands for BLIGHT! His farmer was about to pick his goathorns when he discovered that his whole crop had been decimated by a disease that had blown over from a neighbor's tomato field. By the time I heard about it, his whole goathorn pepper crop had been plowed under.

Luckily, we had a plan B for the California goathorns, with Raffi's friend Arman growing three acres of them. I had even shipped a pair of Bobbitrons to Raffi so we could do the production right there at his facility without using preservatives. But when Raffi returned my call, I heard the concern in his voice when he suggested I fly down and look at his friend's crop.

I hopped on a plane the next day, and Raffi and I drove to his friend's cute little farm where we were greeted by equally cute little pygmy goats bounding around his yard. But when Arman rather sheepishly showed me the peppers that he'd grown for Mama Lil's, I couldn't believe my eyes. They were shaped like goathorns, but they were very, very small goathorns.

I said, "These peppers couldn't be from the seeds I sent you. They're usually six inches."

Arman scratched his head, "Or, maybe they didn't like the goat manure I used on them."

Raffi started laughing uproariously. "Ha! That's gotta be it. The pygmy goat shit turned the goathorn peppers into pygmy goathorn peppers."

I bemoaned, "This is not funny! I need these peppers."

"It is funny. In a tragic way," Raffi said. "And there's nothing we can do about it now."

They call them goathorns because of their shape.

We picked a hundred pounds of these pygmy goathorn peppers, that I futilely prepped with Raffi's crew for four hours, barely making a dent as the peppers which are normally six inches long were at best two inches long. I gave up and paid Armon not to pick his crop. Until next year's harvest, I was back to using the impostor peppers to supply half of the Panera cafés.

Lesson learned, yet again. Never trust someone whose trust hasn't been earned. In both cases, I was relying on California farmers I'd never met. And you can never trust Nature.

Meanwhile, in mid-September, the Yakima Valley underwent a hot spell that sent the temperature soaring to 108 degrees for eight straight days. As I drove peppers back and forth to Seattle, I kept my eye on a parched field of goathorns on Lateral A Road in Wapato. I wasn't even sure which farmer was growing this unirrigated field or why he wasn't watering them. The next time I arrived at Calhoun's to drop off buckets and pick up my next load of fresh peppers, Miggy pointed out to me six bins of goathorns, of 500 pounds each, that he'd separated from the others. "Señor, these chiles, they different."

"Really? They sure look the same," I said. "In fact, these peppers look really healthy."

"Different farmer." Then Miggy said with a daring smile, "Try them." On my way out of the warehouse, I grabbed one of those *different* goathorns and took a bite out of it. By the time I walked into the 108-degree heat, I had a four-alarm fire in my mouth that dropped me to my knees. I went back inside and asked Miggy, "What farmer grew those peppers?"

"Benedicto!" Miggy confessed.

These peppers were from the field that wasn't being watered. The combination of extreme heat and lack of water elevated their capsaicin load. I knew they were too hot for Panera's customers, so I took them to Wolf Pack and made the best Kick Butt Peppers I'd ever made. (I stashed away four of those cases in my pepper cellar, and for years they became the crème de la crème of my pepper gifts to friends.)

On my very next trip to the farm, I was greeted by a frowning Leonard Calhoun, who showed me some freshly picked goathorns that had not fared well in the drought. They all had black spots on them. I asked him if the spots were from a blight like the one that wiped out the California peppers. He had no idea. The peppers had been perfectly healthy just a week earlier. I researched pepper diseases, and the only photo that matched Calhoun's spotted peppers was one that depicted a simple root rot. As it turned out, Max Benedicto was a very intuitive farmer. He knew what he was doing by *not* watering his peppers during the drought. Sure, the peppers got hot, but at least their roots were healthy. But I needed Calhoun's peppers, spots and all, so Jan and I and our crew buckled down and meticulously cut those dark spots out of every single pepper. Luckily, within a week the peppers were healthy again and we were back on track.

On my next drive to the farm with a van load of buckets to drop off, I was but a mile from Calhoun's place when Gayle Krueger phoned me. He was almost laughing when he asked, "Where are you storing your buckets, Howard?"

"In Calhoun's refrigerated warehouse. I'm on my way there now."

"Yeah, I knew you *were* storing buckets at Calhoun's warehouse."

"Gayle, why did you phrase that in the past tense?"

"Because I'm at the warehouse now, watching a fire burn it to the ground." On the horizon, plumes of smoke were rising into the deep blue sky.

"A fire! I have pallets of buckets in there shipping out tomorrow."

Gayle laughed. "You could be in luck. Here's Miggy bringing your buckets out now."

When I arrived at the smoldering warehouse, firetrucks were still spraying it down. Miggy was racing around on his forklift, but when he spotted me, he led me to where he'd put the eight pallets that were to be shipped tomorrow. The buckets had melted into each other. What had once been four feet tall was now two feet tall. It was a complete disaster. But Miggy, ever the jolly soul, reached into a bucket, and grabbed a handful of roasted, pickled peppers, ate them, then boasted, "Mama Lil's! They're still *GOOD!*"

Luckily, I was able to fill the next Panera order with the buckets I had brought with me. And eventually Calhoun's insurance covered the cost of the buckets I lost. But I needed every bucket of the real Mama Lil's Peppers to provide Panera, so it was a huge loss. But undeterred, Jan and I stayed on task until late October and every goathorn pepper was picked. Despite all the catastrophes, at Wolf Pack we increased my output of retail jars by 33 %. And at Real Foods we made 8000 buckets of the real Mama Lil's Peppers, enough to provide 50 % of the Panera cafés.

Soon thereafter, I got a phone call from a Panera distributor who informed me that a café had found mold growing in a bucket. This was the first instance mold had ever been detected in a bucket of peppers in oil, so I had that pallet shipped back to Real Foods so we could inspect it. My biggest concern was that some of the pickling barrels hadn't been cleaned well enough. Upon opening a few of those buckets and seeing what indeed looked like dark mold, I realized I had a major crisis on my hands. I brought 6,000 buckets back from a cold-storage facility to Real Foods, where for five days straight we inspected every one of those buckets from 5 a.m. to 7 a.m.

After a while we detected on the surface of the peppers, but not below it, that the mold had formed grid-like patterns. But this mold didn't seem to be growing, which was odd, as mold spreads quickly. When the lab's report came back, it revealed that it wasn't even mold we were seeing; they were ferrous (iron) molecules leaching from one of the six fryer baskets that we used to press the peppers into the oil. That basket was a non-stainless-steel knockoff that had found its way onto the wrong shelf in the restaurant supply store, and I bought without recognizing it. After weeks of use the peppers' acidity dissolved its aluminum outer coating, so wherever that bad basket's wire mesh touched the peppers, it had left those dark grid patterns.

After scraping all the ferrous molecules off the peppers, we lost fewer than a hundred buckets. What could've been a potential deep-dive disaster was averted. And the distributor didn't tell the Panera's Quality Assurance manager about the mold scare as I feared it would. But it was such a headache for the folks at Real Foods I was not invited back for the next harvest.

At this point in the game, I'd been supplying Panera with basically two different pepper products for more than eighteen months—sixteen thousand buckets in all—and I hadn't heard a negative word from anyone. With twelve thousand buckets remaining on our contract, I felt safe. That is, until I heard through the grapevine that Scott, the executive who had initially okayed the samples sourced from peppers with preservatives, was no longer working at Panera. Then I found out that the buyer who had written my contract was no longer employed by Panera either. These were the only people at Panera who knew that I was using two sources of peppers. And Scott was the only person who knew that one of the sources had a "trace" of preservatives in them. Should I have told somebody at Panera that half of its cafés were getting a different product that had preservatives in it? I didn't even know who that somebody would be anymore.

Even though Panera was opening cafés at a record rate, I soon discerned that instead of my orders going up, they were in fact slowing down, if ever so slightly. Then I heard from Paul Gilroy, the mayonnaise man who always seemed to be in the know, that Panera had dropped the steak sandwich from the menu. Was it due to my impostor peppers? It's what I suspected. The whole point of franchises was that all its products would be consistent in every location. Whether you ate a steak sandwich in North Carolina, St. Louis, Michigan, or Texas, it had better taste the same at every cafe. But more than half of the Panera cafés were using the impostor peppers on that sandwich that I knew didn't taste nearly as good.

If Panera thought my product was going downhill (which it had for half the buckets), it could certainly wriggle out of that contract, couldn't they? But perhaps that contract that bound Panera to buy twelve thousand more buckets from Mama Lil's was what kept the peppers on its lesser-selling vegetarian sandwich for which they were ordering a thousand buckets a month. It was still good business. I just needed to keep the charade going for eight more months until the next harvest, when I was determined to supply all its cafes, and all of its customers, with the most delicious peppers on the planet—the ones that passed their test with such flying colors.

That is—if only I had a place to make them. And if only I had farmers to grow them. After the warehouse fire, the Calhouns were gladly out of the farming business. Then Gayle Krueger informed me that a grocery store chain had reneged on buying a quarter of a million dollars' worth of melons he'd grown for them, and he'd lost his will to farm. Krueger's had been an institution in the Yakima Valley since the 1950s, so it broke my heart to hear of its demise. For twelve years, Gayle Krueger had grown goathorns for Mama Lil's. I trusted Gayle, and trust isn't earned overnight.

In February of 2004, with a case of Mama Lil's Peppers in the seat beside me, I drove down Lateral A Road in the town of Wapato and started introducing myself to farmers and passing out jars. The first place I stopped was Imperial's Garden, where I met Manuel Imperial, who took my jar and happily shared it with his four other siblings. They had taken over the farm

Three generations of Krueger Pepper Gardens.

from their parents, who had immigrated to Wapato from the Philippines in 1983. Some of the Imperial cousins, the Dagdagans and Benedictos, also moved to Wapato and leased farmland off Lateral A Road. Manuel then told me that a few miles away was Wayne Inaba's farm. "Wayne," he said, "is not only the best organic farmer in the state, but hands down the best farmer."

I drove over to Inaba's farm and met Wayne, who along with his two brothers Lon and Norm and sister Diane, had been running the family farm that their Japanese immigrant parents started when they were released from an internment camp in 1947. Their father and mother Shiz—who worked in the office into her nineties— had leased their land from the only people who would let them: the Yakama Nation, the original Native American tribe from that area. I wasn't sure what these hard-working farmers thought of *me*, but every one of them loved the peppers I gave them, and it thrilled me to no end that they wanted to grow for Mama Lil's.

By springtime, twenty acres of peppers were being planted for Mama Lil's in Wapato. But I still had no place lined up yet where I could make and store the buckets. If worse came to worst, I figured I could ship the Washington-grown peppers to Raffi's in Fresno and pack the buckets there. But Raffi wasn't sure if the California Department of Agriculture would even allow him to make the peppers at his place without using preservatives.

Then I recalled at a grocery store demo having met a man named Hess, the CFO from Hogue Cellars Winery who mentioned there was a cannery in the town of Sunnyside in the heart of the Yakima Valley. I found Hess's card. Three calls later, I was calling Gary Stonemetz, the operations manager of Johnson Foods, who owned the cannery. It went to Gary's voicemail message.

When I hadn't heard back from Gary after a few days, I sent him a jar of the formerly embargoed peppers, which, at four years old, I thought were still the best I'd ever made.

A week or so later, I was in line to board my plane heading back to Seattle from yet another fancy food show. It was an encouraging show but now I was focused on my anxiety about the upcoming harvest. In those days, I lived in fear of bad news from Panera, so when my phone rang and I didn't recognize the area code or the number, I hesitated before answering it.

"Hi. I'm a producer for the Food Network. When and where do you make your peppers?"

"The harvest begins in five or six weeks in the Yakima Valley." I cheerfully told the man.

"Can we film in the pepper fields? And where you make your jars?"

"Sure. But we only have an eight-week harvest beginning in late August."

"Good to know. It's still iffy on our end. But if the timing works, I'll contact you."

As I made my way to my seat, I was absorbing the potential marketing windfall when I got another call. It was from an Eastern Washington area code, so I answered. "Mama Lil's!"

"You sure don't sound like someone's mama. I'm Gary Stonemetz. I tried your peppers. They're pretty good. You should come to our cannery to discuss if this is even feasible for us."

"By chance is your cannery kosher certified?'

"It sure is."

In my excitement to win him over, I told Gary, "Great! Food TV will be coming out to film us. You like being on camera?"

"You folks from Seattle are such bullshitters! Come see me at the cannery, let's talk."

Those two synchronous phone calls were very promising indeed. As I fastened my seatbelt and closed my eyes, I could feel my habitual dread about the upcoming harvest melting away. If it worked out with this cannery, not only would I not have to schlep the peppers over the mountains, but it could make Mama Lil's look like a legitimate enterprise as opposed to the guerrilla operation I'd been finagling for years. And if the Food Network filmed us out in the pepper fields and inside the cannery, it would depict that legitimacy. And I'm sure someone at Panera would be bound to see us in action pickling and packing buckets of the most delicious peppers on the planet for them. Panera was now 80 percent of Mama Lil's business, and I needed to impress those people, badly. As we taxied down the runway and picked up speed, I was feeling confident that my little-business-that-could was about to take off, too.

Spicy Greek Shrimp with Mama Lil's

Lisa Gordanier, chef, musician, and copyeditor

This dish is jam-packed with intense flavors, thanks to sweet prawns, briny feta cheese, fresh and dried herbs, and a generous portion of Mama Lil's Peppers in Oil. It's constructed in two stages: first in your sauté pan and then under the broiler, using a blast of heat that renders the feta a little melty and brown and brings all the flavors together. You can serve it with pasta or roasted potatoes, but I prefer the taste and texture of a couple of kinds of artisan bread or rolls (olive, rosemary, sourdough, whole-grain) that have been buttered, then toasted under that same broiler.

Serves 2

Several tablespoons olive oil (Greek, if possible)
Salt and freshly ground black pepper
8 ounces medium-large prawns, peeled and deveined
½ small yellow onion, thinly sliced
2 to 4 garlic cloves, chopped
½ teaspoon cayenne pepper
1 teaspoon dried Greek oregano
1/3 cup dry white wine
1/3 cup chicken stock
½ cup canned chopped tomatoes, preferably fire-roasted
½ cup Mama Lil's Peppers in Oil (mostly pepper rings, but reserve some oil as well)
About 2 tablespoons sliced fresh basil leaves
3 ounces feta cheese, crumbled

Prepare a small ceramic or Pyrex baking dish (3- to 4-cup capacity) by coating its surface with olive oil.

In a small sauté pan, heat 1 tablespoon of the olive oil over medium heat. Salt and pepper the prawns lightly, then cook them for just a few minutes, turning once, until they are opaque and almost cooked through. Remove the pan from the heat.

Warm another tablespoon or so of the olive oil in a medium sauté pan over medium heat, then add the sliced onions. When they soften, add the garlic, cayenne, and oregano. Stir until the onions turn soft and fragrant, being careful not to brown the garlic.

Add the white wine and chicken stock; simmer until the alcohol has evaporated and the liquid is slightly reduced. Add the tomatoes, Mama Lil's Peppers, and fresh basil; stir to combine. Taste for salt and pepper, adding some as desired—but keep in mind that the feta is quite salty. Increase the heat and cook, stirring, until the mixture comes to a simmer.

Meanwhile, set a rack on the second-highest shelf of your oven; heat the broiler to high.

Transfer the prawns to the prepared baking dish, spreading them evenly; then pour the tomato mixture over the top, coating the prawns. Crumble the feta cheese over the top. Broil for about 5 minutes, or until the feta is golden and the mixture is bubbling hot.

THE SUNNY SIDE OF LIFE

THE VERY NEXT DAY, I DROVE TO THE YAKIMA VALLEY to check out the cannery. The abundant orchards that carpeted the Rattlesnake Hills were laden with still-ripening peaches, pears, and apples. But juicy, fragrant apricots were being picked, and farmstands were selling them by the bushel. As I drove along the Yakima Valley Highway toward Sunnyside sucking on a meltingly sweet apricot, I passed a cattle feedlot that went on for miles. Smelling this foulness, I remembered when I'd been to Sunnyside before.

Five years prior, I did a promotional event, the Yakima Valley Asparagus Festival, at Washington Hills Winery. A Dixieland band was entertaining the wine-swilling crowd in the tents set up outside the winery, where a half dozen of us vendors were grilling asparagus and selling our wares. When the winds suddenly changed, bringing that potent blast of manure with it, within a blink, all the attendees vanished from the party. Which left us vendors and the band with a dozen open bottles of wine that needed to be drunk. We then escaped inside the wine cellar where, free of fumes, we all had a very merry time.

When I walked into the Johnson Foods cannery, a middle-aged white man was stirring a kettle of vinegar with a paddle. When he saw long-haired me, he shot me a look of suspicion that he quickly covered up before shaking my hand and introducing himself. Gary Stonemetz had the sun-hardened skin of a farmer, and the way he held his shoulders, I assumed he'd twisted ten million lids onto jars in his life. I followed Gary inside the office to his desk with a view over the cannery. The first thing I asked him was, "Those fumes from the feedlot ever make it over here?"

Gary smiled, "Puts out a stink, doesn't it? We've been told they'll be moving that lot further out of town soon. So, I tried that jar you sent me. They were pretty good."

"You know why they're so good? Because we drain the pickled peppers of their brine so thoroughly, which takes upwards of twenty-four hours."

And like every manufacturer I'd ever explained this to, Gary gave me a pained look. "You're telling me you put the vinegar in, then you drain it all out? For twenty-four hours?! That's a lotta peppers occupying a lotta space for a whole lotta time."

"Sure, it's a lotta time. But we'll be having a lotta fun. We'll be dancing." With a straight face, I looked him in the eye and let my body sway to imaginary music. "*You put the vinegar in. And you take the vinegar out. And you do the hokey pokey.* If we get the whole crew dancing, it's like a drain dance."

Gary raised an eyebrow. "Yeah, you going to demonstrate this dance for us?"

"Damn straight! I'll be working right with the crew, and at some point, I'm bound to break into a dance. Especially if the Cleveland Indians are winning."

Gary chuckled then asked me, "What have you been smoking?"

That's when Gary's wife, Margie, walked in. She had a sneer on her face as she handed her husband a bag. "I hate to shop there," she said. "With their kids running around out of control, it drives me batty." Gary glanced at me with a look of embarrassment, wondering if I had picked up on what his wife was referring to. I hadn't. Until I saw the bag that she gave him was from Walmart. That moment foreshadowed what I'd soon learn about the slowly evolving relationships in Eastern Washington between white business owners and their Hispanic labor force. (Interestingly, this didn't seem to be the case with farmers of Asian heritage, whose family members worked right alongside their Hispanic crews, forming strong familial bonds.)

Gary then gave me a tour of the cannery. It was a step up for Mama Lil's—that was for sure. It had a large hydrocooling station to wash 500 pounds of peppers at one time, a lidding machine, and a space-age pasteurization tunnel with lots of sensors and flashing lights. As opposed to the steam tunnels at Wolf Pack, these jars got cooked in a tunnel with a hot water shower. The moment the jars hit the desired temperature, it became a cold shower, stopping the cooking process. By the time the jars emerged from the tunnel, they were squeaky clean and at room temperature. (No worries about soft peppers anymore. And no juggling those crazy-hot jars!) If this cannery worked out, Mama Lil's would be entering the twenty-first century.

As Gary walked me to my car, I could tell he was still trying to make up his mind about me. "No doubt your product is good. But to tell you the truth, your process sounds like an expensive pain in the ass." I'd heard that all before and could understand why he wouldn't want to take the peppers on. But when Gary saw me climb into my old van and not a Bimmer, I saw him smile. I might be a hippie, but at least I wasn't a yuppie. That's when he told me, "Our season is over after we run the beans in mid-August. Which is when your peppers start coming in. *If* we did your peppers, we could keep our crew working two months longer." A few weeks later, those vibrantly colorful goathorns were coming into the cannery by the truckload.

Another piece of equipment Johnson Foods had was a state-of-the-art slicing machine, which made slicing the peppers so much more efficient than in the past. Pepper rings were run through water sprays and a shaker table on a conveyor belt, and by the time they dropped into the vats of pickling brine, there was nary a seed to be found. What didn't change was that we were still using apple corers to remove the stems and scoop out the seeds.

Right off the bat, Gary Stonemetz was complaining about all this intensive hand labor. I told him that in California and Mexico, where most chiles are grown, the pickers cut the peppers right off the plant using a thumb knife, leaving the stem to rot on the plant. In the Yakima Valley, we'd always picked peppers with their stems on. It's healthier for the pepper and for the plant so to keep producing peppers for us. Nevertheless, I had Chris Bruno send me some thumb knives. But Imperial's pickers soundly rejected them. Nevertheless, Gary kept coming up with one ingenious idea after another to mechanize this laborious process of slicing of the stems and removing the seeds. But none of them worked. We used apple corers for years to come.

By this time, I'd become quite adept with this little tool, and during the three days a week we were slicing peppers, I enjoyed spearheading the crew of Hispanic women. I'd like to believe I added some joie de vivre to the chore, and I especially enjoyed working alongside the vivacious, pixie-like Elena, who was not only an energetic and conscientious worker, but on Fridays, brought the most delicious tamales for lunch that I simply couldn't get enough of.

Johnson Foods, Sunnyside, Washington, 2004.

That first year at the cannery in Sunnyside, I slept in the spare bedroom of Gary's house and usually ate dinner with Gary and his wife Margie. Then after dinner, along with Chip, Gary's apple-loving black lab, I'd walk the rows of his Pink Lady apple orchard with him pruning the limbs. At 4 a.m., before going to work at the cannery, I'd spot Gary and Chip right back in the orchard. Man, he worked so hard on his farm and yet took such joy in it. And in witnessing him doing so, Gary Stonemetz earned my complete respect and trust.

What also made me feel like I was in the right hands with Gary was how much he appreciated the jar of peppers I sent him. I emphasized to him that the reason they'd held up so well after four years was in part because they weren't over pasteurized. Gary made a confession. "I used to pickle sugar snap peas. Fabulous product that won awards at food shows. Then the Department of Agriculture told me there was some new bacteria out there that can withstand more heat, so they insisted I cook the peas four degrees hotter. The snap peas got soft, and folks didn't like them. Next year those jars of snap peas were off the market."

The other aspect of the peppers that was such a pain in the ass was the amount of time it took to drain the pickled peppers adequately. I told Gary, "If the peppers aren't drained well, the oil won't be absorbed into the cell structure of the peppers." Despite what I told him, he hoped for efficiency's sake that we could drain the peppers before the end of the workday, and they'd be ready to pack in buckets or jars when the crew returned to work sixteen hours later.

The very next day I was with Stonemetz at his desk discussing the strangest foods he'd ever pickled (hop shoots) when his attention was diverted out the window to the production area. While the crew was at lunch, the pickled peppers had been packed into the four-gallon translucent buckets, waiting to be mixed with the oil. Gary trained his binoculars on the buckets, then handed them to me. "See that line halfway down the bucket? That line is the brine still draining into the peppers. The line wasn't there when the crew went to lunch. The peppers haven't drained well enough." And that's all Gary needed to see to be convinced how long the process of draining the peppers took.

Five weeks into the 2004 production, the Food Network producer of *Roker on the Road* informed me that it had finally come together, and they were ready to film. When their crew and I arrived at Imperial's farm, they insisted on getting a shot of me picking peppers. This wasn't total fiction, as I'd done my share of picking in my day. But unfortunately, Marcelo Imperial hadn't gotten the word that we'd be filming in the pepper fields that had been irrigated earlier that morning. After they filmed me picking peppers it took two men to pull me out of the mud.

I was barefoot when I arrived at the cannery, where the film crew wanted to capture the whole pain in the ass process from start to finish. I showed the cameraman where the peppers were draining in pallet-sized colanders. "The

single most important step in the process of making Mama Lil's, is draining the peppers."

The cameraman looked at the slow drip of brine. "That'd be like watching paint dry."

That got Gary grinning. "Howard, isn't that where the hokey pokey dance comes in?" No, I didn't do my drain dance, but there was a joyful vibe in the cannery that afternoon. The next day, they interviewed me sitting in front of a stack of my unsold screenplays as Roker laments, "Hollywood's loss is a hot pepper lover's gain." Then after filming me at a farmers' market, we went to the Swingside Café, where Brad Inserra was the star of the show. His frying pans shot out celebratory flames as he cooked up a five-course feast for thirty of my friends and family.

Filming the making of the finest product that can be packed in a jar.

When I look back on that first year Mama Lil's Peppers was made at Johnson Foods, what I treasure most were the friendships I formed, not only with Gary and other white-collar staff, but also the Hispanic blue-collar employees. By joining them on the prep line and at the lunch table, we ingratiated ourselves with one another over the course of nine intense weeks. My sweetest memory from that time was when I called out, "Gracias, señoritas!" to Elena and a few of her colleagues as they were leaving the cannery at the end of their shift. The women turned and curtseyed in unison, then harmoniously uttered the sweetest "De nada!" I'd ever heard.

The most difficult aspect of the fruitful 2004 harvest was that it was an election year. I was aghast at the Swift Boat political ads that they wouldn't dare show on the west side of the mountains where we Democrats lived. Nevertheless, twelve years after I started making peppers, Mama Lil's had finally found a home at Johnson Foods. Not that Wolf Pack was out of the equation. I loved George, and I still made my sweet pickles in his fifty-five-gallon kettles.

The weather in the Yakima Valley that summer of 2004 was so ideal that we picked every single goathorn pepper in the fields before the first frost hit in early November. In all, those 250 tons of Hungarian goathorn peppers filled five thousand cases of jars and ten thousand buckets. This was enough to supply more than 70 percent of the Panera cafés with the real Mama Lil's until the next harvest. In Fresno, Raffi was still cranking out buckets for the other 30 % of the cafes. But for the following year's harvest, I was confident I could reach my goal of phasing out the preservative-laden peppers altogether, so that every single Panera Bread café would be receiving the real Mama Lil's Peppers with all the goathorns grown, pickled, and packed to perfection in the Yakima Valley.

When the *Roker on the Road* episode, "Goathorns of Plenty," came out, it was a fantastic six-minute infomercial starring me, my crew, Brad Inserra, and a lot of people saying, "Yum!" My favorite shot in the video was of my favorite employee, the sharp and lovely Elena, smiling with confidence as she hammers a lid on a bucket of peppers. That show was in constant rotation from Thanksgiving to Christmas on the Food Network, and my retail website lit up with orders. I'd pack those boxes at night by myself where I'd write short notes to each recipient, signing off with a Kurt Vonnegut blessing, "*Peace and Plenty, Mama Lil.*"

But despite feeling the sting of defeat in the presidential election—which cost me dinner at the Space Needle in a bet I'd made with Manuel Imperial—I felt optimistic about the future of Mama Lil's. It was in a good place. And in good hands. I trusted everyone whom I was working with. We were all committed to making the best Mama Lil's Peppers that had ever been made.

Masala Eggs with Mama Lil's Peppers

Nitin Manchanda, (grudging) tech support for Howard Lev

Eggs are consumed all over India, and each region has adapted them to suit their preferences. This recipe is a fusion of these egg recipes. After all, "I am he as you are he as you are me and we are all together. Goo goo g'joob."

Serves 2

> 1 tablespoon ghee or neutral oil
> ½ tablespoon cumin seeds
> 1 to 2 shallots or ½ small red onion, chopped
> 1 tablespoon oil from a jar of Mama Lil's Peppers in Oil
> 2 to 3 garlic cloves, chopped
> 1 tablespoon peeled, chopped fresh ginger
> ½ teaspoon turmeric
> ½ teaspoon garam masala
> ½ teaspoon cayenne pepper or mirchi powder
> Salt
> 2 slices sourdough bread
> 1 smallish tomato
> 2 fine fresh eggs
> 2 tablespoons or more Mama Lil's Peppers in Oil, coarsely chopped
> 2 tablespoons chopped fresh cilantro
> Lime juice

Preheat the oven to 300°F.

In a medium sauté pan over medium-high heat, warm the ghee, then add the cumin seeds. After a few minutes (when the cumin seeds just start to sizzle), add the shallots or red onion, stirring to combine. After a few more minutes, add a little of the Mama Lil's pepper oil, then the garlic and ginger. Stir.

Cook for a few more minutes. Lower the heat to medium-low and mix in the turmeric, garam masala, cayenne pepper, and some salt.

Let the onion masala cook for yet another few minutes, then

spread the mixture in an even layer on the bottom of the pan. Remove from the heat while you make the toast and tomatoes.

Heat a cast-iron griddle or another pan over high heat. Place the sourdough bread slices on the griddle and cook for a couple of minutes. Flip them over and spread some butter on the cooked side. Grill the second side for a couple of minutes, then set aside.

Slice the tomato in half. Drizzle with neutral oil or some of the Mama Lil's pepper oil and sprinkle with salt. Place the cut sides down on the same griddle and let them sizzle for a few minutes, until charred. Place the bread next to the charred tomatoes on the griddle. Transfer them to the oven.

Now, warm the original sauté pan with the onion masala over medium heat and crack the eggs on top of the masala. Drizzle them with some Mama Lil's pepper oil, and sprinkle with a little salt. Scatter the Mama Lil's Peppers on top of everything, especially the eggs.

Cover and let cook for about 5 minutes (more or less, depending on how runny you like your yolks). Finish the eggs with chopped cilantro and a dash of lime juice. Serve alongside the grilled sourdough toast and tomato halves.

THE CAT'S OUT OF THE BAG

In December of 2004 I was stocking jars on a grocery shelf when I received a phone call from the familiar St. Louis area code, which always made me nervous. And this time I had reason to be. The woman on the line was the quality assurance manager at Panera Bread. Without raising any concern, she politely told me that a customer in one of its cafés had experienced an allergic reaction to the vegetarian cheese sandwich that contained Mama Lil's Peppers. Now she was trying to isolate what ingredient had triggered the customer's reaction.

"None of your products have any allergens in them—like nitrates—do they?" she asked.

There was silence on my end as I didn't want to incriminate myself. I had shipped the real Mama Lil's to the same four Panera distributors, while Raffi shipped the buckets he made—the ones with a trace of preservatives—to four other distributors. I had to say something, so I asked her as innocuously as I could, "What region of cafés?"

The QA manager raised her voice. "Howard, why would it matter what region of cafés she ate that sandwich at? All the cafés in all the regions get the very same peppers, right?

I almost swallowed my tongue. I had no idea what to tell her. "Not exactly," I stammered. After my hesitant pause, there had to have been something better for me to say than *not exactly.*

She certainly had no hesitation when she screamed, "What?!"

I started talking fast, probably too fast. "Your executive chef and the buyer knew…that I had…two sources of peppers…at least they knew two years ago—"

"Two years ago. Two sources? What's the difference between the two sources?"

"I'm just trying to get to next year, when all of our peppers—"

"Howard, what's the difference between the two sources of peppers?"

I exhaled, then confessed, "The labels on the buckets made from a blend of yellow wax and red Fresnos state they have a trace of nitrates…and sulfites in them. Mind you, a trace—"

"What?! Why didn't I know about this until now?"

"I certainly informed Scott—"

"But Scott no longer works here. For over a year now!"

"Or so I heard. Scott knew that the peppers sourced from California, which went to half of your cafes, have listed on their labels a trace of sodium benzoate and sodium nitrate."

"Fax me the lab reports on these. I'd like to know how much a *trace* is."

Before she hung up, I asked her again, in which café the customer had the reaction. When she told me it was in Indiana, I knew those buckets had been made at Johnson Foods from Yakima Valley-grown peppers—using no preservatives whatsoever. The allergic reaction was *not* from the peppers. And even though I sent her the lab report that showed just how small a trace it was, she was now deeply suspicious of me.

It was just a few months later that I ordered enough of Bruno's preservative laden peppers to fulfill one order of eighty buckets for the Panera cafés in Florida. But Chris Bruno informed me that he'd temporarily run out of his supply of red Fresno peppers. He had hoped for this one order, that the peppers could be reversed so that the red ones would be mild, and the yellow peppers would be hot. He sent me some samples of the two peppers.

My beatnik, chef friend, Todd Preston, happened to be at my house when the samples arrived. We tasted the peppers together. Wow—those yellow peppers were very hot—too hot, according to Todd. I wasn't so sure, and I really wanted these peppers to work out for this one last time before I shifted these cafes to the real Mama Lil's. I told Todd, "When they open this bucket, the peppers will look like all the other ones they've gotten from me. Besides, over time a heat exchange occurs between the mild and hot peppers."

Todd wasn't buying it. "Right. When will that heat exchange occur? A year from now? Two years?"

I didn't want Rafi to be responsible for making these buckets, so I had the barrels of peppers shipped to San Gennaro Foods so I could pack them myself. And even though I didn't heed his advice, Todd was willing to help me make these buckets. Todd was a good chef and an intelligent man who was sent to me by the gods for a reason—to be the voice of reason. Todd kept trying to get me to change my mind. But I was the fool who kept telling him, "For over two years, I've been supplying Panera cafés with these peppers, and I've never missed an order. I want its employees to see the same dull peppers, so they don't think it's a different product."

But when we got toward the end of packing the eighty buckets, I realized I'd been too cautious in using the hot yellow peppers and now I was running out of red ones. To fill the last two buckets, we had to use more hot yellow ones than I would've liked. Todd tried to put his foot down one last time. "At least give those cafés the real Mama Lil's for the last two buckets." It was 2 a.m.—

not the best time to make decisions, and I stubbornly held my ground until the end. I packed those last two buckets with too many yellow hot peppers and put them on the pallet that would be bound for Florida at 6 a.m.

At 5 a.m., I awoke with a start. To give the peppers more time for the heat exchange to take place—if such a phenomenon even happens—I should've at least buried those last two buckets at the bottom of the pallet, not at the top. Minutes later I was racing back to San Gennaro to rearrange the pallet. As I approached the building, I saw a truck pull out of its loading dock—with that pallet on it that we'd packed last night, now bound for Florida.

A week later, my phone woke me up at 6 a.m. When I groggily answered, "Mama Lil's," the Panera QA manager's scream of "Howard!" may have emulated the shriek of the elderly woman in Florida whose first bite of her cheese sandwich made her shriek in pain. I sat up in bed and tried to explain the situation to the QA manager, but I'd completely lost her trust. I finally heeded Todd's advice and shipped out a pallet of the real Mama Lil's Peppers to Florida and had the other one still with 75 buckets sent back to Johnson Foods. But I now had two strikes against me with the QA manager. And that last one was a real doozie, like swinging at a ball in the dirt.

A month later while out making deliveries, I got another call from a St. Louis area code. I took a deep breath and answered with a bubbly, "Mama Lil's."

"Hi. I'm Mike, the new buyer at Panera. As you know, we've been growing very fast."

When I realized he wasn't calling about quality issues, I told him enthusiastically, "That's so great to hear! And I'm so glad you called. We're just about to plant seeds in our greenhouses. We anticipate growing five hundred tons of goathorn peppers in the Yakima Valley for Panera alone! That's a million pounds of goathorn peppers—"

"And how many peppers did you grow for us last year?"

"About half of that."

"So, if we're making you grow that fast, what are you going to do for us?"

"This year all the peppers will be grown in the Yakima valley. This year, we'll be making the highest quality peppers for Panera ever."

"Mr. Lev, we expect the highest *quality* from all our suppliers. What I'm asking you is how much are you going to lower your price for us?"

I didn't see that coming. Even though I knew I had wiggle room on pricing, I stuck with the cards in my hand. "Mike, I have a contract with Panera. The pricing is within the contract."

"Impossible. We don't give contracts with pricing to our suppliers."

"Well, Mama Lil's has a contract. Written by the head buyer."

"But I'm the head buyer now."

"I realize. But Mike, I need to plan months ahead. We're about to plant—"

"Have your secretary fax me that contract." *Click.*

Secretary? Who did he think Mama Lil's was?

I faxed him the contract. Mike called the next day. "This is the strangest contract I've ever seen. Why was the estimate for usage so far off? I'm going to our legal department to get us out of this." *Click.*

I didn't want this to become more adversarial than it already was, but I was advised to hire a contract lawyer. We called Panera's legal department from his office. As our lawyers jostled, I could hear Mike's perturbed voice in the background advising Panera's in-house legal team. But once my lawyer mentioned the Uniform Commercial Code—put in place in 1952 to protect suppliers and farmers from exactly these sorts of situations—the conversation shifted in my favor. We could still hear Mike protesting when the call ended. My lawyer boasted to me, "I bet Mike walked out with his tail between his legs." I winced when he told me this. The last thing I wanted was for Buyer Mike to dislike me more than he already did.

The upshot was that the contract with Panera was left in place, and they were still paying a premium price of $70 a bucket. But only five thousand buckets were left in that contract. Then what? Mike was the kind of buyer I'd been warned about, one who had all the power and was going to use it to get what he wanted from me. I wrote to Buyer Mike and explained to him again about our short growing season and how we had to make a year's supply in two months. I got no response. I didn't know what to do or how many peppers to have planted. A few weeks later, I built up the nerve to call him yet again. He picked up the phone this time.

"What can I do for you Mr. Lev?"

"Mike, I'm open to renegotiate pricing, but we need to know now how many peppers to grow to supply Panera from September of this year until September of next year."

"We don't have these issues with any other suppliers. Look, Panera has no plans to stop using Mama Lil's. And I'll honor the contract. But only until it ends. Then we'll revisit pricing."

From his dismissive tone, I knew I was on his shitlist. Not knowing what to say to him, I figured I'd give good old-fashioned *truth* a shot. "Mike, here's our reality. In January, farmers purchase seeds for the greenhouses. Late April is when the plants are committed to the fields. Mid-August through late October, we'll harvest, pickle, and pack over a million pounds of Yakima Valley goathorn peppers for—"

"You've told me all this before." *Click.* I immediately knew not only had I misplayed my hand, but I'd revealed all my cards. I just told Buyer Mike all the best times to screw me over.

When I asked my businessman father what I should do, he said it was just too big a risk to supply Panera without a contract, especially considering that I'd be paying for a chunk of this inventory with a fully leveraged line of credit on my home. He suggested, "Hedge your bet. Pack half a year's supply for Panera." My dad was a wiser businessman and a better gambler than I. But then what? If Panera kept ordering, I'd be back to square one by using impostor peppers.

I discussed my predicament with all my friends in the food business, but their products—polenta chubs, pasta, crackers, mayonnaise, vegetarian sausages—were made when the purchase orders came in. None of them were dependent on fresh produce to make all their inventory for twelve months in two months' time. The consensus I got from them was that there was too much risk without some semblance of a contract.

I was becoming all too aware of the conundrum I was facing of quality versus profits. I couldn't make the real Mama Lil's Peppers from peppers I sourced from Bruno's. But it was certainly better from the business angle to use them; they were a commodity I could order as needed—so no need to stock up on a year's inventory.

In 2005, by shifting all the production to the Yakima Valley, where the peppers grew best and could be packed to perfection, I took a leap of faith. Or was it a dive into the unknown? When I asked my farmers to plant enough seeds in their greenhouses to grow 1.3 million pounds of goathorns for Mama Lil's—the amount I'd need to provide peppers for all the Panera cafés and my other accounts for the entire year ahead— it felt like I entered a dark tunnel of fear. This year I'd have twice the work, thrice the investment, and ten times the risk.

Why did I take this risk, knowing that I couldn't trust Buyer Mike to be fair with me? One explanation is for the same reason I bet on the Cleveland Indians every year: a self-deceptive tendency toward wishful thinking. *Maybe Mike will end up being a good guy after all.* Now any business adviser will tell you it's a bad strategy to have so many eggs in one basket. But maybe I took this risk simply because I didn't want this good business to stop. Because I knew there was so much risk involved, I offered to have a contract written up with the farmers. But Manuel Imperial told me, "On this side of the mountains, we shake hands."

When the seedlings in the greenhouses were ready to be planted in the fields in late April, I emailed Buyer Mike to notify him. I didn't expect to hear back, and I didn't. But no news is good news, right? I knew Mike didn't like me, but that was no reason to stop using my peppers, was it? Then while going over my books, I realized I'd reached a milestone: *I'd surpassed the twenty-nine thousand buckets in the contract, and Panera was no longer beholden to buy any more buckets from Mama Lil's.* Yet its orders kept increasing as it opened more cafés. I had reason to feel confident about the upcoming harvest. There was never an issue of quality from the Yakima Valley-grown peppers, the ones that had passed that test with flying colors. For the first time in three years, there'd be no more impostor peppers. And I'd be harboring no secrets.

In early August, after scouting the five large peppers fields, I left Buyer Mike a voicemail. "We're about to start picking and packing peppers. We estimate that twenty-two thousand buckets will meet your needs. Please give me the go-ahead whether to proceed."

This time he called back. "Mr. Lev, your peppers are still on our menu. We've no other plans—as of now. If we change our minds, we'll give you sixty days' notice." *Click.*

Where did Buyer Mike learn his phone etiquette? Wharton Business School? That bastard was asking me to gamble on how many peppers to grow, with no safety net of a contract. Sixty days' notice is not very long when I'd be making them a twelve-month supply in two months' time. By moving *all* the growing and production of the peppers to the Yakima Valley to make my product uniformly great, I'd have twice the work, thrice the investment, and ten times the risk.

As I lay in bed that night, I tried to dream my way forward with positive thoughts. *This year's peppers will be packed to such perfection that, of course, Panera will keep ordering those buckets. Maybe it'll bring back the steak sandwich with the peppers on it. Or better yet, maybe it'll put them on its top-selling chicken sandwich! Who knows, maybe we should've planted even more peppers?"*

The next day I went to the bank and increased the line of credit on my home to $250K.

Mama's Vinaigrette

(or what to do with the dregs of the jar)

Todd Preston

This makes one cup of salad dressing that's wonderful drizzled over greens and grilled veggies.

Once all the Mama Lil's Mildly Spicy or Kick Butt Peppers have been eaten, pour the remaining oil from the jar into a measuring cup. Add enough extra-virgin olive oil to make ½ cup total.

Pour this oil mixture back into the Mama Lil's jar and add the following ingredients:

  2 ounces sherry vinegar
  1 tablespoon Dijon mustard
  2 teaspoons honey
  Salt and freshly ground black pepper to taste
  Optional: Finely chopped herbs—tarragon, basil, parsley, chives, etc.
  Optional: For a creamy dressing, add 2 tablespoons mayonnaise.

Put the lid back on. Shake the jar vigorously to thoroughly emulsify the ingredients.

THE GREATEST HARVEST OF THEM ALL

WHEN THE 2005 HARVEST BEGAN, the Cleveland Indians were in the thick of a pennant race, so I bought a new one-ton van with a satellite radio to listen to the baseball games for the thousands of miles I'd be putting on it. Why had it taken me so long to make this upgrade? I sat tall in my seat as I inspected the pepper fields just starting to show some yellow color. Then it took but one cold night and abracadabra, it was like Mother Nature called "Action!"—and those peppers started turning orange and red right before our eyes. Soon truckloads of those peppers were being brought to the Johnson Foods cannery.

With Gary Stonemetz, Sunnyside, Washington, 2005. Photo © Jean Sherrard.

When I wasn't in Sunnyside making peppers, I was at Wolf Pack making PeppaLilli and bread-and-butter pickles in George's kettles. I'd go home on weekends to make local deliveries and peddle peppers at a couple of farmers' markets in Seattle. Then on Sunday, I'd drive back to Sunnyside with the setting sun behind me so to be back on the prep line on Monday morning.

Looking back on that harvest, I'm not so sure where I got the energy, especially after the Cleveland Indians were eliminated from the post-season.

I feared it was another omen for an early frost that would end the pepper season as well. But that did not happen. Then in late September, I got a huge shot of encouragement when *Newsweek* magazine did a feature article about artisan foods made in America and ranked Mama Lil's Peppers in the top five—with a photo of Mama Lil's jars smack dab in the middle of the magazine. Talk about getting noticed seven times! That issue was delivered to over three million mailboxes that week.

When my father, ever the realist, saw the *Newsweek* article, he said to me, "Don't get your hopes up, son. People read *Newsweek* in the dentist's office. No one is thinking of buying peppers while waiting to get a root canal." He was probably right. But I was so encouraged by this moonshot of publicity that as long as the goathorns kept ripening in the fields, we kept pickling them. To make sure Buyer Mike and the CEO of Panera saw the article, I sent them each an autographed copy, along with jars and a slightly sardonic note congratulating them on using such stellar ingredients on the company's sandwiches. Neither of them responded.

But when my old friend Patrick Lango, who I hadn't spoken to in eight years since I hosed him down in the cannery, saw the *Newsweek* article, he wrote me a note: "The Al Roker bit was great, but the *Newsweek* thing is absolutely galactic." And Patrick and I became instant friends again. Patrick, it is worth mentioning, makes the greatest yogurt known to man with his White Cow Dairy brand sold at his Farm Shop in Buffalo.

I have so many wonderful memories from the 2005 harvest that play out in my imagination like a movie montage depicting the splendor when all is going well for the hero or heroine: I loved walking the rows of Gary Stonemetz's Pink Lady apple trees in the evenings as he'd wait for the day when they, too, fully ripened and could be picked. Scouting the colorful pepper fields below Mount Adams after work. The many delicious Filipino dinners I enjoyed with the Imperial family at their communal table. And how satiated I felt as I drove back to Sunnyside past acres of plump winter squash glowing orange and gold at sunset.

Although my baseball team didn't go far that year, the local soccer team that Mama Lil's sponsored—Mama Lil's Manchester United—was playing for the Yakima Valley championship on a warm mid-October evening at the Grandview soccer field. With the clock ticking down, we were tied when the opposing team knocked our best player, Jesus, out of bounds and held him down so he couldn't get back in the game. As the team's sponsor, I had my Mark Cuban moment when I ran down from the stands to help free Jesus so he could score the winning goal!

The only word I heard from Panera was that it planned to do an audit of the cannery. Stonemetz said it was a very good sign. "Why would it pay to do an audit if it had plans to stop using Mama Lil's? Its customers are going to love these peppers we're making for them." By the end of that harvest of 2005, we processed more than 1.3 million pounds of goathorns—two hundred million pepper rings dancing on the shaker table as they surrendered their seeds—that were packed into twenty-two thousand buckets and eight thousand cases of jars. And we just got better at making them as we went. Gary and I had been so fastidious in all aspects of production that we were confident that every bucket and jar was made to perfection.

On the last day of processing, I brought out the cash I'd saved from farmers' markets and tipped the whole crew for their vaunted effort. When I passed out Mama Lil's T-shirts and everyone put them on right over their clothing, I saw they were as proud of the fruits of their labor as I was. With two pallets of peppers behind me and a box of Gary's Pink Lady apples and the soccer championship trophy beside me, I set out for Seattle.

My first stop was twenty miles away at Imperials' farm stand, to splurge at their Filipino harvest feast attended by two hundred of their friends, family, and employees. When I couldn't eat one more lumpia or slice of cow spinning on the barbecue spit—where surely, I took a nip or two off a bottle of Johnnie Walker Red Label being passed around by Marcelo Imperial—I drank some coffee and started driving home. Not only had I survived my most intense harvest yet, but I felt like I was emerging out of a dark tunnel of uncertainty and had arrived at the place that I'd been striving to get to for the last four years. Now, only the *real* Mama Lil's Peppers existed. Two hours later, I was gliding down Snoqualmie Pass in moonlit snow flurries. An early snow was a good sign as it boded well for a deep snowpack that would keep filling the Yakima River for all of next year's harvest.

Then after the unprecedented harvest of 2005, life's bounty kept coming my way when in mid-November, Jerry Mascio from San Gennaro Foods took me and my friend Jeffrey squid jigging at least a dozen times below the bright skyline on Seattle's downtown waterfront. We caught so many of those translucent squirmers that I took buckets of squid to my favorite restaurant friends, who in exchange would cook me and my friends a wonderful calamari dish.

Brad at the Swingside Café certainly knew what to do with squid. As did Mike Easton when he was the chef at Bizarro, and Dylan Giordan at Serafina. But it was at the 1200 Bistro (long gone) where chef Chet Wallenstein made one of the most spectacular plates of food my uncle Dan, aunt Arlene, and I had ever seen or eaten. With yellow, orange and red pepper rings floating in the black squid-ink sauce, it was so colorful we couldn't stop staring at it. And when we dug in, we didn't stop until we soaked up every last drop of its sauce. *Yum, yum, yum!*

Calamari Cooked in Its Own Ink
with Mama Lil's Peppers

Chet Wallenstein, former private chef for Paul Allen and Jeff Bezos

Portuguese sausage is a dry-cured, smoked, highly flavorful sausage that is similar in texture to a salami. It is definitely not a fresh, raw sausage in casings like you'd find at the meat counter of your grocery store. A reasonable substitute for Portuguese sausage would be a dry-cured chorizo or linguiça. Black garlic is available online or in gourmet grocery stores. If you can't catch your own, the squid and ink (bought separately) should be available in an Asian grocery store and online.

Serves 2

1 tablespoon oil from a jar of Mama Lil's Peppers in Oil
½ cup finely diced sweet yellow onion
2 teaspoons minced garlic (2 to 3 cloves)
2 black garlic cloves, mashed (if available)
1 cup large-diced Portuguese sausage (about 2 medium links) (see headnote)
1 teaspoon smoked paprika
1 teaspoon kosher salt
½ teaspoon freshly ground black pepper
⅓ cup dry white wine
1 tablespoon tomato paste
½ cup crushed canned tomatoes, preferably fire-roasted
¼ cup Mama Lil's Peppers in Oil
½ cup clam juice
1 tablespoon squid ink
1½ cups thinly sliced calamari rings, along with some tentacles
2 tablespoons chopped Italian parsley

In a large sauté pan over medium heat, warm the Mama Lil's pepper oil. Add the onion and minced garlic and sauté for about 3 minutes. Add the black garlic, sausage, smoked paprika, salt, and black pepper and cook for another 3 minutes, stirring gently.

Add white wine and tomato paste; stir to combine. Cook until liquid is reduced by about half.

Add the crushed tomatoes, Mama Lil's Peppers, clam juice, and squid ink; simmer 2 minutes. Add calamari and simmer for another several minutes, or just until the squid is cooked through.

Remove the pan from the heat and add parsley. Adjust with salt and black pepper as needed.

THE DESCENT

I WAS ON JERRY'S BOAT JIGGING FOR squid in December of 2006 when I received the news from my brother that my dad had been admitted to the hospital. It wasn't urgent, but the next day I flew to Ohio to see him. When I got to the hospital, Harry was about to have a colonoscopy to see if he had diverticulitis, and my job was to make sure he drank the laxative prep. After a few sips, he handed me the bottle. "If you really love me, *you* finish it." I regretted that I made him drink that vile-tasting stuff that made for an extremely uncomfortable two hours. The results were negative, so it seemed silly the doctor wanted Harry to spend the night in the hospital for observation.

When I went to his room, he was enjoying the company of his roommate, who Harry loudly introduced. "This is Ted. I was telling Ted about your peppers. Ted's a chef."

Ted corrected my nearly deaf dad, "My name's Ed. And I'm not a chef. I'm a sheriff."

The next morning, as I walked into my dad's room, the sheriff was being moved out, having come down with pneumonia. I sat down on my dad's bed. He was weaker than he'd been the night before and wistfully sentimental. "Son, what they say is true. Life does go by fast." Then he pulled me closer so he could kiss me on the cheek, then held my head and looked at me more deeply than he ever had. "Are you going to be okay, son?"

"I'm great dad. Because you made me meet that trucker, Santisi, I'm about to make real money."

"Money can't buy you happiness, son," he said, his eyes emoting a weary wisdom.

"I hear it can't buy you love either." I said, hoping for a laugh out of my dad.

But he didn't even crack a smile, which was unlike him. My dad wearily said, "I used to be strong, I feel so weak." That's when I realized he was sinking and most likely coming down with pneumonia himself. I alerted the nurse, and Harry was moved into the ICU. When his condition stabilized, I flew back home to tend to business and pack for the next Fancy Food Show in San Francisco. It was on the last busy day of the show that my father died. So here I was again, sobbing my eyes out as I packed up my booth.

In the eulogy I wrote for Harry on the plane, I recalled a trip when my dad came to see me in Seattle after Lil died. He'd read an article in the in-flight magazine about a gluttonous sea lion named Herschel who, no matter how many times he was transported to California, kept swimming back to Seattle to feast on the salmon at the fish ladder at the Ballard Locks. Since Harry's nickname was Herschel, he identified with him and wanted to see this voracious sea lion for himself. When Harry spotted Herschel through binoculars, he made a face like a ravenous beast then demanded, "Let's have salmon for dinner!"

After Harry's memorial service, I diligently got to work on the most thankless task of running my business: following up on sales leads. First, stuff envelopes with sales literature to remind the potential buyers we met at the show. Wait one week, then call them to (hopefully) make a sale. Here's a trick of the trade about phone sales that I learned too late in the game: *Sitting is a submissive posture. When making sales calls on the phone, stand up. You feel more in charge, so it's easier to get someone to acquiesce and say, "I'll take a case of each."*

Right after taking an order for a new store, four purchase orders from Panera appeared on my fax machine. One thousand buckets were to be shipped out next week for a total of $70,000! I took these orders as a blessing from Harry. But this bout of hopefulness in the dead of winter lasted only a few days. My uncle Dan, my very favorite person in the world, informed me that he had lung cancer. Many more sad months lay ahead.

On a February morning I was listening to voicemails to begin my workday. The first one was from Wayne Inaba, letting me know that the seeds for next year's pepper crop had been planted in his greenhouses. Next, was a large order from the West Point Market, which was always nice to see come in. And lastly, a curt message from Buyer Mike. "Call me back."

I felt a familiar sense of dread at the sound of his voice, like I'd been told to call my oncologist. I didn't call him. Instead, I called Gary Stonemetz and let him know how much I dreaded making that call. But Gary was nonchalant. "They've gotta be loving these peppers. Call that buyer back. And ask him when they're doing that audit. We're ready for them."

I dialed. Buyer Mike picked up on the first ring. Before I had a chance to stand up, he dropped the bomb. "We're going in a different direction. By May 1, Mama Lil's Peppers will officially be off Panera's menu." Just like that, Buyer Mike shot my soaring business out of the sky. I imagined him in his office, licking his trigger finger, proud of his aim. And I was his victim, willing to play it to the hilt.

"Mike, I have more than fifteen thousand buckets that I made *just for Panera*. My dad died two weeks ago. My uncle was diagnosed with cancer. Now you're telling me that you won't be buying them?"

"Sell them to someone else. In sixty days, Mama Lil's Peppers are off our menu." *Click*. I'd been given my prognosis. It was terminal.

I sat there frozen, unable to move, until I remembered my four farmers had already stocked their greenhouses for this year's crop. Which Mama Lil's no longer needed! I called Stonemetz to tell him the news. He was devastated too, as he was looking forward to the challenge of the next harvest when we planned to make more than thirty-three thousand buckets for Panera. But he'd been in the business long enough to know that despite the Uniform Commercial Code, this happens to farmers all the time. He called two of the farmers he knew best, and I called Wayne Inaba and Manuel Imperial. Luckily, it was early enough that they could restock their greenhouses with late crops like eggplant and winter squash.

The next day, I drove to the mammoth cold storage facility in Grandview, Washington, to see for myself what more than fifteen thousand buckets looked like in one place. I was given a hard hat, hopped on a forklift and was driven to the furthest building. The driver pointed to the row with my buckets. "We call it Pepper Lane. You know, like in that song, 'Penny Lane.'"

I began my walk down the length of the lane, lined with pallets of eighty buckets each. Every bucket had two goats on the label. I'd never seen so many of those goats in my life, three pallets deep, stacked on racks reaching to the top of the twenty-foot ceiling all the way down the long row. As I walked down the aisle, it all went into slow motion. Then it hit me. I'd entered the nightmare I'd feared all along.

I was walking into a TUNNEL of BUCKETS! With no end in sight.

These fifteen thousand buckets would've been enough to supply Panera for nine months. But at the present rate of sales for all my other accounts, it would take more than nine *years* to find the mouths to eat those peppers. And I wanted nothing more than to escape this tunnel—if not forward, then backward. It was just one exit over on the freeway to get to Johnson Foods.

When I was loading up a couple pallets to bring to Seattle, I ran into its young owner Gary Johnson. I still owed them $150,000 from last year's harvest. Without giving it much thought, I offered to sell him Mama Lil's for the cost of goods of my inventory, if they paid me right on the spot. But Johnson told me his family business was in a downturn, and they couldn't afford it. That was the end of that conversation.

As I drove back to Seattle, I could hear Lil's voice scolding me when as a kid I'd always get stuck with too many points in my gin rummy hand. I knew I was a bad gambler, but there I was sitting at the card table, losing again. And I wasn't learning from my mistakes. I was losing, again. If I'd listened to my dad, who told me to make only half a year's supply for Panera, I'd be in good shape right now. As I drove, I thought a lot about Harry. Just as I associated Lil's death with the floodgates opening and manna from heaven flowing Mama Lil's way, I now wondered in the grand scheme of a family's spiritual matters whether Harry's last words to me—"*Money doesn't buy you happiness, son*"— was his foreshadowed warning: "*Son, the spigot will be turned off.*"

I probably had this inventory nightmare coming to me—because for years I was keeping secrets from Panera and living in constant anxiety that they would be exposed. Even though I'd finally moved beyond those impostor peppers, was I now being punished for my past sins? Sure, I felt some guilt that Panera had overpaid for the forty thousand buckets I'd sold it these past four years. But look, I didn't tell its buyer to choose the seedless peppers with the inflated price. It just worked out that way, to my very good fortune. Until now.

I couldn't help but think that if I were truly ethical, I should've somehow renegotiated the contract with Panera back in the beginning. And on a purely business-savvy note, instead of being fearful of Panera, I should've made a bigger effort to stay in closer contact with its QA manager from the outset. If I had, chances are I'd be in a better place. Because now, every dime that Mama Lil's had was invested in this tunnel of buckets! And so was my home!

Panera did order two thousand more buckets before the orders (and checks) stopped. I was able to fully pay Johnson Foods and almost all the production bills, that is, except for the largest of them all: the line of credit on my home. The only victory I had in all this was a sneaky one. Ramon, who knew the cannery and its warehouses better than anyone, found hiding in the walk-in refrigerator those seventy-five buckets made with the very hot yellow impostor peppers that I had shipped back from Florida. I suppose I could've donated those buckets to the food bank, but heck, they were now a year old and had had plenty of time for that heat transfer to occur. Those buckets were on my very last Panera order. When they got loaded on the truck, not only was it good riddance, but a satisfyingly immoral "fuck you!"

When the Panera orders stopped for good, I owned 12,862 buckets. This number of buckets was so astronomical I just couldn't face it, as I had no clue who would buy them. Instead, I spent as much time as I could with my uncle Dan in the last months of his life. Like my friend Jonny, my uncle was a mentor to me. When I came to Seattle for college, I knew Dan would facilitate my education more than any teacher could. But Dan showed no interest in Mama Lil's whatsoever. He just didn't see me as a businessman. But when I pulled into his driveway one day with two pallets of peppers in my van, Dan was so impressed by all those cases he demanded, "Give me a case!" In my eulogy for Dan I wrote, "Considering what most father-son, father-daughter, mother-son, mother-daughter relationships are like, what you really want in life is a great uncle."

After Dan's memorial service, I couldn't ignore the reality of my bucket inventory any longer. Not only was I paying more than $2,000 a month in cold-storage fees, but an accountant informed me that my inventory was now considered an asset—that I had to start paying taxes on! No matter what metaphor I assigned to Mama Lil's predicament—be it a dying bird, a sinking boat, or a slow bumpy ride in an empty boxcar heaving backward, then forward through an endless tunnel—what I felt most was the sheer weight of those buckets on top of me. And since I couldn't get out from under it, I'd tell everyone I met about my predicament, hoping a little gallows humor would lessen the load.

While delivering a bucket to the charcuterie shop, Salumi, I practically cried into wise, old Armondino Batali's shoulder when I told him how many buckets I owned. But Dino just laughed, put his arm around my shoulder, and then started singing, "12,450 buckets on the wall, 12,450 buckets. If one of those buckets would happen to fall, Howard will still have 12,449 buckets on the wall." It's a drinking song. But I also knew it as a camp song that we'd sing on the bus until we got to our faraway destination. But man, I owned so many buckets that I'd be singing it all the way to the moon. And back.

When I told the screenwriter Tony Gilroy, about the 160 pallets of buckets I got stuck with, he started laughing at me too. I asked him, "Why do you find my predicament so funny?"

"It reminds me of a comedy my brother and I wrote, called *Dimes*. Bank robbers break out of jail, and when they go to retrieve their loot, all $50,000 is in dimes. These idiots had to buy a forklift to move those two pallets of dimes around."

"But this idiot has 160 pallets! And every dime I have is in them buckets. And unlike your dimes, my buckets have a shelf life!"

Tony was now laughing harder. "That makes it even funnier!"

Then I ran into another Gilroy, Paul Gilroy, the mayonnaise man, who was always in the know about the latest food business gossip. When I told him how many buckets Panera stuck me with, he started cackling.

"Why the hell does everybody think this is so fuckin' funny?" I implored.

Between belly laughs, Paul said, "I was on an industry booze cruise on Lake Washington chatting up this woman when the topic of Mama Lil's Peppers came up. I was bragging to her that you were pulling it off with smoke and mirrors! Hell, I didn't know she worked at Panera."

"You're kidding me, right?!"

"When I saw you making buckets, you *were* pulling it off with smoke and mirrors."

"That was three years ago! This year's buckets are the best we've ever made! Christ, what else did you tell her?"

"It's what *she* told me. Panera didn't drop that steak sandwich your peppers were on. That sandwich is still on the menu. Your peppers were replaced by another pepper product."

"Someone else makes pickled peppers in oil?"

"No, I think they're using some peppers called…Peppapews or something…"

"Not the Peppadews!" I moaned.

He snapped his fingers. "That's it. Peppadews."

Mama Lil's! The most delicious peppers on the planet.

Gilbano Grinder with Mama Lil's Peppers and Artichoke Aioli

Mitch Gilbert

This was the Sicilian steak grinder featured at Grinders Hot Sands in Shoreline, Washington that was considered a must-try by *Sunset* magazine. I ate so many Gilbanos after making deliveries to Grinders that I was starting to look like Mitch. So, I switched to his whack-whack salad, loaded with meat, chicken, and cheese and dressed with Mama Lil's oil. I was always in a rush, so I ate fast. Mitch told me that when I'd walk out, half of that salad was still on my face.

Makes 2 big fat grinders

Artichoke Aioli

    1 (14-ounce) can quartered artichoke hearts in water, drained

    4 tablespoons mayonnaise

    4 tablespoons grated Parmesan cheese

    Juice from ½ large lemon

    ½ teaspoon red pepper flakes

    Salt and coarsely ground black pepper to taste

    1 tablespoon Mama Lil's pepper oil

Gilbano Grinder Filling

    Oil from 3 tablespoons Mama Lil's Peppers in Oil

    1 pound beef tri-tip steak, thinly sliced

    Salt and freshly ground black pepper

    8 garlic cloves, chopped

    1 teaspoon capers

    2 anchovy fillets (optional)

    3 tablespoons Mama Lil's Peppers

    1 onion, thinly sliced

    1 green bell pepper, thinly sliced

    1 teaspoon red pepper flakes

    1 tablespoon Marsala wine

12 slices aged provolone or Asiago cheese

1/4 cup crumbled Gorgonzola cheese

1/4 cup chopped basil

1 (12- to 16-inch-long) baguette

8 fresh basil leaves, julienned

2 ounces grated Parmesan cheese

To make the aioli:

Add the artichoke hearts, mayonnaise, Parmesan cheese, lemon juice, red pepper flakes, salt, black pepper, and Mama Lil's pepper oil to a blender. Blend until thoroughly combined and smooth. Set aside.

To make the grinder filling:

Preheat the oven to 325°F. In a large skillet over medium heat, warm the Mama Lil's pepper oil. Add steak, salt, and black pepper. Cook 2 minutes, then add the garlic, capers, and anchovies. Flake and smash the anchovies with a fork until they dissolve. Add Mama Lil's Peppers, onion, bell pepper, red pepper flakes, and the Marsala wine. Stir to combine and cook for 3 minutes. Now add the provolone, Gorgonzola, and chopped basil. Cook a little longer, say a minute or so, stirring to combine until the cheeses have melted. Remove from the heat, then set aside.

To assemble the grinder:

Place the baguette in the preheated oven, bake until its exterior turns slightly crunchy (about 3 minutes). Cut the baguette crosswise in half. Then slice the baguette lengthwise, but not all the way through, so it opens like a book. Spread generous smear of the artichoke aioli on the bottom half of the baguette, add the meat filling from the skillet, spreading it evenly over the bread. Sprinkle with julienned basil and grated Parmesan cheese and close up the sandwiches.

BACKWARDS, FORWARDS, UNDER, OVER, SIDEWAYS, DOWN

I COULDN'T BELIEVE THAT MY PRODUCT—one of the five best gourmet foods in the country, according to the fine editors of *Newsweek* magazine—had been replaced by a pepper product that, in my totally biased opinion, was mediocre at best. I had never thought much of the Peppadews to begin with, but now I downright despised them. But I learned two important lessons about the business I was in: It wasn't necessarily fair, and there was no accounting for taste.

I had no choice but to attend more food shows, primarily in search of new markets for these buckets. At the 2006 NYC Summer Fancy Food Show, a posse of buyers from BJ's Wholesale Club lingered at my booth, tasting each of my products as they watched the Food Network episode on a monitor. One of the buyers had a mother named Lil, and he was interested (or so he said) "in bringing the Peppers in Oil and the Sweet Hot Peppas to all fifty of our stores! And if you show this video while doing demos to support the jars, I think they'll do quite well."

"How well?" I asked. "How many cases you think your stores would sell over a year?"

When he responded, "Thousands," I knew this was the lead I was searching for!

When I got back to the cannery, Stonemetz and I experimented with filling pint jars for BJ's straight out of the premade Panera buckets, with good enough results I felt that I could supply BJ's with jars filled from those buckets. Meanwhile, the thirty tons of goathorns we had growing in the Yakima Valley would fill five thousand cases of Sweet Hot Peppas. I then made ten thousand display boxes for those two products and one hundred CD copies of the Food Network episode for all the demos I planned to do. When I shipped out twelve hundred cases of my two products on a four-day truck ride bound for BJ's East Coast warehouse, I was ecstatic.

Ten days passed, and I never got confirmation from BJ's that the twelve pallets of jars had been received at its loading dock. The trucking company hadn't heard from the truck driver either. It was a total mystery. No one had a clue where my 1,200 cases were.

As it turns out, a forecasted snowstorm had caused a logjam at BJ's receiving dock. When it started snowing, my truck driver unhitched the container carrying our peppers in the distributor's parking lot, then skedaddled in his truck before he got stuck in the snow. It *was* a huge snowstorm. That snow completely covered the container in the corner of the lot. My jars weren't found until twelve days later when the snow finally melted. Thankfully, despite the freeze, the peppers were in good shape, and they eventually got checked in. But the demo schedule I had arranged was thrown out of whack and no one would call me back to reschedule the demos.

I flew out to New Jersey to check on the BJ's stores and hopefully arrange to do some demos. Contrary to its buyer's promise of high visibility for the product, BJ's had merely put out a few jars that were hidden on some out-of-the-way shelf. They weren't even placed in the beautiful display boxes, of which I'd made seven entire pallets just for them. I called its offices to discuss the situation, but no one took my calls. In fact, I never heard from BJ's again.

Considering my run of bad luck, for all I know the buyer got fired for even deeming to do business with Mama Lil's in the first place.

So, instead of shortening the tunnel of buckets, I now had a mountain range of forty pallets of Sweet Hot Peppas that I didn't have a market for either. (Not to mention seven useless pallets of display boxes and a hundred CDs of that Food Network episode.) Mama Lil's, which I had been devotedly married to for fifteen years—I slept at my business, I woke up at my business—was in the toilet. And I was going down with the flush. And I had that drinking song playing on an endless tape loop in my head, taunting me. I'd awaken in the middle of the night to the dream of a bucket falling and bursting open, spilling its oil. *Still ten thousand buckets on the wall? I'll never fall asleep.*

Compared to 2005 when we grew more than five hundred tons of goathorn peppers, in 2007 we were down to growing just fifteen tons, all of which we packed into retail jars. At the end of that short harvest, I brought home thirty pounds of colorful goathorns that my artist friend Don, who sometimes lived in my basement, strung up with twine, then hung along the exposed pipes that ran below the basement's ceiling. A few months later, Don and I were chatting in my office when we heard a *rat-a-tat, rat-a-tat* chomping noise. Perched on a pipe in plain view was a rat gnawing on a dried pepper. On further inspection, we saw that many of the dried goathorns had already been chewed on.

Don scratched his head. "Howard, think it might be time to take these peppers down?"

A few days later, Don stepped on a dead rat near his bedroom door. A day later, I found another rat carcass in the doorway to my office. But who had left them for us? Certainly not my blind cat Marion. Then Don and I caught a glimpse of another large rat stealthily moving about in the shadows. I had no tolerance for rats whatsoever, so I promptly moved my computer out of my basement office and up to my kitchen. The next day, Don came upstairs and put a dictionary on the kitchen table. "This rat isn't a rat," he said. Then he opened the dictionary to a page, pulled out a magnifying glass, and held it over a small drawing. "We got one of these."

I squinted through the magnifier at the drawing of a rodent. "We got a chinchilla?"

"I don't know how we do, but we do. And he's quite at home in your office."

Now willing to venture back down, I peered into my office, and yes, the chinchilla was sitting on his haunches looking quite at home on my desk. He took two hops toward me, paused as if to say hello, then scampered out. At the time, Chile was focused on catching the last of the goathorn pepper-eating rats living on what was now his turf. When the chase was on in the ceilings and walls, it sounded like an all-out brawl. But now we were down to just one rat. When that last squeal ended in abrupt silence, and a proud Chile appeared a minute later, Don told me, "He just might be a keeper." When he urinated in the empty Mama Lil's box that I'd set out with kitty litter, I knew Chile was a keeper.

This chinchilla was playful in a peek-a-boo kind of way. When a friend of my uncle's, the Southeast Asian scholar Benedict Anderson, was at my house in transit to his winter home in Thailand, he was excited to meet my pet chinchilla. Ben told me, "In most Southeast Asian cultures, not only would the appearance of this mysterious creature be seen as a sign of good luck, but they'd assume it was inhabited by one of their ancestral spirits." Ben and I were standing below Chile's favorite ceiling pipe when the chinchilla appeared. Ben offered him an almond and shuddered with happiness as Chile took the nut from him with his dainty fingers and quickly chewed it up.

I told Ben, "Gauging by his appetite, he's a Lev. But is he Harry? Or Dan?"

Ben fed Chile another almond then endearingly whispered to him, "Good to see you again, Dan."

Whoever Chile was, he felt like family. And whether this creature who appeared out of thin air was there to bring me luck or not, he made my time in my office feel less lonely when doing my books and making futile sales calls. With my home's line of credit gnawing at me, I'd dig through my business cards, searching for someone, anyone, who could take my inventory off my hands. At food shows, buyers of distressed goods (often wearing yarmulkes) would ask if I had any product nearing the end of its shelf life. I'd typically shoo them away. "You shvindler! My peppers just get better as they age." Then I'd usually toss their cards in the trash.

But now I needed one of these shvindlers.

I found a few cards to choose from, but it was Big Lots, the national mega-bargain store that buys and sells distressed products—not because they're bad but because the producer had inventory issues and needed the cash flow—who were most enthusiastic about the Sweet Hot Peppas and said they would buy my entire inventory of jars in one fell swoop. Mind you, the buyer wasn't interested enough to offer me a fair price. This buyer dealt only with people who were stuck between a rock and a hard place. Her best offer meant I'd lose 75 cents on each jar. And I just couldn't go that low.

But after ten days of nervous waiting, I called her back. I made sure to stand up before she answered, but I'm sure I was sitting down by the time I caved in and accepted her pathetic offer. When I shipped out those four thousand cases of perfectly good Sweet Hot Peppas at a net loss of $36,000, I was embarrassed. I'd never been inside a Big Lots store before and was just hoping that none of my customers shopped there either. Once someone pays $2.49 for a jar that normally sells for $7.99, it will be a while before they're willing to pay full price again.

A month later, I was eating lunch at Matt's in the Market when its chef, Chet Gerl (now of Gracia in Ballard), came over to me, smiling ear to ear. "You won't believe where I found your Sweet Hot Peppas? I bought every jar on the shelf! What a steal." True confession. Ever since, I've have been known to shop at Big Lots scouting for awesome deals.

With those 50,000 jars of Sweet Hot Peppas I made for BJ's gone, I could now focus on finding new customers for the 9,000 buckets of peppers in oil I had left. The next show Mama Lil's exhibited at targeted the dairy, bakery, and deli sections of grocery stores, which included olive bars. While Mama Lil's sold well in olive bars in the Pacific Northwest, I was still trying to figure out how to crack the national market for olive bars. At the show I learned from people in the business that two middlemen companies held exclusive arrangements with the major grocery store chains. If I wasn't doing business with either of them, I was told my products stood no chance of getting into olive bars outside of the Pacific Northwest. The Peppadews, for instance, were being sold by one of these companies, while a Peppadews knock-off made in Peru was being displayed at the booth of the other middleman. Since there apparently was room for only one crock of peppers at olive bars, this left no space for Mama Lil's in olive bars outside of the Pacific Northwest.

But at the next trade show I did, the buyer of one of those middlemen companies stopped by my booth and showed interest in the buckets he tasted from. The peppers were sixteen months old by then, and I swear they were becoming more delicious. He wasn't concerned that their best-by date was only eight months away, as he thought he could sell them before they expired. But we couldn't work out a deal. Besides not agreeing on a price, he wanted to affix his company's own label right over the Mama Lil's label on the bucket. The nerve of him! Considering I was still sitting on more than 8,500 buckets with a limited shelf life, I'm surprised I held my ground. But darn it, if I allowed him to cover my label, it would've eliminated my hard-earned brand recognition. My mom would never have forgiven me. Even Lil knew: *Brand is everything*.

As my father once told me, "Sometimes the best deals are the ones you don't make."

Aioli

(What to do with Mama Lil's leftover oil)
Erik Brett Cannella, former chef at Matt's in the Market

One of my favorite ways to serve this aioli is on a fish cake with grilled asparagus on the side. This tangy, rich, orange-red aioli is the best possible complement to the fish and veg. I also recommend using it liberally on any kind of sandwich. Note that this recipe calls for only the oil from a jar of Mama Lil's Peppers; put the peppers back in the jar for another use.

Makes about 1 cup

1 (12-ounce) jar of Mama Lil's Peppers in Oil (plus additional as needed)
1/3 cup neutral oil, such as vegetable, avocado, or mild-flavored olive oil
1 to 3 garlic cloves
1 tablespoon fresh lemon juice
½ teaspoon Dijon mustard
Salt
1 egg yolk

Place a strainer in a small bowl. Drain what's left of what's left of a jar of Mama Lil's Peppers through the strainer, into a bowl, and pour the oil into a measuring cup. You should have about ½ cup. Add enough neutral oil to fill the quantity to ¾ cup. (Or, if you're starting with a full jar of peppers, strain off the oil and put the peppers back in the jar and save for tomorrow's pizza.)

Put the garlic, lemon juice, mustard, and a pinch of salt in a food processor (or use a hand blender with a narrow container or jar), and blend until the ingredients are thoroughly combined and the garlic is finely minced.

Add the egg yolk to the garlic mixture and blend. Slowly drizzle in the oil and watch the aioli change into a creamy, unctuous mayonnaise. If it seems too thick, add a few drops of water and blend.

Taste and correct the seasoning with more lemon juice, mustard, or salt as needed.

WHERE THERE'S A WILL

I WAS IN MY OFFICE FOLLOWING UP ON SALES leads after the show, with Chile on my desk keeping me company. Having witnessed me doing this tedious task before, Chile must've wondered why I was wasting my time. He knew that, like himself, luck just appears from thin air. *It's true,* I thought—*all my best accounts found me, not the other way around.* When the phone rang, Chile was startled and looked at me as if to say, "Look, it's luck."

And it *was* luck. The person on the other end of the line was the buyer from Burgerville, a highly regarded Oregon fast-food hamburger chain with forty locations in Oregon and southern Washington. They designed a cheeseburger that featured Oregon's famous Tillamook cheese and Mama Lil's Peppers. What really excited me was they also made an aioli from the leftover oil to spread on the bun! Now the company wanted to put the burger on its seasonal menu.

I excitedly asked the buyer, "How long will the burger be on your menu?"

"Two months."

"Only two months?" This was disheartening. I had a lot of buckets I'd like to sell to these guys. I asked him, "But what if that burger becomes like, a hit?"

"If that burger does especially well, yes, it could become a fixture on our menu."

Now that's what I wanted to hear! My favorite burger in Seattle back then was Zippy's Giant Burgers's No. 11, named for the nearby No. 11 fire station. I did the math: if each of the 40 Burgervilles did as well as Zippy's, that would take me a long way through my tunnel of buckets. (Luckily for my waistline, I delivered four buckets, or four weeks' worth of peppers to Zippy's at a time. That No. 11 burger was so good I'd eat two of them on my drive home.)

Weeks later, my childhood friend Jonny Katz informed me he was in Portland with his sister, Kathy, attending a trade show for her lighting business. Could I come see them? I checked out the Burgerville website. This was the perfect time to drive to Portland. The Mama Lil's cheeseburger had just been put on the menu, and I'd be passing three Burgervilles on the way. Six cheeseburgers later when I crossed the Columbia River into Portland, I was belching up a storm. But I drove right to a Whole Foods store and did a demo where I told everyone, "Burgerville's Mama Lil's cheeseburger is da bomb!"

That evening, starting out from the Pearl District, Jonny led me on an aimless walking tour of the town he'd grown to love over the past several days. As we crossed over a couple of bridges, we passed through several of Portland's leafy neighborhoods, where I'd point out the restaurants that used Mama Lil's Peppers. "It's a toss-up. Does Apizza Scholls or Nostrana have the best pizza in town? ... Le Pigeon's seared foie gras is to die for... You'd love Navarre's cassoulet?" Jonny asked if I'd like to grab a bite at one of these great looking spots, but I told him, "I'm not hungry yet. Let's keep walking."

Jonny and I hadn't spoken in years, so we had a lot to catch up on. He'd just seen an exhibit of African art in Portland that he was especially excited about. It was the first I'd heard that he was not only collecting African ceremonial artifacts himself, but that he'd applied to become the curator of Getty's African collection. I knew Jonny to be an expert in Renaissance art, so it seemed like a major identity shift. "Why African art?" I asked. "It seems so unlike you."

With a look of awe and admiration on his face, Jonny told me, "So much soul has been imparted into these objects that if you spend time with them, they'll speak to you."

"Like how that Grecian urn spoke to Keats?" I was referring to Keats's great ode that Jonny had introduced me to when I was a teenager.

"Exactly. An object so imbued with meaning that its past is alive in the present. It's as if these drums or clubs or whatever used in these ancestral ceremonies, they accumulate magical powers from all the souls who've held them in the past."

"I feel the same way about Lil's meat grinder," I said wistfully. "Every time I cinch it up to the countertop, it performs some magic trick. I'll find my wallet. Or my cat, who I haven't seen in days, will announce herself with a loud meow! Or Mama Lil's will land a huge account."

Jonny laughed his way through some memories of Lil. One vignette that stuck with him was when his family was leaving our house after a bounteous Chanukah feast, Lil slipped Jonny a folded $10 bill, making him feel very special. When he got in the car with his four siblings, they all pulled out their $10 bills that Lil had given them without the others knowing. "Lil loved nothing more than giving gifts to people."

"It's true. It's why she made the peppers. She loved giving them away to the people she loved."

Jonny smiled warmly as he mused, "I wouldn't want to be her enemy, but if Lil loved you, watch out."

Four hours into our walk, I caught a whiff of an all-too-familiar smell and tugged at Jonny's arm, jaywalking us across the street. He didn't know where I was taking him until we walked right into a Burgerville franchise. Jonny was incredulous. "You showed me all those great restaurants that use Mama Lil's, and now you want to eat a burger?"

A minute later, I put two cheeseburgers on our table. I lifted his bun to show off the peppers. "They use them too! I've eaten six of them today. And I'll most likely eat six more on my drive back to Seattle. Two years ago, I got stuck with thirteen thousand buckets. I still own over eight thousand buckets of these peppers that are costing me a fortune to warehouse. I need this burger to be successful and stay on the menu for a year."

Jonny started laughing. "Howie, only you would think you could eat your way out of this. As a kid, you were always getting in trouble. But as I recall, you always got out of it. You'll survive this too. And be a better man for it. It's all been written."

"Did you say, it's all been eaten?"

Jonny laughed. "Yes, all those peppers *will* get eaten. It's been written."

On my way home, I did stop at those same three Burgervilles. I ate my share, but that burger stayed on the menu for only two months. In the end, I sold them a mere two hundred buckets that got me below 7,500.

But Burgerville, I'm telling you now, you quit me too soon.

The Canard Steam Burger
Origin Story

As told by chef-owner Gabriel Rucker
of Portland's Le Pigeon and Canard

The steam burger story starts with a staff meal (or "family meal" in the restaurant biz). I was cruising through the bread aisle in Safeway, thinking about how much I love King's Hawaiian Sweet Rolls and how I wished I could eat more of them, when I thought to myself, "I bet that bread would make one hell of a slider."

I threw eight or nine packs of Hawaiian rolls in the cart, along with a few packages of American cheese and some nice fatty ground chuck. I headed back to the shop and realized I had forgotten pickles!! Luckily, I had a jar of Mama Lil's Bread & Butter Pickles & Peppers on the shelf from a previous beef tartare dish. A quick chop-chop and we had our spicy sweet-pickle relish.

While looking around for the pickles, I came across a package of Lipton's Onion Soup Mix, which seemed like the most perfect thing to season the hamburger with. The aroma coming out of the oven of the meat baking with the rich onion soup was almost too much to take. I wanted to capture that moment, so after pulling the hamburger from the oven, I diced up some white onion and stewed it with the onion soup–flavored beef fat. Imagine the most amazing cheeseburger-flavored onions!!

I knew I was on to something because the interest in the kitchen was high, and people kept commenting on how ready for lunch they were. I might have been a little excited myself as well. Once the burgers were assembled, we all ate way too many to get back to work.

Before the invention of the steam burgers, the idea of opening a third restaurant sounded horrible. But after making and eating them, this germ of an idea started to form in my head. In about three weeks, I had a plan. We could open a low-class-meets-high-class steam burger and oyster bar where my partner, Andy Fortgang, could sell the most amazing bottles of Champagne and Burgundy to go along with my dirty little steamed cheeseburgers, and...Canard was born. Of course, it has turned into so much more. But I always say that the steam burger is the sun that all the other flavor planets revolve around.

Canard Steam Burgers

As **Chef Rucker** notes, "It is sacrilege to eat these with ketchup. Also, they're killer the next day heated in a steamer or the microwave—that's why I've scaled this recipe to make so much. 'Cause leftovers are a beautiful thing." (Feeds 4 to 12 people depending on how hungry they are.)

4 pounds ground beef chuck, 80 percent lean

2 packages Lipton Onion Soup Mix

1 tablespoon salt

3 eggs

1 onion, finely minced

24 slices yellow American cheese

1 cup Mama Lil's Bread & Butter Pickles & Peppers, chopped

1 cup Mama Lil's Peppers in oil (chopped if you like them that way)

2 packages (12 each) King's Hawaiian Sweet Rolls

Yellow mustard

Preheat the oven to 400°F.

In a large mixing bowl, thoroughly combine the ground beef, onion soup mix, salt, and eggs. Spread the mixture onto a baking sheet in an even layer (about ½ inch thick is great).

Bake for 10 to 13 minutes, until the beef is cooked through.

Set a medium saucepan on the stove. Holding the meat in place (you can use the flat of your hand, a pot lid, or another baking sheet to do this), carefully drain the excess fat from the sheet into the pan. Add the minced onions to the pan and simmer over medium heat for 5 or 6 minutes, or until they become tender.

To build the burgers, layer the beef "sheet" with the onions, then top with the cheese slices. Return the baking sheet to the oven and bake for 5 minutes, or until the cheese is mostly melted. Remove from the oven and spread your desired amount of Mama Lil's Bread and Butter Pickles and Mama Lil's Peppers on top of the meat-onion-cheese sheet. Cut the sheet into burger-size squares that roughly match the dimensions of the King's Hawaiian rolls, then place a patty on each of the bottom halves of the rolls.

Squeeze some yellow mustard on the top halves of the rolls, then place these halves atop the burgers.

If you have a steamer (most home kitchens don't—we're spoiled in the restaurant kitchen), pop them in for 30 seconds. If not, put the burgers on a plate, cover them with a slightly damp paper towel, pop them into the oven for a minute or two. Or microwave for 30 seconds.

CLIMBING THAT HILL

JONNY'S ENCOURAGING SPIN ON MY INVENTORY predicament gave me the courage to believe that I had it within me to pull a Houdini and escape out of this tunnel alive. When I returned to Seattle, it *was* easier to sell those buckets. And sell them I did. Not only did I keep ten buckets in a second refrigerator so I could start my day by making deliveries, but I had a two-gallon bucket in my main fridge. And I put the peppers on everything. My favorite quick sauce for pasta was pesto mixed with Mama Lil's Peppers, cherry tomatoes, and canned salmon. The sandwich that I couldn't get enough of was a toasted bagel with goat cheese, smoked salmon, a slice of tomato, and a few pepper rings. To hell with capers. Mama Lil's Peppers with lox *rocks*!

Perhaps most importantly for my bucket sales, Seattle's popular pizzeria chain, Pagliacci, started designing pies that featured Mama Lil's. Its first pizzeria opened in 1979, the same year I went AWOL on the Mississippi River and moved back to Seattle for good. Over the years, I'd spent thousands of dollars on its pizza—many of them while driving a cab, holding a slice in one hand and the steering wheel in the other. So, it was about time Pagliacci was my customer, too.

But so many of these buckets remained in expensive storage that I had no choice but to keep searching for a market for them beyond the Pacific Northwest. I bought a booth space at the National Restaurant Association Show (the other NRA), held at the largest convention center of all—Chicago's McCormick Place. I'd always loved Chicago when as a kid my family would drive there to visit Lil's relatives. Besides all the gussied-up toy stores on Michigan Avenue, what I loved most about Chicago were its hot dogs called *Red Hots*. (They really were red back then.) If anyone asked me what my favorite food was as a kid, I'd say, "A Red Hot with mustard and a pickle in a warm sesame-seed bun."

With this thought in mind, I hoped to accomplish two things at the show. The first was to promote my Honkin' Hot PeppaLilli as the ultimate hot dog relish. (Though the peppers in oil are good on dogs, too!) Second, considering that Chicago is a steak-and-chops town, I wanted to plant the seed for using Mama Lil's Peppers as a condiment to be served with steak. I discovered soon enough that Chicago is set in its ways of what you dare put on a hot dog. But on the first day of the show, I shared my peppers with the fine folks from Niman Ranch, a famous meat company that produces top-quality, humanely raised animals. They loved the peppers and happily grilled some cuts of steak for me to demo with my peppers.

By now, I knew the best way to attract people was through their noses. For this purpose, I opened three buckets of peppers in oil on my display table. If you were within twenty yards of my booth and loved savory food, you couldn't help but be lured over by the tangy, garlicky, peppery aroma. I was multi-tasking, slicing meat, making hors d'oeuvres, scanning badges, taking orders, while those bites of steak with pepper rings swiftly met their fate with the grazers walking the floor.

On the second day of the show, a woman I'd never met before walked up to my booth and gave me a hug. "I'm so glad you're here!" she said, grinning at me. "I've missed Mama Lil's since I moved from Seattle. I'm Rita Dever, the creative director of a group of fifty Chicago restaurants called Lettuce Entertain You. Do you have distribution in Chicago? If not, maybe I can help."

Oh, lovely Rita, where would I be without you? After the show, she took a couple of cases of jars and what remained of those three buckets to her test kitchen where all the Lettuce Entertain You chefs, who were each responsible for the menus at their own restaurants, could try them. Before long, many of these chefs began using the peppers in creative ways—blending them into a sauce for a layer in lasagna, a dip for calamari, or as a condiment for myriads of entrées. In the end, Mama Lil's gained three distributors while I was in Chicago.

Next up, I rented a booth at the Summer Fancy Food Show in New York City. To save on hotel expenses, I'd often book red-eye flights, and arrive on the morning of the show to set up my booth. But this time I got stuck in the security line and missed my flight. This meant I'd be absent on the busiest day of the three-day show, and, for all I know, be fined for not being there.

Then I thought of my friend Joshua Smith, who often asked me to take him to the Fancy Food Show sometime. Joshua, a young chef of boundless energy, had been a devoted friend ever since I met him when he was a teenage cheese monger. Now ten years later he was living in Boston and had worked his way up the ladder to become a chef at Boston's Four Seasons Hotel. Even though it was 2 a.m. in Boston and I knew Joshua was in bed next to his pregnant wife, I was desperate, so I called him.

"How you doin', bro?" Joshua groggily answered.

"Well, you know how you've asked me to take you to the Fancy Food Show sometime? Now would be a really good time. But here's the deal: You've gotta get out of bed, like right now, drive to Manhattan, sneak into the show without a badge, and set up my booth by 9 a.m." It was a huge ask and I did not take him seriously when he said he'd think it over.

The next afternoon, I was wheeling my luggage through the bustling aisles of the food show when I saw people swarming around the space where my booth was supposed to be. But as I fought through the crowd, I realized that all those people were clamoring to get the attention of the people working at the booth next to me. But there was Joshua in front of my booth among these people who were paying no attention to him as he offered them samples of Mama Lil's peppers.

I slapped Josh on the back. "Wow! Thanks for coming, Josh! But what the hell is going on in the booth next door?"

Joshua held up an aluminum foil pouch. "Black garlic. And this here is liquid black garlic. I only slept an hour last night, but this stuff has kept me going all day."

Black garlic had just been introduced to the market, and this was its very first tradeshow, but apparently it was already the rage. For the next two days, those black garlic drinks, placebo effect or not, kept me going as I fended off the people obscuring my products as they tried to place orders or get their badges scanned at the black garlic booth. To combat the crowd, I stood in front of my booth like a bear in a stream of salmon, casting my array of cheesy lines to lure somebody—*anybody*—to try my peppers. "A peppa for your thoughts? The peppatunities are endless! You gotta mama, I gotta mama…" When I barked for the hundredth time, "Who would like to try the most delicious peppers on the planet?" I caught a live one.

Making his way through the crowd was a short, well-dressed man in a slick suit, thin stylish tie, and bright red shirt with ruffles on his cuffs. He immediately picked up one of my jars and examined it, then asked me with a strong French accent, "Are zeez zee most delicious peppers on zee planet?"

"Yes, the spicy peppers in oil are our most popular product."

"Sure, let me try zoze."

I put some peppers on a cracker, handed it to him on a napkin, then gave him my well-practiced spiel. "These come in foodservice sizes too. Just awesome on pizza and sandwiches…"

"On sandwiches, you say?" With a smirk on his face, he took a dainty bite. Then he spit the peppers into a napkin, wiped off his lips, and then tried to give the napkin back to me. Barely disguising a sneer, he told me, "Zeez are not zee most delicious peppers on the planet! *I* have zee most delicious peppers on zee planet! Everyone on zee planet knows zat."

"Really? What peppers do you have?"

"My Peppadews are zee most delicious peppers on zee planet!"

Holy shit. I'd heard this South African company was owned by a Frenchman. And here was Count Peppadew himself standing right in front of me—or was he Pepé le Pew dressed as a musketeer, ruffles and all. I imagined his hand was on his sword. I know my hand was on my sword when I asked him, "What's in that brine of yours anyway?"

Pepé puffed out his chest. "Zat brine is our *secret sauce!*"

It was as if I'd been waiting my whole life to tell him, "Pal, people with secrets have got something to hide! Your secret sauce is sucrose. Or is there corn syrup in there, too?"

When Count Peppadew's heels clapped together, I thought he might be readying himself for a duel. But he just dropped the napkin at my feet and did an about face. I stared daggers at him as he brusquely squirmed his way through the crowd of black garlic admirers. He tripped on someone's foot and almost fell. But no such luck.

By the harvest of 2007, I still owned 7,000 buckets. So even with the new foodservice business, it would be a while, if ever, before I needed to make more of them. Only the Imperials still grew goathorn peppers for Mama Lil's, all of which went into making retail jars for Mama Lil's product line.

In mid-November 2007, I delivered a bucket of peppers to Brad's Swingside Café. While he was writing me a check, he happened to look at its lid. "Hey, this bucket is expired. As of yesterday." Brad pulled off its lid. "What that date means is—" He dipped his nose into the bucket, and said as if overwhelmed by the fragrance, "—they've acquired *soul.*"

When Gary Stonemetz and I made those buckets in 2005, I had expected all of them to be eaten by Panera customers within a year, not still sitting in cold storage after two years. We only gave them a two-year shelf life. Gary told me we could've added another year if I had saved accurate records of the four-gallon buckets I made in 2000—which were better than ever at three years old. So Gary, being the adult in the room, refused to extend the best-by date. Just as I was starting to think I was going to make it through this suffocating tunnel alive, I had a new issue keeping me awake at night.

Since this happened almost twenty years ago, I assume it's safe to divulge that as I made my way through those thousands of buckets, Stonemetz turned his back when I slyly printed new best by labels, with the same production codes but with two more years added to their shelf life. On my bi-weekly trips to Sunnyside to pick up more buckets, often with Jean Sherrard beside me snapping photographs, we'd take Canyon Road through the stunningly tranquil landscape the Yakima River carved out. When we arrived at the cannery Jean would distract Stonemetz at his desk, while I surreptitiously slapped two more years of shelf life onto 160 buckets before loading them in my van.

To vary the scenery, I sometimes took Chinook Pass on the way back to Seattle. It added to the length of the trip—but how could I not be emboldened when suddenly I'd turn a corner and there it was—the grandeur of the godlike Mount Rainier? As I recall, the music I listened to most during these many drives (when ball games weren't on) was Lucinda Williams' album *Car Wheels on a Gravel Road* and Bob Dylan's *Blood on the Tracks.* My much-overplayed theme song was "Buckets of Rain."

As I pounded the pavement in search of new customers, with *all of them buckets comin' out of my ears,* slowly but surely, more local restaurants and grocery stores that made sandwiches, pizza, salads, and pasta dishes started using Mama Lil's, and were now naming the peppers as an ingredient on their signboards and menus. After fifteen years, Mama Lil's was now well known enough that there was no better way to describe its flavor than by using its brand name—the best advertising I could have ever hoped for. Then Joshua Smith found two more distributors for Mama Lil's in New England. And the speed of that drinking song had accelerated so it sounded like a soulful Irish jig. And I can only think this was because the peppers *were* just getting better with age. They *were* acquiring more soul!

In January 2008, I attended yet another Winter Fancy Food Show in San Francisco where I was approached by two major foodservice distributors in Northern California who wanted to stock the buckets. But my favorite new account was Lombardi's Gourmet Deli & BBQ in Petaluma, California. Lee Lombardi noticed my peppers and instantly fell in love with them—not only because he liked their flavor, but also because his own beloved mother was named Lil. (Yes, I've noticed that Mama Lil's are very popular with sons of Lil.) Soon, Lee was telling his customers that Mama Lil's was his own brand, named after his own Mama Lil! Which was fine by me, as he ordered buckets by the pallet for his popular #8 Mama Lil's Tri-tip sandwich.

At this show, I often wandered over to the booth across the aisle from me, where an Iowa hog farmer and his wife were serving the most delicious white bacon I'd ever tasted. As we munched on each other's products, we talked about the Iowa caucuses, stoking our irrational exuberance that the young, eloquent upstart, Obama, might just win the nomination. By the time we packed up, I had three pounds of their bacon, and they had a case of Honkin' Hot PeppaLilli. When I returned home from the 2008 show, I was encouraged enough by my foodservice sales that even though I still had over 4,000 two-gallon buckets from 2005 sitting in cold storage, I asked Manuel Imperial and Wayne Inaba to increase their goathorn yield for the upcoming harvest by 50 percent.

Then in May 2008, I went back to the Chicago restaurant show. While slicing Niman steaks behind my booth, I spotted four young women relishing my steak appetizers while watching the Mama Lil's Food Network episode on a monitor. I overheard one of them say, "I loved Mama Lil's on our steak sandwich! Why don't we use them anymore?" Then I noticed her badge. She worked at Panera Bread's corporate office in St. Louis. In fact, all these women worked there, where they would've eaten only the real Mama Lil's Peppers on their sandwiches. "Hey, you're the guy in the video!" one of them said. "I'd love to buy a jar and have you sign it for me."

"Hey, do any of you know why Panera stopped using Mama Lil's on your steak sandwich?" I asked them. None of them knew, but they all said they missed the peppers, and asked if they could buy some jars from me. These women were not my enemies. All four of them walked away with free jars.

Panera Bread was obviously out to make its presence known at this year's restaurant show. I spotted dozens of people with Panera on their badges. A well-dressed, kindly, middle-aged man appeared and wanted to shake my hand. "I own thirty Panera Breads in Minnesota. Whenever I'd visit one of my cafés, I'd always make a sandwich for myself. And I always put Mama Lil's on it. I miss Mama Lil's Peppers." This guy was certainly not my enemy.

"Any idea why you stopped using Mama Lil's?" I asked him as he ate a sample.

"Not entirely. But I complained to the folks in corporate when they did! Not that they listen to us independent cafe owners. But what I will say is that in the world of food franchises, there is a triumvirate of authority. The buyer. The quality assurance manager. And the head chef. In that order. Word has it that the QA manager and the buyer teamed up against Mama Lil's. Buyers don't like dealing with single-source suppliers in part because they can't play vendors against one another. The chefs seemed to want Mama Lil's, but they don't have the clout of the buyer. Hey, can I buy a jar from you to bring as a gift to my wife?"

That very kind and very decent man walked away with two gifts.

In the last hour of the show, I was starting to pack up when I noticed two smartly dressed, corporate country-club types watching the Roker episode at my booth. One seemed to be enjoying it while the other had a smirk on his face. As I got closer, I could read their badges. They were also from Panera. Then I stepped in front of them so I could read their names.

The smirking man was none other than my own true enemy, Buyer Mike.

From his point of view, I must've looked like the fool he took me for, with my pepper-themed apron, Mama Lil's T-shirt, olive oil-stained hat, and long hair that he made go gray! Without pause, I walked out of my booth and extended my hand to him. He was hesitant, for good reason. As we shook hands, I forced a smile and looked him in the eye, so he had no choice but to smile back. Then I tightened my grip, as if channeling Jake LaMotta, itching for a fight.

"Mike, I can't tell you how much misery you've brought me over the last few years of my life. Even in business, God damn it, you've got to be kind."

Mike sneered at me as he tried to pull his hand away.

With my left hand, I took a jar from my display. "Mike, would you like to take a jar home with you for your wife?" He pulled his hand away from me, abruptly turned and walked away, shaking out his sore fingers. I saw him utter one word to his colleague walking beside him: "Asshole." Hearing this, I cathartically cackled to myself. I'd gained weight since I started eating my way through all those buckets. But after encountering my two greatest nemeses, Count Peppadew and now Buyer Mike, at least my spirit felt lighter.

Like I'd shed twenty pounds of old-fashioned piss and vinegar.

After the restaurant show, I went to Ohio to visit Lil's friend, Ellie Katz, as her children, my childhood friends Nicky and Kathy Katz, would also be in town. When I arrived, I gave Ellie some jars of Kick Butt Peppers. As she put them in her pantry, she told me in her gentle, soft-spoken voice, "Howie, every time I eat your peppers, it brings Lil back."

Over dinner, I overheard Nick and Kathy discuss their older brother Jonny's health. Kathy said, "His disease is so rare it doesn't even have a name. It's an orphan disease."

"I'm an orphan now—I hope I don't get it," I joked rather insensitively, to some eye rolls. But Ellie put a positive spin on my thoughtlessness. "Howie, the only antidote for orphanhood is having your own children."

"Fat chance that. I'm 52 years old."

As I picked up tidbits of the Katz family discussing Jonny's mysterious illness, I flashed on "The Extraction of the Stone," an imaginatively ambitious story of Jonny's that I'd read thirty years ago. I could even recite its opening epigraph taken from some Arabic text: "A foolish man rides here. With my saddle. And on my camel!" The story is about a man who has a terrible head-ache, and we follow him through Paris on his way to meet the doctor who can diagnose his condition. The doctor, who may be Lazarus himself, discovers an object growing inside his head, but it's not a tumor—it's a rare stone that grew "from the ingrown follicle of human folly itself." Just like the character in his story, Jonny had developed a disease so rare that it couldn't be identified. Jonny, has it all been written? And did you write it?

My phone rang, and I stepped away from the dinner table to take the call. It was from Gary Johnson, who owned the cannery in Sunnyside, informing me that Gary Stonemetz's wife, Margie, had suddenly passed away. My heart sank. My parents were gone, and now I realized that stage of life had begun when friends started dying, too.

Later that year, Gary Stonemetz took a month off work to go to Kenya with his pastor to visit an orphanage sponsored by his church. I was nervous he wasn't going to make it back for the 2008 pepper harvest, where an estimated fifty tons of goathorns were ripening in the fields. But men like Gary were born to produce, and he made sure to return in time.

But how was I going to allocate the fifty tons of peppers my farmers ex-pected to yield this year? It was a gamble I was forced to take every year. The three thousand expired buckets still in cold storage were holding up well, but since I was now selling on average four hundred buckets a month, for the first time in four years I needed to make more buckets. As for what to do with the remaining tonnage of peppers, I gambled by quadrupling the number of half-gallon jars of Sweet Hot Peppas over what I'd made the year before. I hoped that this product, with its higher profit margin and no waste product, would catch on as a foodservice item for restaurants. Then, bingo! Right after the harvest, two local gourmet pizza chains, Zeeks and Tutta Bella, each designed pies featuring them. Before long, both of those pizzas were selling like gangbusters.

After fifteen years in business, finally I'd correctly predicted the future.

If Panera Bread represented 80 percent of my business when I lost that account, in three years' time the other 20 percent of my business had now more than doubled. Mama Lil's also achieved a healthier balance between the foodservice and retail sides of the business. And since I was now selling half of my jars directly to customers via farmers' markets and off the website, Mama Lil's was profitable again, albeit with me as the only full-time employee.

But now, from my perspective, the whole country had been led on a bumpy ride through a long, nightmarish tunnel that included a pointless war in Iraq and now a deep recession. At the end of the 2008 harvest, I made a bet with my farmer friend Manuel Imperial that Barack Obama would beat John McCain in the 2008 election, with the loser buying dinner at the restaurant of the loser's choice. It only seemed right that I brought along a jar of Mama Lil's up to the top of the Space Needle's famous spinning restaurant with the greatest view in town. Manuel and I both ordered New York steaks. But wouldn't you know I was beaten to the punch as those perfectly grilled steaks were already garnished with the most perfectly aged, three-year-old spicy pickled goathorns in oil.

Who Needs Pimentos?

Rita Dever

Mama Lil's gives a bright, spicy kick to this dip with its mildly spicy goathorn peppers. This makes a great appetizer dip with crackers and crudités, but it has multiple uses—try putting a dollop in your scrambled eggs or mac and cheese. And it's awesome on a toasted cheese sandwich or your favorite burger!

Makes about 3 cups

¾ cup Hellmann's mayonnaise
¼ cup cream cheese
3 cups freshly shredded sharp cheddar cheese
¼ cup, plus 1 tablespoon Mama Lil's Mildly Spicy Peppers in Oil, drained and finely chopped
1½ teaspoons canned finely chopped chipotle pepper
1 tablespoon thinly sliced scallions

Place the mayonnaise and cream cheese in the bowl of a food processor and blend until smooth. Add the cheddar cheese, ¼ cup of the Mama Lil's Peppers, and the chipotle pepper. Pulse until blended but not smooth; it should still be chunky.

Transfer the dip to a bowl. Stir in the scallions and the remaining 1 tablespoon of Mama Lil's Peppers if you want a little more kick. Enjoy!

Photos of Yakima River by Jean Sherrard

THE AUDACITY OF HOPE

Right after that momentous presidential election in 2008, I went on a date with an acquaintance named Lisa, who told me a sad story about her adopting an infant whose birth mom changed her mind and then took him back. I could tell that Lisa was still grieving her loss, so I took her down to the basement to meet Chile. When that magical creature appeared on the ceiling pipes to appreciatively take his almond, I told her, "I had a rough patch in business, then my luck changed. Maybe my luck will rub off on you."

A week later, Lisa received a photo of a boy she'd been matched with. He had been born a month earlier in Bahir Dar, Ethiopia, on the shores of Lake Tana. Now he was in an orphanage in Gondar on the other side of the lake. Lisa and I were just getting to know each other, but I was intrigued by this baby she was adopting. I couldn't help but believe that my luck, Chile's luck, or, for all I know, Reverend Franklin James's blessing *had* rubbed off, facilitating her match.

It was Martin Luther King Jr. Day weekend of 2009, the last day of the Winter Fancy Food Show in San Francisco. As vendors were arriving at the convention center, we all came to a standstill, transfixed by President Obama's inauguration speech broadcast on large screens above the escalators leading down to the show. Had the escalators come to a stop? That's how I remember it. As all of us stood there watching this monumental moment, I couldn't help but peek at the photo on my phone of this baby boy Lisa was adopting, also of East African descent. When Obama was sworn in, a cheer went up, and throngs of happy attendees descended into the halls of commerce. A recession was going on, but at that show, the buyers were buying.

When the time finally came for Lisa to retrieve her five-month-old baby boy, she asked me to go to Ethiopia with her. I was certainly tempted, but it was hard enough to escape my business for a few days, let alone for two whole weeks. Besides, although we discussed the possibility of me becoming his dad, we hadn't made any firm decision yet. But I found myself very involved in helping choose his name. Since she'd be bringing him back on Passover, when the custom is to save a seat at the seder for the prophet Elijah, and since Lisa's Aunt Elizabeth had just died and left her with the money to pay for the adoption, I suggested we name him Elijah, with his Ethiopian name Getachew becoming his middle name.

I dropped off Lisa and her friend at the airport, and then *abracadabra*, two weeks later she walked out of the terminal with a baby boy strapped to her belly. When I stuck out my hand toward Elijah, he grabbed my thumb and put it in his mouth like he owned it. And I fell in love.

Six weeks later, in May 2009, I was getting ready to go back to the National Restaurant Association Show in Chicago. I still wasn't sure if I was going to become Elijah's father or not—I felt conflicted. Lisa and I were just getting to know each other, and like Lil had told me, wasn't I too old to be a dad? Before I left for the show, Lisa insinuated (rightfully so) that Chicago would be a good place and time to make up my mind about committing to becoming Elijah Getachew's father. Or not.

How wonderful it was to be in sunny Chicago in early May. The city was still abuzz with pride that its native son had become the first Black president of the United States! Inside McCormick, I was once again serving steak-and-pepper bites at my booth to great fanfare. But admittedly, I found myself less interested in scanning badges than in flipping open my phone and showing off Elijah's photo. Whether I knew it or not, I fell more in love with this boy every time I saw his face. But when Chef Myron saw his photo, he looked at me askance. "They're cute now. But you have no idea what you're getting yourself into. You're no spring chicken, mama."

After the second day of the show, Myron and I attempted to nab a cab at McCormick Place's front entrance amid the chaotic throngs of people trying to get back to their hotels. A cab stopped in front of us to let a person walk by. Seizing the opportunity, I flung the door open and both of us slid in. This completely surprised a smartly dressed sixty-year-old woman sitting in the backseat. I told her we'd drop her off first and pay for her fare, and we were off. Making small talk, I asked her what I asked everybody at the show: "Are you attending? Or exhibiting?"

Without a drop of irony, she answered, "I'm here because…I'm Betty Crocker."

Myron acted starstruck. "You're *Betty Crocker*? Wow! What an illustrious trio we have here. I'm Chef Myron and this is Mama Lil himself."

I said, "Betty, I have a very important question, since you might be one of the most famous people I've ever met," I then pulled out my phone, which she must've assumed was because I wanted to take a selfie with her. So, she was happily surprised when instead I showed her Elijah's photo. "Could you tell me if I should become this boy's dad? Or not?"

She gazed thoughtfully at Elijah. "I can recommend what cake to bake for his birthday. But I can't tell you whether to become his daddy. That's a lifelong commitment."

Myron added, "That's what I've been telling him. He has no idea what he's getting into."

Before getting out of the cab, Betty said to me, "But he sure is a beauty."

As the door shut, Myron said, "Don't listen to her. Betsy never baked a cake in her life." Betty Crocker, like Jane Withers' character of Josephine the Plumber, was baked up by an advertising firm in 1921. This Betty was a calligrapher who'd been signing Betty Crocker's name in General Mills' cookbooks for twenty years.

Despite my distraction with this big decision that I hadn't made up my mind about yet, Mama Lil's had a decent show. My best lead was from the buyer for the Midwest region of Whole Foods; she ordered Mama Lil's Peppers for all thirty of its stores' salad bars, where she planned to mix them in with mozzarella cheese balls. (A nice combo!)

At the end of the last day, I was weaving my hand truck through the madhouse of people flocking to the convention center's exits. As always, I'd made my flight reservations too close for comfort. Knowing there'd be a quagmire at the main entrance, I redirected my hand truck toward a distant exit sign in hopes of catching a cab there. But when I opened the door, I realized I'd picked the wrong exit entirely. I was in a tunnel used exclusively for tradeshow buses. Taxis weren't allowed here. I was going to miss my flight! Turning tail, I frantically wheeled my boxes back into the convention center when, out of the corner of my eye, I spotted a yellow cab racing through the tunnel, and ran back in. "Stop!" I screamed.

The cab came to a screeching halt. The driver jumped out and yelled, "Quick, quick!" We threw my stuff in the trunk, and I jumped in. "To O'Hare." I told him. "And if you get me there on time," I then dropped a $100 bill on his seat, "You can keep the change."

"Really?" he said, inspecting the $100 bill. Then we were on our way.

I could tell from my cab driving days that my driver had Ethiopian facial features, like many of my cabbie colleagues. I leaned forward to show him Elijah's photo on my phone. "My girlfriend adopted this boy from Ethiopia. I'm thinking of becoming his dad."

The cab driver looked intently at the photo on my phone, then broke into a jubilant smile. "Really? You're thinking of becoming this boy's father? Where in Ethiopia is this boy from?"

"Uh, I think, Gondar."

The cabbie looked at me in the rearview mirror with his eyes gleaming. "Really?! That boy is from Gondar. Let me see him again." As he looked at the photo more closely, he smiled even more joyously. "This beautiful boy even looks like he's from Gondar." I sat back in my seat and enjoyed the ride as the cabbie, smiling the whole way, weaved around cars, determined to earn his tip. As we approached the airport terminal, he looked at me in the mirror again. "I'm curious. This boy from Gondar, what's his name?"

"His first name is now Elijah. But his Ethiopian name was Getachew."

The cabbie was pulling up to the curb when he whipped his head around to look at me right in the eye. "*Really*? This boy is from Gondar, and his name is Getachew?"

"*Was* Getachew. Getachew is now his middle name."

"That's close enough for me," the cabbie said as he hopped out and helped me load my heavy boxes onto a cart. Then he wanted to shake my hand, which I assumed was because of the $50 tip I gave him. But I was wrong. He'd put the $100 bill back into my palm.

"I can't take your money," he said, staring at me with wide eyes.

I guffawed, "Why can't you take my money?"

"Because *my* name is Getachew. And I am from Gondar!"

"*Really*?!" I said, my jaw dropping dumbstruck.

He looked at me as if he had just witnessed a miracle. Then I dropped the $100 bill back onto his seat and told him, "You gave me the best cab ride of my life. And I've had a few. Thank you!"

When I got home that night, it was just in time to give Elijah and his mother a hug and kiss before she put him to bed. When Lisa came out of his room, I couldn't wait to tell her, "I thought I was going to miss my flight. Then this cabbie appeared, like an angel. His name was Getachew. And like our Getachew, he was born in Gondar!"

Lisa wasn't impressed. "Elijah wasn't born in Gondar. He was born in Bahir Dar on the south side of Lake Tana. His first orphanage was in Gondar, on the north side of Lake Tana."

I pondered this fact for a life-spanning second, then confidently told her. "Born in Bahir Dar. First home in Gondar. Both towns are on Lake Tana. That's close enough for me."

Puttanesca Sauce á la Mama Lil's

Brad Inserra

Brad's Swingside Café was a legendary small Italian restaurant in Fremont (Seattle's funky, hip "Center of the Universe" neighborhood) that closed in 2014 after twenty-five years of serving Italian soul food and dishing out great music to his loyal customers.

Serves 4

⅓ cup olive oil

⅓ cup chopped shallots

¼ cup chopped garlic

¼ cup capers, rinsed

1 (2-ounce) can anchovy fillets, chopped, oil reserved

⅓ cup sliced kalamata olives

⅓ cup sliced green olives

½ cup Mama Lil's Peppers in Oil, oil reserved

1 teaspoon dried thyme

1 teaspoon dried oregano

½ cup dry red wine

1 (14-ounce) can fire-roasted tomatoes with juice

2 tablespoons tomato paste

¼ cup chopped flat-leaf parsley

1 teaspoon dried basil

In a 2-quart stainless steel pot or saucepan over medium-low heat, warm the olive oil. Add the chopped shallots and sauté for 2 minutes, stirring. Add the chopped garlic and sauté another 4 minutes. Then add the capers, anchovies, and the reserved anchovy oil. Stir for about 3 minutes, then add the kalamata olives, green olives, Mama Lil's Peppers, and—why not?—some of the pepper oil from the jar. Sauté for 3 or 4 more minutes; add the thyme and oregano and sauté for 1 more minute.

Add the red wine, stir, and simmer for 3 to 5 minutes to reduce the sauce slightly and cook off the alcohol. Add the tomatoes, tomato paste, parsley, and basil. Sauté on low heat for an additional 15 to 20 minutes, stirring occasionally. Now your Mama Lil's puttanesca sauce is ready for your favorite pasta! It pairs well with seafood—particularly prawns. Buono appetite!

MAMA LIL'S LAST GIFT

December 2009. I was out making deliveries on a dark rainy late afternoon. But I was in a joyful mood for a couple of reasons. When I delivered the very last bucket from 2005, to Brad's Swingside Café, I had reached the light at the end of the tunnel. I hope I gave that bucket to Brad for free as no one enjoyed serving those vintage peppers more than he.

The other reason I was happy was at my next stop, my fourteen-month-old son came crawling toward me when he saw me walk through the nanny's door. With Elijah safely buckled in the seat behind me, we were happily singing and bouncing along to a Paul Simon song, *We brought a brand-new baby back from mainland China... Beautiful."* When my phone rang, I turned the music off. Elijah frowned at me in the mirror as if to say, *how dare you*? But it was Jonny's sister, Kathy. I had to take her call and put it on speaker phone.

When I told Kathy that Elijah was in the car, she said, "Howie, Jonny has been talking a lot about Elijah. When I showed him the photo of him you sent me, Jonny stared at it intently, like he was studying a painting. Then he said, 'Tell Howie that Elijah has a very happy spirit.'"

I chortled, "Doesn't take a perceptive art critic to see that. Elijah's smiling in the photo."

"I suppose not." Kathy said. "But Jonny also said, even though Howie is white, and Elijah is Black, Elijah will grow up to look like Howie."

"Hah! The reason Elijah will be happy is because he knows I'm his dad and he won't have to look like me!" When Kathy laughed, Elijah laughed too, as if he were in on the joke.

Kathy mused over the phone, "Perhaps Jonny enjoys thinking about Elijah because your son is entering Jonny's orbit of family and friends just as Jonny might be departing it."

I asked Kathy, "So, you think Jonny will be hitchhiking on Elijah's spirit?"

Kathy sighed, "It's a beautiful thought, isn't it?" In the mirror, I could see Elijah's thoughtful expression as if he'd been contemplating our conversation. Kathy's voice then became dire. "I'm standing outside Jonny's ICU room. He's been intubated for a week now and has been missing the pleasure of food. Or even a sip of cola on his lips. But this morning I appealed to his imagination. I asked him, 'When we get this fuckin' tube out of your throat, what's the first thing you want to eat? Your favorite Cuban food?' Kathy giggled as she repeated Jonny's answer: 'The first food I want to eat is… Mama Lil's Kick Butt Peppers!"

When Kathy spoke Jonny's words, not only did it elicit a chuckle and joyful tear or two out of me, but I could see in the mirror that Elijah's eyes had squeezed out a tear as well.

By late January of 2010, the toll of being Mama Lil's schlep for so many years had finally caught up with me. On the same day I had triple hernia surgery, Jonny passed away. Even though Ohio was in the grip of a nasty snowstorm, and I hadn't yet been given permission to travel, I booked a flight to attend his memorial service that would be held at the Rodef Sholom synagogue in Youngstown, Ohio, this coming weekend.

As I packed for the trip, I found a photograph I'd taken of Jonny thirty-five years before, when he must've been twenty-three years old. I couldn't even remember having taken the photo. With his thick David-like curls, Jonny is wearing an overcoat standing amid piles of snow in front of the Rodef Sholom synagogue where the service would be held. As I studied the image, I wondered if maybe I'd taken it so Jonny could be standing at that same spot in front of the synagogue thirty-five years later, fixed in time, so he could say goodbye to his family and friends who would be walking past him on their way to his own memorial service. There's a Jonny thought if I ever had one—straight out of a story by one of his favorite writers, Jorge Luis Borges.

As I studied the photographic image it almost felt like Jonny was looking over my shoulder as if pointing out hidden details. What I noted was that Jonny's hands were not tucked into his coat pockets as they'd normally be on a winter's day. Rather, his arms were thrust forward slightly. The way Jonny's black leather gloved fingers were splayed out, it gave the impression that Jonny was getting ready to take flight.

Then I had an idea of how to commemorate Jonny. Since I knew it would be snowing in Ohio, I decided to dress like Jonny in the photo and wear an overcoat and black leather gloves. Going through my closet, I found a moth-eaten wool coat that would suffice. Then I started looking for a pair of black leather gloves. I found three of them—but they were all left-handed! What are the odds of that? I surmised that I kept my keys in my right pocket and lost the right-hand gloves when digging for my keys. Lesson learned: *Don't bring any keys*. I kept searching for a right-hand glove.

In the guest room, Reverend James's former bedroom, I looked in the top drawer of my tall dresser, where I kept precious keepsakes. Hidden under one of my mother's scarves, I found a flat box that looked vaguely familiar. When I opened it, there was a pair of fine black leather gloves that looked like they had never been worn. Then I recalled that Lil had given them to me as a gift on her eightieth birthday just before she had her brain aneurysm. When I put the pair of gloves on my hands and felt just how soft they were, I understood why I had never worn them. They were just too nice, and I must have known I'd lose one. But it was freezing in Ohio, so I stuffed the gloves deep into my overcoat pockets.

Ten hours later, I parked my rental car at the end of the long, snowy Katz driveway lined with cars. I put on the leather gloves, grabbed two jars of Kick Butt Peppers from my suitcase, and shuffled through the snow to the Katz home. I entered through the mudroom door, but the mudroom was filled to the brim with coats, so I hung my coat in the hallway closet inside the house, making sure to stuff the gloves deep inside the pockets again. I didn't want to lose my hat either, so I kept it on my head while I greeted my friends milling around Ellie Katz's kitchen.

The first person to approach me was Ellie, Jonny's still beautiful eighty-four-year-old mother. I offered my condolences and handed her a jar of Kick Butt Peppers. In her soft voice, she told me, "Thank you, Howie. How'd you know I was running low on jars?"

"Like you said, every time you eat the peppers, Lil comes back," I told her tenderly. "And I want to make sure she keeps coming back." I was showing Ellie photos of Elijah when someone pulled my hat off my head. It was my childhood friend, Deacon, the handsome one, whom I hadn't seen in ten years.

"I thought you'd gone bald," Deacon said, primping his own full head of hair.

I told Deacon, "I'm wearing my hat, so I don't lose it. I almost wore my gloves for the same reason."

Then I greeted Nicky, Jonny's younger brother and my best friend from kindergarten. He was a gastroenterologist, and without asking, he pulled up my shirt to examine my sutures from the hernia surgery. "They did a good job," he said as he handed me a copy of the eulogy he'd written for his older brother's memorial service. "Let me know if you have anything to add."

After reading it, I had only one suggestion for his spot-on portrayal of his older brother. "Jonny had no ego. He saw the world so clearly because he had no ego to obscure his view."

I found Jonny's sister, Kathy, in an upstairs bedroom hanging out with her two younger brothers, Jeffrey and Daniel. The room was lit by only a dim lamp and had a séance-like atmosphere. It felt too intimate to enter. But as I closed the door, I swear I caught a glimpse of Jonny sitting with them.

At midnight, I said my goodbyes, then grabbed my coat from the hall closet, and walked through the mudroom door and out into the lovely snow flurries where several high-spirited friends, ambled down the driveway to their cars. As I walked to my rental, I dug into my overcoat pockets. But I only pulled out my left-hand glove. My right pocket was empty.

I'd lost my right-hand glove!

How could I have dropped it? I'd been so careful to stuff both gloves deep into my overcoat pockets. As I frantically searched for the missing glove on the snowy driveway, I had visions of how angry my mom would get when, as a kid, I'd lose scarves, gloves, rings, and mezuzahs she'd given me. How many times had she told me, "You'd lose your head if it weren't screwed on."

I went back into the Katz home through the mudroom door to retrace my steps. I spotted a black glove. But it was left-handed, and not my glove! Flustered, I went to the hallway closet where my coat had been hung and rustled through the coats, hoping my glove would fall to the floor. But no such luck. I was just opening the front door—a door I hadn't passed through all night—when a friend called "goodbye!" from the kitchen. As I waved to them with the left glove in my hand, someone behind me bumped my arm, and the glove fell out of my hand. I turned around to see who bumped into me. No one was there. I then reached down to pick up my dropped glove. There on the floor was—

The left-hand glove, placed perfectly on top of the lost right-hand glove. It looked like the two gloves had reunited and were holding hands.

I hadn't walked through this door before that moment, so this was very mysterious. Like a magic trick that really was magic! I walked straight up to the bedroom where Kathy and her brothers were. "I think Jonny is here," I whispered, as I showed her the two reunited gloves.

Kathy smiled. "Because stuff is being moved around? He's here."

As I walked down the snowy driveway to my car I was still mystified by the reappearance of that glove, so when I sat down behind the wheel, it didn't surprise me that Jonny's presence was waiting for me. With joyful tears streaming down my face, I asked him out loud, "How'd you pull off that magic trick with the glove? And what is the meaning of it?"

His answer came quickly: *When it comes to our imaginations, our most authentic selves, nothing is truly lost.* As I slowly drove to my motel on the snowy, vacant roads of my youth, I found myself still talking out loud to Jonny. "Will I ever hear from you again?"

His spirit chuckled and told me, *"Beats me, I'm new at this."*

Suddenly Lil's spirit spoke up from the back seat. *"You've been to memorial services before. Or weren't you listening to that prayer?"*

I had listened. *As long as we're held in the hearts of the living, none of us truly dies.* And nothing helps to hold people in our hearts more than if we keep saying their names out loud. Isn't that

Jonny Katz, 1973.

right, Mama Lil? And Bobbi, and Harry. And you too, Jonny, who knew more than anyone about the power that can be vested in names and words.

In preparation for my eulogy at Jonny's memorial service I recalled the last stanza of a poem Jonny introduced me to at his house forty years ago—"Ode on a Grecian Urn," by John Keats. And it all came back to me.

When old age shall this generation waste,
Thou shalt remain, in midst of other woe than ours,
A friend to man, to whom thou say'st,
"Beauty is truth, truth beauty,—that is all
Ye know on earth, and all ye need to know."

After the memorial service the following morning, I drove to the cemetery where Jonny's ashes would be placed in a drawer in the small stone chapel. Once the Katz family departed the chapel, I went inside. I'd almost forgotten the two times I'd been to the chapel before. It was such a comforting surprise that the drawer for Jonny's ashes was so close to where my mother's and father's ashes rested. As if to measure the distance between these new neighbors, I touched Lil's and Jonny's drawers with my black leather–gloved hands. Then I had the thought, "*You two were in my car with me last night. Maybe you'll keep each other company. Snack on salata and peppers. Play a little gin rummy.*"

When I got back home to Seattle that evening, it was just before Elijah's bedtime. I was still in recovery from surgery, so he was too heavy for me to lift. With Lisa carrying Elijah we went down to the basement. Chile heard us and appeared on the exposed pipe, patiently waiting for his treat. When Elijah's tiny fingers reached up to offer him an almond, the chinchilla gently took it with his own diminutive fingers. Elijah then clasped his hands in joy and spoke the first word—besides "Mama" and "Dada"—that we'd ever heard come out of his mouth.

"Chile!"

With two-year-old Elijah.

Grilled Eggplant Panini

**Jason Kunkel, fellow baseball dad
and former sous chef of Lampreia**

Grilling the marinated eggplant on a panini grill before you build your sandwich is what makes this panini so awesome, so quick to make, and one of my favorites. You can do this one panini at a time or do what I do: Make a larger supply of the pre-grilled eggplant slices, then keep them in the fridge for up to a week. If you don't use all the eggplant for this sandwich, cut the slices into smaller pieces and add them to a pasta sauce or a grain-based salad. Or dip them in some hummus and eat 'em for a snack.

For this recipe, I buy 2 or 3 large, very dense, firm eggplants, then peel and marinate them (as described below) for several days. Then I grill them all and repackage them for later use. Once the slices are pre-grilled, this panini sandwich can be ready in 2 or 3 minutes.

Makes 1 sandwich.

¼ cup Mama Lil's Peppers in Oil (from one 12-ounce jar), oil included

1 medium globe eggplant, Salt

Handful of fresh arugula or mixed greens

Extra-virgin olive oil

Champagne vinegar

2 tablespoons basil pesto or goat cheese

2 thick slices country bread

To marinate the eggplant (takes 2 to 3 days): Place a small bowl under a colander. Drain the Mama Lil's Peppers into the colander and shake out all the oil into the bowl. Save the peppers for making the sandwich later. Peel the eggplant and slice it into rounds about ½ inch thick. Sprinkle both sides with salt, and drizzle both sides with the Mama Lil's pepper oil. Put the slices into a container with a tight-fitting lid. Turn the container a few times to coat them evenly with the oil. Refrigerate for 2 to 3 days, turning the container occasionally.

To make the panini: When you're ready to make your sandwich, preheat a panini grill and place the eggplant slices on it in a single layer. Grill for 7 to 10 minutes, or until they are cooked through with nice char marks from the grill. Remove from the heat and let cool. Wipe the grill clean.

In a bowl, toss arugula with a drizzle of olive oil and a splash of Champagne vinegar. Set aside.

Spread a little pesto or goat cheese on the bottom slice of bread. Top with a layer of grilled eggplant, then the peppers. Top with the other slice of bread. Grill for 5 minutes, or until the panini is golden and nicely crisped. Remove from grill and let cool slightly. Lift off the top slice of bread, then pile on some of the lightly dressed greens. Reassemble, cut into halves, and serve hot.

BACK ON TRACK

THE NEXT MORNING, I WENT DOWN TO MY OFFICE. Chile was waiting for me by the phone as if to forewarn me that several voicemails had come in. One of them was from Wayne Inaba, who was wondering how many peppers he should plant in his greenhouses. I hadn't been thinking about my business since I made over a dozen deliveries in one day before my hernia surgery. For more than four and a half years, all I'd ever thought about was selling those thousands of buckets. But as Jonny had predicted, those peppers did get eaten and they were now in the past. But I had to confront the future and become a fortune teller again. How many peppers to grow this year?

I consulted my QuickBooks to see if it could provide any clues. Its numbers confirmed my intuition: It was my local business—where shipping costs were taken out of the equation—that was accelerating. Every aspect of my local sales—retail, wholesale, foodservice, gift baskets—was showing steady growth of 50 percent over the previous year. Why wouldn't it? In eighteen years, I'd never let up on getting the peppers into people's mouths. The sweat equity of all those demos and farmers markets had accumulatively added up and now were paying off. So, in 2010, I asked all my farmers to increase their yields by another 50 percent.

I would've asked them to grow more if my QuickBooks hadn't also revealed that I was failing in my efforts to expand the Mama Lil's brand in any significant way beyond the Pacific Northwest. Now, Mom, I know you fantasized about your name being on grocery shelves throughout the whole country. But dream on. At one point, Mama Lil's whole line was in every Whole Foods store in the country. But no matter how many demos I did, it was never enough. Those jars just got lost amid the thousands of other brands crowded onto the shelves—which were also inevitably discontinued. There was no way to win this game. The House always wins.

Naming my business after Lil certainly gave me that extra oomph of motivation to make the brand be associated with the highest quality. And maybe, just maybe, Lil pulled a string or two for me from the great beyond in a last-ditch effort to make her son successful. But then the magic ended. Her name didn't help sell jars outside of the Pacific Northwest any more than Jane

Withers' endorsement did. Nor, for that matter, did Julie Paschkis' gorgeous labels that made Mama Lil's line the most attractive jars on anybody's shelves. (Although her labels may have to do with why folks *keep* buying them. And of course, it's why they make such beautiful gifts.)

But outside the Pacific Northwest I was bleeding stores, as grocery chains weren't reordering the jars.

The problem wasn't the product, it was the market. When I sold my jars to select stores outside the Pacific Northwest that put their own branded labels on them (in other words, to *private label*)—such as Joe Leone's store in Point Pleasant Beach, New Jersey (still doing it), or Chris Cosentino's salumeria Boccalone (now defunct)—those stores were motivated to sell pallets of those jars. (It's worth noting that, to protect my brand, I agreed to private label only if the label stated somewhere, made for them by Mama Lil's.)

That might be the biggest lesson to be taken from my experience, and I may as well divulge it now so I can get on with the story. *Despite everyone's initial ambitions, your products don't have to go national to be successful. Due to the nature of grocery stores' demands for free fills and chargebacks, it is nearly impossible to succeed in them nationally. But it's okay to be a local gourmet foods business with a regional market, often based on regional cuisine.* In Mama Lil's case, the real raison d'être was how well the goathorn peppers grow in the Yakima Valley.

While exhibiting at the National Fiery Foods and Barbecue Show in Albuquerque, I encountered several jarred products that featured the exceptional New Mexican Hatch chile peppers. But you will rarely find these jars on grocery shelves outside of the Southwest. Not that it wasn't attempted, as at one point I saw jars of Hatch chiles in Seattle grocery stores. But not for long, because no matter how good they were, they just didn't sell that well. (But like everything else, luckily those fabulous products now can be found on the Internet.) The point is that regional gourmet food businesses can exist and flourish in the same way as local microbreweries can, where being small—and devoted to quality above all else—can be a recipe for success. You may not become rich, but you can make an honest and gratifying living.

I knew of many local one-man (and woman) brands whose products were canned at Wolf Pack but sold only at farmers' markets. These producers made a decent living and got the extra social benefit of being outdoors amid an appreciative community. Some of these small producers made the same products I did from the Pickles and Relish chapter in the *Joy of Cooking* book.

And why not? Those recipes are tried-and-true American classics that are beyond yum—especially if made the old-fashioned way. In fact, since cucumbers and onions grow well in most regions of the country, I urge people to make these same pickle and relish recipes, not only for themselves, but also even to sell at their local farmers' markets. For that reason, I've included the recipe for our Honkin' Hot PeppaLilli on these pages. It is fun to make. And beyond yum. And who knows? Maybe you'll be inspired.

Although I was now content to be a local brand, I continued to attend trade shows to court national business. But by this stage, with twenty years under my belt, I was far more discriminating about which stores I was willing to sell my products to. Before I said yes, I'd ask them if they'd display the jars on their cheese or meat counters, so they stood half a chance of getting noticed. Otherwise, if they would just be gathering dust high on the condiment shelves, what was the point? There's another lesson I learned too late in the game: *When I started saying no to unpromising accounts, I increased my profit margins.*

By the pepper harvest of 2011, I was determined to make enough of my product to grow by yet another 50 percent, albeit locally. We packed seven thousand buckets of Peppers in Oil, two thousand cases of half-gallon jars of Sweet Hot Peppas, and several thousand cases of retail-size jars. I also increased the PeppaLilli and Bread & Butter Pickles over the year before in Wolf Pack's kettles. And Mama Lil's paid for all of it without my taking a loan against my house.

Photo © Jean Sherrard

Near the end of the harvest, I was beyond honored when one of Seattle's favorite local gourmet pizzeria chains, Pagliacci, held its corporate retreat at a winery in Zillah in the heart of the Yakima Valley and I was asked to be its tour guide. I'd been doing business with Pagliacci for five years and they always praised Mama Lil's consistent quality. I'd say the same thing back, as I'd been eating their pizza for thirty years.

Our first stop on the tour was the Inaba pepper fields. With Mount Adams looming like a scoop of luscious ice cream melting on the horizon, the thirty pizzeria managers watched the bucolic sight of the pepper pickers walking with full buckets of peppers balanced on their heads. When minutes later, I pointed out where the organic onion fields were, Matt Galvin, the enthusiastic CEO and co-owner of Pagliacci, called out like a Boy Scout leader to his loyal staff, "Follow me to the onions!" Before I could stop them, his troops eagerly followed their general into the Valley of "SHIT"! They all got an ankle-deep lesson in organic farming—where steer manure was used as fertilizer.

Gary Stonemetz had the cannery set up so the "Pizza Pie People" would witness the three-day process of making Mama Lil's from start to finish. I convinced a manager to give the apple corer a whirl, and the eight women on the line giggled at his ineptitude. When Ramon emptied bins of pickled peppers from a forklift into pallet-sized colanders, I got to explain to the observant managers how important it was to let the peppers drain for at least twenty-four hours.

Minutes later we moved to where our crew, led by lovely Elena, was filling the buckets of pickled peppers with oil. When someone asked, "How long do the peppers need to be in the oil to achieve its flavor?"

Elena said with a chuckle, "I'll defer to Howard for that one."

I said, "Ideally, at least three years—"

Gary, smiling ear to ear, butted in, "But four is even better."

Between 2006 and 2012, Mama Lil's didn't attract another national restaurant customer the likes of Panera Bread, and I didn't want one. I was fearful of cutthroat corporate buyers, and whether it was true or not, I had this suspicion that an unseen hand of corruption factored into buyers' decisions. I wanted the foodservice portion of my business to grow again, but now I focused my full attention on growing it locally, which included Northern California. By 2012, enough chefs were asking for Mama Lil's that soon every major food distributor in Seattle, Portland, and, to a lesser extent, San Francisco, and Chicago, were carrying our buckets. (When Mama Lil's garnered new restaurant accounts outside of these regions, it was attributable, not surprisingly, to chefs sharing the peppers with their colleagues in other cities in the country.)

With Mama Lil's popularity spreading like gossip, I wasn't totally surprised when a producer from the Food Network's Cooking Channel informed me that it was interested in doing an episode on Mama Lil's. Getting more free advertising on TV was great—but if I could help it, I didn't want this to be like every other food show with people standing around saying, "Yum!" I wanted it to be different, and when I was told filming would take place on September 19, I knew how to make it different. September 19 was the date in 1819 when John Keats, while walking near Winchester Cathedral, paused to sit up against a tree and write his ode "To Autumn."

Back then, five mornings a week, I'd hoist Elijah on my shoulders and walk him to daycare. Right when we came to the same spot where we'd picked blackberries, he'd squeeze my shoulders and demand, "Poem, daddy." I recited "To Autumn" so many times to Elijah that I could stop at any place in the poem, and he'd chime in with the next word.

"To bend with…*apples*! And fill all fruit with ripeness to the…*core*!"

Since this was my show, I told the director I wanted to recite "To Autumn" while sitting in the pepper fields. She wasn't so keen on my idea. For good reason—her job was getting people to say "Yum!" But she told me if I gave her one or two usable lines, sure, I could say what I wished. So, there I was sitting in the middle of the pepper field with one hand holding an orange goathorn pepper and the other proudly holding a jar of Lil's fifteen-year-old homemade peppers. The director must've asked me to kiss the jar because that's what I did. Then I quoted my mother's dear friend, Ellie Katz: "Every time I eat the peppers, Lil comes back!"

I could see the director was pleased she got at least one line from me that she could use. Then I did it my way.

"Season of mists and mellow fruitfulness… To bend with apples the moss'd cottage trees, and fill all fruit with ripeness to the core…" I swooned through two stanzas of "To Autumn." I hope Keats was watching from above with his pal, Peter Piper, and getting a peck of laughs at my expense. When I came to the line, "Where are the songs of spring?" I looked up to see: the camera-man stifling a yawn, the soundman squinting to read his watch, the director making cross-eyes, and my friend Jean blowing his cheeks out to keep from breaking into stitches. He met me forty years ago in a poetry class and it had come to this.

I snapped out of it, stopped reciting, made a 'cut!' gesture to the direc-tor, and said, "That's enough!" putting an end to the filming that afternoon. (When the spot aired two months later, poor Keats got cut out completely. But they used my words "That's enough!" quite cleverly to end the episode.)

On October 9, 2011, a weather alert was issued for an early frost that would effectively end the harvest. I needed a mere two hundred pounds of goathorns to make my last batch of Honkin' Hot PeppaLilli at Wolf Pack. But there were more important orders needing to be picked that day than mine and, if I wanted those peppers, I'd have to pick them myself. Picking is back-breaking work, but I got through it as I was flashing on Lil in her own garden at dusk, telling me how fun it was to find the peppers hiding among their leaves.

Over the next two days at Wolf Pack, I made seven hundred gallons of PeppaLilli in that kettle whose crank lifted and lowered like a heavy draw-bridge. On the drive home, my right shoulder started spasming and I couldn't feel my hands on the steering wheel. It took an hour before my fingers started working again and I could resume driving home. I enjoyed the intensity of the harvest, but it was taking its toll on me. Call me a fool—but I didn't know how to run my business any other way.

A week later, on Halloween day, I had just loaded two pallets of peppers in my van to take back to Seattle when Gary Stonemetz pulled up in his beat-up old SUV. "Last year, it was the pizza pie people. This year, more TV cameras. And I really liked meeting Elijah. I hope you're counting your blessings. Because *someone* is blessing you. And maybe not just your mom."

"The Reverend Franklin James blessed my house. That counts, right?"

"Right, the towers of Crisco cans that came down like the walls of Jericho." We'd spent so much time together Gary had heard *all* my stories by now. Then Gary got out of his car and put a box of Pink Lady apples on the passenger seat. "Finally ripe," he told me. "And I got them all picked before it freezes tonight. Drive safe, it's supposed to snow on the pass."

As I drove down the Yakima Valley Highway out of Sunnyside, I pondered that box of Gary's Pink Lady apples beside me. I'd eaten many of these tart apples on evenings after work walking Gary's orchard with him as he tested his apples with a Brix meter (a handheld tool that measures sugar and sweetness levels in vegetables and fruit). The apples were deliciously tart with a hint of sweetness. I thought they were ripe. But Gary refused to harvest his apples until their sweetness reached its peak—a phenomenon triggered by one cold night. Then it was the race against time to pick the apples before the first freeze hits.

I grabbed a Pink Lady and took a bite. So juicy but still tart. But as I chewed a magical transformation took place in my mouth: the juice of the apple was becoming seductively and vivaciously sweet. Gary often talked to me about his faith in Jesus, but from my point of view, his true spirituality is a Keatsian embrace of cyclical Nature, as evoked in his ode, *To Autumn*: "to bend with apples the moss'd cottage-trees and fill all fruit with ripeness to the core."

After my Pink Lady appetizer I stopped on Lateral A. Road in Wapato to attend the Imperials' end-of-harvest feast held at their large open air farmstand overflowing with hundreds of people in the process of being very well fed. After standing at the barbeque spit slicing off bites of steak alongside Marcelo and Mel Imperial—eaten with a jar of peppers they grew, and Gary and I made—I bid adieu to the Yakima Valley and drove back to Seattle. And just as the poem *To Autumn* ends on the line as "gathering swallows twitter in the sky" forecasting the onset of winter, it did snow on Snoqualmie Pass that night. But with the *balasto* of two pallets of peppers, I put the van into low gear and fearlessly drove down that long hill without touching my brakes.

One of the biggest problems for sole-proprietor business owners like me was plain and simple burnout. And if I wasn't minding the store, who was? For this reason, I could never get away from Mama Lil's long enough to recharge my batteries. Could I have hired an assistant? If I could have found the right person, sure. The truth was, Mama Lil's was now making me a decent living, but was there enough profit in it to provide a living for someone else, too? Not yet. In the meantime, as business increased, it was mostly on my shoulders packing up pallets, shipping out boxes, and hand-trucking buckets and heavy cases into stores and restaurants.

One wet and cold December night, to avoid daytime traffic, I was making a delivery to one of my favorite restaurants, Dinette, (now but a fond memory) when a speeding car ran a stop sign and T-boned me right between the two driver-side doors. When my car stopped spinning, I was surprised that I wasn't badly injured. Knowing my car was totaled and would be towed away, I hid the buckets and cases I kept in my car (miraculously intact) behind some bushes.

Then with a bucket in hand I walked the few blocks to Dinette. When Dinette's lovely owner Melissa Nyffeler brought me a plate of her liver terrine on toast, she asked me, "Ah, where's Elijah?" When making deliveries I'd often bring my four-year old son to eat at Dinette where inevitably he'd find his way into the kitchen to play with the knobs on the stove.

"Ah, now there's a blessing in disguise," I said. "A car just crashed into me —right where Elijah would've been sitting." Later, when a cab driver helped me retrieve the peppers that I stashed in the bushes, I noticed that my body was now feeling sore. And by the time I carried those boxes and buckets into my mudroom, my neck and shoulder were throbbing with pain, adding to the prolonged abuse of twenty years of being Mama Lil's schlep.

That car that came out of nowhere was like a wicked messenger (or was it the angel of death?) telling me in the most dramatic of ways to "STOP!"

Dinette's Chicken Liver Mousse

Melissa Nyffeler

Makes about 4 cups

1 pound chicken livers, rinsed and patted dry
Salt and freshly ground black pepper
2 tablespoons neutral oil, plus more as needed
2 tablespoons minced shallots
1 tablespoon capers
1 tablespoon fresh thyme
1 teaspoon minced garlic
2/3 cup good port or sherry
4 tablespoons unsalted butter
2/3 cup heavy cream
Toast, for serving
Mama Lil's Kick Butt Peppers in Oil, for serving

Season the chicken livers with salt and black pepper. In a large sauté pan over medium heat, warm 2 tablespoons of the oil until very hot. Add the livers and brown them on both sides until they turn medium rare, about 2 minutes on each side. The livers should be firm but still pink in the center.

Add the shallots, capers, and thyme to the chicken liver and continue to sauté until the shallots become soft, adding more oil if necessary.

Add the garlic and port and stir to combine. Cook for 2 minutes to reduce the liquid.

Transfer the liver and shallot mixture to a plate and let cool slightly. Then transfer to the bowl of a food processor and blend for 1 minute.

With the processor running, add the butter 1 tablespoon at a time, then slowly pour in the cream until well incorporated. The mousse should be creamy.

Pour the mousse into an airtight container, cover, and chill in the refrigerator until it has set and is completely firm, about 1 hour.

To serve, spread the mousse on toast and top with Mama Lil's spicy pickled peppers!

PASSING THE TORCH

IN EARLY 2013, JUST AFTER I ASKED MY FARMERS to increase their goathorn pepper yields for Mama Lil's by yet another 50 percent, I was approached by a brother and sister from Portland, Oregon, Marty and Carolyn Marks, who made me a serious proposal to buy a majority stake in Mama Lil's. Like almost every small business owner, I'd had fantasies of selling my business, as in some ways that was the biggest marker of success. But now I had to face what that meant.

Mama Lil's had been my baby for more than twenty years. Was it time for the baby to kick its mama out of the nest? My brand's popularity was on a steep upward arc (locally anyway), so it was probably not the best time to sell. If I could wait longer and build up the brand in California, my business would be worth considerably more. Yet I was old enough to know that my energy was finite. And as an older dad, I wanted to spend as much time as I could with my son—with a body that still functioned and an arm that could still throw him a ball.

But who was I without Mama Lil's Peppers? What I was most fearful of losing was the fun identity I'd created for myself. Could I still hold on to who I was? I still had two drawers of Mama Lil's T-shirts, so if nothing else, I could always dress the part. Finally, I told the potential new owners that on the condition they kept everything the same—and I meant *everything* about the production—I'd consider selling. Were they going to use the same farmers whose trust I'd cultivated for more than a decade? And even more importantly, would they keep the production at Johnson Foods's first-rate cannery under the trustworthy supervision of Gary Stonemetz? When they agreed to this and said that they'd hire me for a year to oversee the transition, I agreed to sell a majority stake of Mama Lil's.

The day after I became a minority owner and officially moved Mama Lil's office out of my basement, Chile snuck out of my house to take a quick moonlit frolic around the neighborhood. He'd escaped before but always came home after he had his adventure. This time he didn't come back. But when we found his body in the neighbor's yard, he seemed at peace. That creature had mysteriously arrived at Mama Lil's darkest hour and continued to keep me amused for years as I performed the boring chores of running a business. Perhaps his job was done? But how I mourned that softest of creatures, and how I missed his mysterious presence in my life.

What I missed most about Mama Lil's was seeing my friends while making those deliveries to stores and restaurants, where inevitably I'd pause for a plate of food and a glass of beer or wine or be handed a sandwich on my way out the door. What I didn't miss about running a gourmet food business was promoting my products. It's true that those countless farmers markets and demos I did had made Mama Lil's the local success it was. But I hadn't quite realized how much the act of *selling* wore my spirit down. For years afterward, I'd get a panic attack just walking into a grocery store. And I couldn't even go near a farmers' market.

To keep the connections alive with the agricultural community of the Yakima Valley, I'd visit Stonemetz at the cannery and bring back to Seattle hauls of vegetables and fruit for my friends. I also got in the habit of gleaning the fields to pickle and pack goathorns in my own kitchen.

I also picked some goathorns for a neighbor of mine, Kirby Kallas-Lewis of OOLA Distillery, so he could experiment with using the goathorns to make a chile pepper vodka. It worked! His pepper vodka, which he calls ALOO, even won an award for being the top spirit made in the Northwest. Now when I bring back peppers for my homemade jars, I'll bring a few hundred pounds for Kirby, too. He'll be the first to tell you that what makes his pepper vodka so special are those amazingly sweet and spicy Hungarian goathorns that not only flavor it but also impart a pink tint to the vodka. I know that Gary Stonemetz, Ramon, and the Imperial brothers sure look forward to receiving their bottles of pepper vodka that Kirby gives them every harvest.

With Kirby Kallas-Lewis (far left) of OOLA Distillery and members of the Imperial family: Mel, Marcelo, Manuel, and Vergie at Imperial Gardens in Wapato, WA. 2020.

What to Do with the Brine?

Dick Cantwell, founder of Elysian Brewing
and the author of many books about beer.

As a brewer, I'm known for using some unusual ingredients to make beer. At Elysian, one of our mainstays was an IPA brewed with jasmine flowers, and I'm pretty sure we were the first brewery to put yuzu in a beer. I've written books about using eclectic ingredients in brewing IPAs and the effects and techniques of aging beer in barrels and on wood. We certainly didn't pioneer the use of pumpkin in brewing, but we did take it to pretty ridiculous lengths for our annual Elysian Pumpkinfests.

But I admit that I was stumped when, in one of our earliest conversations, Howard asked if I might have some use in brewing for the brine used in pickling Mama Lil's Peppers. As a responsible and economical user of raw materials in general, he was pained to see all that flavorful, nutrient-rich liquid go down the drain once it had been used to pickle his peppers.

Howard's and my paths have crossed and recrossed over the years. For a short time in the 1970s, we both attended the same hippie college—Hampshire College—in Massachusetts. Decades later, after we'd made our separate ways to Seattle, we recognized each other at the Cancer Lifeline Brewfest. Then we ran each other at the pool at Seattle University, where we both swam our daily laps a handful of blocks from both my brewery and Howard's house. He became a regular at my bar and we became friends, in large part, by discussing the vicissitudes of our respective businesses, usually with a beer in hand and often eating something augmented with Mama Lil's or his mother's eggplant recipe.

Another thing I do is judge beer competitions. In addition to the big ones in this country, such as the Great American Beer Festival and the World Beer Cup, I judge all around the world. One lesson I've learned from one of my brewing friends, Pete Slosberg, who used to make Pete's Wicked Ale, is that when visiting peoples' breweries, wherever they might be, it's nice to take along a little gift from our own local food cultures. I've found Mama Lil's to be just the thing. On a recent trip to Argentina, I learned something else: While Mexicans, Guatemalans, and other Central Americans love a little spice, that just isn't the case once you get farther south. The organizer of the Copa Argentina de Cervezas barely survived his introduction to the Mama Lil's Peppers and Cholula hot sauce that I served with the meat at Los Talas, an incredible churrascaria on the outskirts of Buenos Aires—and they aren't even that hot! But you know what, after a while they adjusted, and dare I say, a little competition ensued between Mama Lil's and Cholula and hands down Mama Lil's won, as soon the whole case I brought got eaten. Howard was especially proud of those peppers, as they were ten years old. He assures me it's draining the brine out of the peppers that's responsible for making them so good.

But back to that. There are beers made with salt—the German style Gose comes to mind—and I've made beers with hot peppers, such as Hot Guava Monster, a double IPA brewed with habaneros and guava. The secret to that one is that the habaneros are in contact with the beer for only an hour. I've never made a beer with Hungarian goathorns, although I should probably try one of these days. But the brine—it's just so, well, salty, that it seems like it just wouldn't work in a beer. When Howard first floated the idea of coming up with something to use it for, I said I'd think about it. I'm still thinking about it.

And I'm still thinking about it, too. So, if any food scientist or home canner out there has an idea or two on what to do with the spent pickling brine, I'm all ears. Worth noting, I have made some decent hot sauces that utilized the pepper brine, but the hot sauce market is saturated. For years I would save the brine to pickle other vegetables in, like Mama Lil's first versions of Asparagini and Lilibeans, which were great. The problem was that the peppers were harvested six months after the asparagus and a month after the beans. I had to save that brine for an inordinate length of time in barrels that were stored in Wolf Pack's walk-in refrigerator. After three months, George witnessed some stuff growing in those barrels that he said, "Looked like it was grown on the dark side of the moon. Get them out of my walk-in." To kill the active enzymes, he said I'd have boil the brine. The next year I boiled hundreds of gallons of brine in Wolfpack's kettles that I packed in five-gallon buckets then stored in Wolf Pack's warehouse. When George saw two pallets of buckets of brine taking up valuable space, he muttered, "What a pain in the ass." And he was right.

Hornblower IPA

Dick Cantwell

Many creative brewers find inspiration in not only the elements traditionally used for making beer, but also in other ingredients that combine well with hops and malt, such as fruits and vegetables, herbs, spices—even Hungarian Goat Horn peppers. When using peppers with any heat at all it's important not to overdo it, to taste frequently and to be able to remove the peppers from the finished beer at the point flavors are bold but not overpowering. This could be a matter of days, or of hours, and require a fermentation vessel with a wide enough lid to be able to remove and gain access. Goathorns have a moderate but present heat, which should combine well with the fruity hop varieties in an IPA. It's tempting as well to consider using fruits such as plums or peaches in combination with peppers, as well as to add a hotter pepper, such as Habañeros, for additional heat. For now, however, we'll consider a fairly basic IPA recipe and move on from there.

Batch Volume: 5 US gallons
   Original Gravity: 16.1° Plato/1.065 Specific Gravity Final Gravity: 2° P/1.008 SG
   Color: 3.9 SRM
   Bitterness: 54 IBU Alcohol: 6.9% by volume
Malts:
   10.5#/5.25 kg Dingeman's Pilsner malt 8 oz./.25 kg Weyermann Cara-hell
Hops:
   13 AAU Warrior @ 90 minutes
   1.5 oz./42 g Citra @ 2 minutes
   .5 oz./7 g Citra @ Whirlpool
Yeast:
   Imperial A30 Corporate Ale Yeast or other serviceable American Ale yeast
Other Ingredients:
   2 oz./56 g Fresh Hungarian Goat Horn Peppers, chopped finely and bagged, but not until fermentation is ended

Brewing Notes:
Mash 60 minutes @ 153°F/67°C Runoff and then Boil 90 minutes
Ferment @ 68°F/20°C until terminal, drop yeast and then chill to 35°F/3°C

Condition @ 35°F/3°C with bagged peppers, tasting every couple of hours for flavor and heat; remove when satisfied and continue chilling for c 1 week until bright
Carbonate to 2.5 volumes/4.6 g/L CO_2

Additional notes: If using fruit in ferment, clean, purée and add with yeast. 2-3 pounds should be sufficient. If using additional, hotter peppers in addition to Goat Horns, use no more than 3/4 oz/21 g and taste every 15 minutes to determine when to remove. As a side note, Loftus Farms in Moxee, WA has grown the peppers for Mama Lil's for the past few years, and wouldn't you know it, are the family behind Bale Breaker, as well as being an original cultivator of Citra hops—a match made in heaven. Heck, the goathorns are ripening as I write this, and Citra hops are coming down from their trellises. I'm going to make this beer, in collaboration with Kevin Quinn of Bale Breaker Brewing and serve it at Howard's book launch!

Dick Cantwell and Kevin Quinn at Bale Breaker Brewery, 2024.

MAMA LIL'S BEST FRIEND

Typically, when businesses change ownership, it's almost a cliché to assume that the new owners put in cost-cutting measures that cause the quality of their products to start going downhill. This has not happened in the least with Mama Lil's. If anything, it's quite the opposite. This is largely because of the continued presence of Gary Stonemetz, the real showrunner of the operation. The new majority owners have been true to their promises and have embraced Gary's authority and precise methods.

Stonemetz once confessed to me, "My whole adult life, I've been working in agriculture in one way or another, but nothing has given me more satisfaction than making Mama Lil's Peppers. I knew they were special the first time I tasted them. And I knew then that I wanted to perfect the process of making them." And during that process, I watched Gary learn from his mistakes, repeatedly. One of the first aspects of pepper production that Gary attempted to refine was how to automate the laborious process of destemming and deseeding the peppers. Over the years, Gary came up with several Rube Goldberg-type contraptions, none of which finally worked. Prepping the peppers still entailed stabbing the stem with an apple corer, giving it a twist to break the seed membrane, then scooping out the seeds.

Meanwhile, in 2015, the debilitating pain in both of my shoulders continued to worsen. An orthopedic surgeon determined my left shoulder had been so badly injured by the car crash that the only way to fix it was to replace it. But it was the right one—my throwing shoulder—about which I was most concerned. I knew it had lots of frayed connective tissue from years of lifting buckets and cases, not to mention turning that stiff kettle's crank at Wolf Pack. But the surgeon said this didn't explain why I could no longer throw a ball to my son. He then had me demonstrate how I used the apple coring tool. His probing fingers followed my arm from my wrist all the way up to my shoulder. Then he told me, "That twisting motion of your wrist and elbow, is why your bicep is holding onto its shoulder tendon by a mere thread."

The next day I drove to the cannery and told Gary, "If we don't figure out a better way to get the seeds out, our whole crew will develop the same shoulder issues as me."

Sometimes all you need to do is plant the seed, then let the imagination take over. Gary called me the next day and told me excitedly, "I dreamt how to take the stems off. I drew it up when I awoke." Within a week, Johnson Foods' engineer was building the first destemming device just as Gary imagined it. Its design was simple but brilliant, consisting of two sharp blades that come together in a V. When you slid a pepper between the blades, the stem and seed membrane were pinched off. Prepping the peppers still involved manual labor because every pepper needs to be touched by someone's hand. But the device sped up the prep process without torquing the workers' arm joints and potentially causing them a lifetime of misery. Within a month, the engineer at Johnson Foods had built twenty of these destemming contraptions.

In 2014, when the *Seattle Weekly* newspaper listed its favorite sandwiches in Seattle, Macrina Bakery's bread and Mama Lil's Peppers were cited as the two ingredients that local chefs used the most to make their sandwiches just a cut above. Shortly thereafter, Starbucks, whose corporate offices are down the street from Macrina Bakery in Seattle, informed us it was developing a breakfast sandwich that included Mama Lil's Sweet Hot Peppas.

For our foodservice containers, we packed the Sweet Hots in half-gallon glass jars that needed to be pasteurized so to be made shelf stable. (This is unlike our buckets of Peppers in Oil, which are doubly preserved, first in vinegar and then again when they sink into the anaerobic environment of the oil.) But since the insurance policies of large restaurant corporations like Starbucks forbid glass in their kitchens—if you've ever seen a slow-motion video of a glass jar breaking into a million sharp shards, you'd know why—we had to figure out a way of packing and pasteurizing those Sweet Hot Peppas that wasn't in glass.

Gary got his hands on a one-gallon, semi-opaque recyclable plastic container that theoretically wouldn't leach chemicals from the heat of pasteurization. He packed some of these plastic jars and set them on his desk to keep an eye on them. He was hopeful—until one month later when the peppers turned dark right before Gary's eyes. After witnessing this oxygenation, Gary told the new owners that there were too many factors about this plastic jar he didn't understand yet. He couldn't guarantee a three-month shelf life, let alone a year. (Or four years, as we give the buckets of peppers in oil!) Gary refused to make the Sweet Hots for Starbucks.

I warned the new majority owners about my experience with Panera when I was forced to grow before I was ready. But just like me, they didn't want to lose this big fish off the hook. They found a farmer in Mexico who said he could grow a winter crop of hot goathorns, then located a cannery in Fresno, California, who guaranteed they could successfully pack those peppers in large plastic jars. Gary and I tasted the samples made for Mama Lil's in Fresno. They were pretty good, but we could detect a trace of chemical preservatives.

They just didn't have that same *je ne sais quoi* as the real Sweet Hot Peppas. But nevertheless, Starbucks accepted those jars for the national rollout of its breakfast sandwich.

Not surprisingly, supplying Starbucks with peppers grown in Mexico and packed in California was fraught with problems. Mexico's winter growing season has less sunlight, so the peppers take longer to ripen. The first farmer got frustrated when his peppers didn't turn color fast enough and he sold his crop to another customer when they were still yellow. The next farmer refused to pick his crop until he got paid first and by the time his peppers arrived at the border, they'd rotted and were turned away. One crop grown for Mama Lil's couldn't be picked because the roads had been blockaded by the Mexican Army when it was hunting for the drug kingpin El Chapo. Within a year Starbucks took that sandwich off the menu. Luckily, we had ample warning and didn't get stuck in an endless tunnel of inventory. But money was lost.

But praise be to the Master of the Universe! In 2016, I placed the largest bet I'd ever wagered on the Cleveland Indians to win the World Series. Rajai Davis had miraculously tied the game with a home run off the most vaunted pitcher in baseball. I was set to win $14,000. Then there was a rainstorm, momentum shifted, and the Indians broke my heart—yet again. I also had a dinner bet with Manuel Imperial on the outcome of the presidential election that I was fully expecting to win. It felt like the country got broken in two when I lost that wager. It wasn't long after that I noticed when playing ball with my son Elijah that my hip was broken and needed to be replaced. Soon afterward, Elijah's mother and I decided to parent him from separate homes. When things get broken, you can try and fix them. And if you can't, well, you just got to be kind.

In March Stonemetz asked me to drive over to the cannery as he wanted me to taste something. When I got there, he opened a large plastic jar and handed me a ringlet of yellow peppers. "I found these goathorns from a farmer in Arkansas." On the first bite, I knew Gary had captured the genuine Sweet Hot Peppas flavor. And I knew it was an all-natural product as there was no aftertaste of preservatives. Gary then bragged, "Think how much better they'll taste when they're made from our own goathorn peppers." (To reveal his process would be giving away trade secrets, so I won't.)

As these things tend to go, a whale of an account swam into the waters of Elliot Bay in the guise of MOD Pizza, a Neapolitan pizza chain founded in Seattle by former Starbucks employees. MOD had national ambitions, but being local, its management was familiar with Mama Lil's and asked us if we could make the Sweet Hot Peppas in foodservice containers. That was five years ago. At MOD's corporate gathering three years ago, Mary Marks reported that the audience of investors and employees applauded when the Sweet Hot Peppas was mentioned. As well they should have—the Sweet Hots had become MOD's customers' favorite pizza topping.

As Stonemetz considered retiring from Johnson Foods so he could focus on farming, he grew close to Elena, who'd been working at the cannery in all facets of production since 2000. Elena's joie de vivre spirit made those grueling hours on the prep and production lines go by faster, and almost seem fun.

In 2018, when Stonemetz told me that he and Elena had gotten married and he had adopted her daughter Frida, it filled me with joy. Considering his deceased wife's negative attitude about Hispanic people, Gary and Elena's marriage not only seemed like an act of rectitude but also a sign of progress between the white and Hispanic cultures of the Yakima Valley.

When Elijah was eight years old, I took him to see Gary's farm, where his organic asparagus field—"*an old man's crop*" which, to my dismay, had replaced his Pink Lady orchard—was yielding

Gary and Elena Stonemetz

its first crop. Gary taught Elijah and me how to use the asparagus-picking tool, and the spears we sliced were so tasty that Elijah and I ate them raw. Gary takes so much satisfaction in pickling and packing the asparagus he grows that a few years back—along with Gary Johnson, who owns the cannery—he started growing Hungarian goathorn peppers at their farms, all of which go in filling the jars and buckets of Mama Lil's Peppers.

At the beginning of the 2019 harvest, I drove to the cannery to check on how production was coming along. In the production room, where normally a crew of twenty-five people wearing gas masks would be standing in front of the destemming devices, there were just a few people—and no destemming devices in sight.

I asked Gary, "Where is everybody? How are you getting the stems off?"

He smiled cunningly. "Look around the room."

After being washed, the peppers were sliced into ringlets, with their stems still on. The sliced peppers—stems and all—fell onto a conveyor belt that passed right through a machine that looked like lightning in a box. Seconds later, when the rings came out of that box, their stems and seed cores were gone. This space-age contraption was a laser sorter equipped with hundreds of lenses that spotted the stems and seed membranes and with a burst of air, discarded them.

By convincing Gary Johnson to invest in this high-tech, quarter-million-dollar gadget—which could also detect and discard cherry pits from the gazillion pounds of cherries that Johnson Foods grows and packs every year—Stonemetz had tackled the worst aspect of making the peppers: the immense repetitive manual labor it required. And folks, we're not talking *great* manual labor jobs here. During the harvest of 2023, we sliced and pickled six million pounds of goathorn peppers. That would be unfathomable if all that hand labor hadn't been eliminated.

During last year's harvest, I was at Gary and Elena' s farm picking up some of his goathorn peppers for my home-made jars when Gary told me a funny story that was still tickling his fancy. An inspector for the Washington State Department of Agriculture had just been out to Gary's farm. He was checking on Gary's organic D'Anjou pear orchard, giving him grief over his organic protocol. The inspector was checking what other crops Gary had growing nearby when he noticed a field below that was brimming with colorful fruit.

The inspector asked Stonemetz, "So what you got growing down there?"

He told him, "Down there. Those are Hungarian goathorn peppers."

The inspector asked, "Not for Mama Lil's, are they? I love those things." When he found out they were, his issues with the pears didn't come up again.

I've often wondered if Stonemetz's commitment to Mama Lil's was in part due to his deep connection to the Yakima Valley, where he has lived and farmed his whole life. As is also the case with the cannery's owner Gary Johnson. Both men know that the hot goathorns grow better in the Yakima Valley than anywhere in the world, and they both grow acres of them on their Sunnyside farms. All those goathorns go into jars and buckets of Mama Lil's.

But don't let me kid you. More than thirty years after I made my first sellable batch of jars in a church kitchen, the whole process of making Mama Lil's Peppers is still a pain in the ass. But it's a hundred times more efficient than it used to be and yet the quality of our products is more consistent than ever. This is due not only to Gary Stonemetz's passion and his pursuit of perfection, but also to his determination to pass on that knowledge to all the other folks who will still be making the peppers at Johnson Foods after he's gone.

From when those peppers are a gleam in Stonemetz's eyes until the jars appear out of the pasteurization tunnel eight months later, he'll baby them just like everything else he bestows his Midas touch upon. I'm eternally grateful for my great friend Gary Stonemetz's dedication in making sure Mama Lil's Peppers remains "the finest product that can be put in a jar. Or bucket."

EPILOGUE

AUGUST 2018. THE DAY BEFORE, I'd been walking Imperial's pepper fields in Wapato, selectively picking some of the very first colorful goathorns of the summer. At its farmstand, I bought some plump eggplants. The next morning, I grilled the eggplants on top of the stove, unleashing their pungent smokiness into the entire neighborhood. An hour or so later I was cinching my grandmother's meat grinder to the countertop to start making salata, when my ten-year-old son Elijah burst in the kitchen. When he saw the peppers in my sink, he asked me sarcastically,

"Does your mom really come back every time you eat your peppers?"

"Not every time I eat them. But *sometimes* she does."

"Like the tooth fairy, right? I'm going to see if Denny's home. Can you make me lunch?"

Elijah grabbed his football and was out the door in a flash. I was multitasking, grilling him a steak and some asparagus, while also feeding eggplants and goathorn peppers into the grinder. Whenever I make this salata recipe, it brings back memories of sitting at the kitchen table doing homework while Lil spun the grinder's crank. The first time I ever used her grinder myself was thirty years ago, when she brought it from Ohio to show me how to make some of my favorite foods (but *not* her chicken and dumplings!)

As I spun the grinder's crank, I realized that this family heirloom had indeed become like Jonny Katz's ceremonial African artifacts, invested with the auras and energies of all the people who'd handled them in the past. As if the very act of spinning that crank teases friendly spirits to come out of hiding. Or perhaps it's the pungent aroma of charred eggplant awakening the dead?

Whoosh! Elijah ran back inside, bursting with joy. "I'm the luckiest boy in the world!"

"Why are you the luckiest boy in the world?"

"I just found this in the alley!" He opened his palm to show me a folded $20 bill. "I'm going to show it to Denny!" Then he flew right back out the door.

But I was suspicious. Who drops $20 bills? And hadn't I just shown Elijah the top drawer of my tall dresser where I'd stash precious keepsakes and cash?

I went into the spare bedroom—Reverend James's former room—and stood on a stool to look inside the top drawer. My five $20 bills were right where I'd put them. But then I glimpsed, peeking out from under one of Lil's scarves, that pair of black leather gloves, my last gift from Lil. I'd tucked them away in this drawer after Jonny's memorial service and forgotten about them. I put the gloves on. Just as their inner softness caressed my fingers, my mind's eye saw *exactly* how Elijah found the $20 bill.

Jonny and Lil are playing gin rummy for a dime a point, with a years-long tabulation of numbers beside them. As Jonny apprehensively sets down a card, Lil raises an eyebrow then snaps the card up, throws down her winning hand and calls, "Gin!"

As Lil victoriously shuffles the cards, she catches a whiff. "Jonny, do you smell that?" Then, there Lil and Jonny are, high atop the flowering horse chestnut tree, with a view of the alley behind my house.

Below them, Elijah and his friend Denny are making acrobatic one-handed catches with the football.

Jonny nudges Lil. "Isn't your grandson a beautiful boy?" When she spots Elijah, she bites on her knuckles to contain her joy. But she's frustrated.

Jonny has an idea. "Lil, give me that twenty you just won from me."

Jonny folds Lil's $20 bill, drops it. They watch its twirling descent.

As Denny tosses the football to Elijah, a crow swoops past, distracting my son just enough that the football slips out of his sure-handed fingers. The football bounces away, going this way and that, then comes to a stop at the fence.

Voilà, the $20 bill lands next to the football.

After reveling in this sweet vision for a few seconds, I put the leather gloves back into the drawer, then returned to the kitchen to slice the steak for Elijah's lunch.

Elijah flew back in, eyes still sparkling. "I'm *still* the luckiest boy in the world!"

As I handed him a plate of steak and asparagus, with a garnish of peppers—from a jar made before he was even born—I told him, "Elijah, luck doesn't come from out of nowhere."

He placed a pepper ring onto his bite of steak. Then, with something between a smirk and a smile, he rolled his eyes and asked me, "So where *does* luck come from?"

For the hundredth time I told him, "When we eat the peppers—"

Elijah beat me to the punch. "Lil really does come back." Then he gobbled up two more bites and was back out the door. As I watched him run down the alley, tossing his football up in the air to himself, I couldn't help but sense Reverend James standing beside me. Having raised several kids, grandkids, and great grandkids in this house, he must've watched them run down this alley a hundred times. I could almost hear him gloating.

"I know I blessed this house, but I didn't think I blessed it this good."

ACKNOWLEDGMENTS

Just as this entrepreneurial memoir begins with origin stories, there's also an origin story about the inspiration to write this book. When my ten-year-old son Elijah Lev and I visited his "uncle" Nicky Katz at his home in Florida, I took this intriguing photograph with my iPhone of Nicky and Elijah playing in the swimming pool at night. I emailed the photo to Kathy Katz, who in turn shared it with their ninety-year-old mother, Ellie. According to Kathy, Ellie looked at this image of our two sons, Nicky and Elijah, for a few seconds, then extemporaneously described it to Kathy in these words.

It's the universal melting of light and dark.

The contact is a rhythmic gentle melting of souls,

Joined together by generations of familial love.

And it's going forwards, not backwards, so it has real energy.

And there's no power of one over the other as they merge.

Ellie's poem so eloquently nailed this image, that it gave me a theme, so I could see the pattern in this necklace of stories that I was about to thread. When a year later I confessed to Ellie that I was writing this book about my business and that Jonny had found his way into it, Ellie demanded, "Howie, finish it before I die. I want to read it." A year on, packed inside a box with a case of peppers, Ellie received a rough first draft of *A Pepper for Your Thoughts?* She called me a few days later. "Howie, I *loved* it. Then after I finished it last night, I dreamt of Jonny. I *saw* Jonny take that glove from the coat closet. And today, he's been following me around wherever I go. He's with me now. Thanks for bringing Jonny back to me."

If no one else reads my book, Ellie's words made the whole enterprise worth it. Ellie passed away peacefully in January of 2023 at the age of ninety-five. Ellie put the peppers on her sandwiches so I'm told, until her last days.

In a similar vein, when I told George Wolf that I was writing this book and since he was in it, he'd better read it in case he wanted to sue me. A week later, George called me. "I just read your book. It's great! And I'm not saying that because I'm in it. You show the grit it takes to make it in this God damn business."

In October of 2022, just as Mama Lil's was making PeppaLilli at Wolf Pack, I was at George Wolf's deathbed in his one-room living quarters near the end of the cannery's pasteurization tunnel. He was eighty-eight years old and in palliative care by then, and I asked him if he knew where he was. He turned to look at me with his eyes closed, then cracked a big smile. "Same room where you were on your knees, screaming to the heavens, 'The Indians are going to the World Series, George!'"

George may have passed away, but Wolf Pack is alive and well. Luckily before he died, George sold his business to Dhanesh Raniga who is running a first-class operation at this rustic gem of a cannery in the foothills of the Cascades.

Since I made all my products for the entire year during the Yakima Valley's two-month pepper harvest, in the other ten months I had the wherewithal to single-handedly perform all the other chores of running my business myself. As my business grew, I didn't hire new employees, since I was barely making a living for myself. Instead, I just increased my capacity to multitask. But who am I kidding? Mama Lil's may have been a one-man brand for its first twenty years, but I gotta lotta foot-stomping help from a rhythm section of friends, friends of friends, sons and daughters of friends. One of the reasons I wrote this book is as a thank-you note to all those people I was so dependent on. If I took but one of them out of the equation, my whole pepper kingdom would have tumbled down like Humpty-Dumpty, never to be put together again.

Thank you to my parents, Lil and Harry, for loving me and instilling in me a strong work ethic.

I can't say enough about what Gary Stonemetz has meant to me and to Mama Lil's since I met him twenty years ago, so I'll just leave it at.

My friend, Gary Johnson, constantly adapted his processing facility in Sunnyside to meet Mama Lil's needs and accommodate for its future growth. Can't ask for more than that.

Jean Sherrard accompanied me on so many of my drives from Seattle to the Yakima Valley, he witnessed half of this book. And whether he knew it or not, he was indispensable in jogging my memory so I could write it. (*How many watermelons did I heave at that tractor?*) Perhaps, what I appreciated most about Jean's presence on those many drives was that I had to stop so he could take his gorgeous photographs—some of which appear in this book—so that I, too, would pause to admire the stunning landscape carved by the Yakima River.

Jean's son, Ethan Sherrard, not only helped me pack my products at Wolf Pack, but when he went off to college on the East Coast, Ethan did dozens of demos at Whole Foods stores around Philadelphia for me. Committing all those hours to Mama Lil's certainly didn't help his grades, but it kept Mama Lil's jars on the shelves—for one year longer, anyway.

From the beginning, David Lee was watching over me and giving me leads and honest advice. He ended up being more successful than all my friends in the business. But what I envy most about his product's success is the Field Roast logo on the Toronto Blue Jays outfield wall.

Mama Lil's wouldn't have made it far without Jerry Mascio. Not only did he do me a hundred favors that enabled Mama Lil's to stay in existence as a phantom business, but he was great companionship at food shows. But what I most appreciate is that he took me on so many squid jigging, crab potting, clam digging, and other fun expeditions on the waterways around Seattle.

My thanks to Jeffrey Baron, who, nearly forty years ago and under the influence of magic mushrooms, (or was it, LSD?) insisted that we start a business making these peppers. At the end of every summer, it's been a tradition that Jeffrey and I (along with our friends Nitin Manchanda, and David Lee) pickle and pack at least two hundred pounds of goathorns in my kitchen. Man, it's a lot of work making those sixteen cases of pint jars. And I'm still finding pepper seeds on my floor months later. But this past year, I talked Jeffrey into buying a Bobbitron, so at least slicing the peppers was easier. When I was helping him carry his stash to his car, I asked Jeffrey, "How many of these jars will you keep for yourself? And how many will you be giving away?"

Jeffrey, a consummate businessman who has greased a few palms in his day, confessed, "About half and half. The peppers aren't crypto, but they are currency."

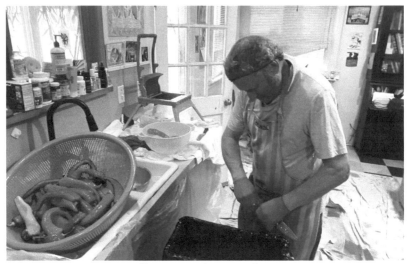
Jeffrey Baron, harvest of 2023

Jan Barton came all the way from Prague three times to help me make Mama Lil's. Yes, he loved living in nature at Wolf Pack, but what he *really* loved were the peppers. At his home outside Prague, he grows enough goathorns each year to make a dozen jars for his private larder.

Don Blevins helped enable Mama Lil's in infinite ways over the last thirty-five years. Not only did Don design Mama Lil's first label and help me glue them on my jars, but heck there were nights when my 75-year-old friend was packing peppers with me past midnight. Most importantly, when I was away, he took care of my pets Marion and Chile.

I can't imagine Mama Lil's without Julie Paschkis's images that so imaginatively epitomized Mama Lil's brand. And to Tom Kleifgen who then turned those images into such beautiful labels.

Kudos to the linguistic wizardry of Ron Dakron and Doug Nufer.

Kimberly Weston gave me technical, aesthetic and emotional support while I was writing this book.

I have such deep gratitude to all the Yakima Valley farmers (and their farmhands) who have grown the Hungarian goathorns for Mama Lil's over the past thirty years. I welcome into the fold, the Smith's from Loftus Farms who now grow peppers for us a mere five miles away from the cannery. As of this writing, Imperial Gardens is going stronger than ever and still growing goathorns for Mama Lil's. But in 2021, the Inabas found the perfect exit strategy when they sold their farm back to the Yakama Nation, then worked alongside them for three years to teach them how to farm.

And I'm certainly thankful to the current majority owners, Carolyn and Marty Marks, for not only keeping Mama Lil's alive these past twelve years, but for ensuring she's kept to the highest standards. And Carolyn, you make some mean PeppaLilli mustard pickles.

Tomas, wherever you are, thank you for keeping my cars running and my knives sharp. In fact, I want to thank all the itinerant workers who helped me slice peppers in those early years.

These people came through for Mama Lil's in ways big and small: Nick Stull, Cynthia Breen, Orion Breen, Jackie Roberts, Tom Douglas, Jay Beattie, Eric Stone, Tikka Sears, Bryan Yeck, Jim German, Santha Cassell, Corrine Kocher, Jimmy Watkins, Tony Cascioppo, Michael Brooks, Scott Smith, Joshua Smith, Pete Vogt, Chris Adams, Terry Lee Hale, Jack at Husky Deli, Steve and Yusuf Shulman from Leschi Market, Mark Takagi, Pam Foster, Matt Janke, Matt Lewis, Matt Galvin, Matthew Hoffman, Mitch Gilbert, Brad Inserra, Daisley Gordon, Melissa Nyffeler, Rita Dever, Antonio Galata, Leonid Ezernitsky, Maggie Laird, Linda Anderson, Deborah Rome, Carla Torgerson, Megan Skinner, Lisa Jones, Grace Daeger, Todd Preston, Mark Wittow, Patrick Lango, Tony and Susan Gilroy, Paul Gilroy, Rick Best, Gayle Krueger, Bruno's Pepper Company, Raffi Santikian, Myron Becker, Sydney Croskery, Donny Santisi, Ramon Ortega, Carlos Alfaro, Max Benedicto, Ryan Calhoun, Wayne Inaba, and Manuel, Marcelo, Mel, and Vergie Imperial. I apologize to the dozens of you I may have left out.

These friends read drafts of this book, then graciously allowed me to quiz them about it: Melissa Borden, Tom Kleifgen, Julie Paschkis, Ron Dakron, Don Blevins, Jan Barton, Alex Beloi, Tarik Burney, Kami Ahmad, Dan Kennedy, Dick Cantwell, David Levy, Sharon Croskery, Terry Lee Hale, Mark Sommer, Jeffrey Gold, Jeffrey Baron, Tommy Kane, Tony Gilroy, Lenny Neimark, Dan Burdick, Doug Nufer, John Shaw, Gnat Shaw, Patrick Lango, Nitin Manchanda, Kim Weston, Frank Lev, Don Creery, Nick Katz, and Deacon Shorr. I had excellent editing help from Matt Bennett, Lisa Gordanier, and Mi Ae Lipe.

On behalf of Mama Lil's Peppers, I want to thank all the restaurant owners and their chefs, as well as all the grocery stores, caterers, and most of all, our customers who continue to use some of the finest products that can be put in a jar. Or a bucket. *If not for you…*

Though Howard Lev claims to have been an excellent cabbie, otherwise his life was a series of misadventures until at the age of 37 he started a pepper business based on his mother's recipe. He claims to have only succeeded in that due to his utter fear of failure, which he believes is the origin of his grit. Either that or as his dentist claims, "Howard has the bite of an ox." He has never won an award or had any acclaim whatsoever but is uniquely qualified to have written this book. Born in Youngstown, Ohio, he has resided in Seattle for fifty years, presently with his handsome teenage son and beloved cat and dog.

RECIPE INDEX

www.ingramcontent.com/pod-product-compliance
Lightning Source LLC
LaVergne TN
LVHW071041220625
814250LV00010B/2